from tragedy to
TRIUMPH

LIVING SANELY SERIES

Books:

Living Sanely In An Insane World: Philosophy for Real People

Life Changing Advice from People You Should Know

From Tragedy to Triumph: 100 Amazing and Inspiring Comebacks

Internet Sites and Email Lists

www.LivingSanelyBooks.com

www.PositivePress.com

Positive Quote of the Day email list

Positive News email list

Living Sanely email list

from tragedy to
TRIUMPH

100 Amazing and Inspiring Comebacks

THE LIVING SANELY SERIES

John F. Groom

with David Noon

ATTITUDE MEDIA

FIRST EDITION

Published in the United States by Attitude Media

2 4 6 8 10 9 7 5 3 1

Printed in the United States of America

ISBN 978-0-9632701-4-6

CONTENTS

INTRODUCTION

Who is this book about?

You. This book covers a very wide variety of people, individuals who have faced a range of obstacles: imprisonment and torture, sickness, rape, business failure, poverty, discrimination, divorce, more business failure, serious car accidents, sudden debilitating disease, political repression, depression, substance abuse, career failure, family tragedy, academic failure, and every sort of rejection. Any sort of serious problem that you may face is probably touched upon in one way or another within these pages. Hopefully, by seeing how others have overcome adversity, you will see a path that can help you, your friends, or your family. You may already know what you need to do, and reading these inspiring profiles will give you the strength to keep moving forward.

Some of the adversity you'll read about in these pages was sudden and dramatic: teenaged surfer Beth Hamilton had her arm ripped off by a shark while surfing, and Max Cleland lost both legs and an arm to a grenade in Vietnam. But for others, their hurdles were much less dramatic, with no "start" date: Paula Deen was simply terrified of leaving her house, so she didn't.

In some of the stories, the subjects are so heroic as to defy belief: John McCain, Nien Cheng, and Armando Valladares were tortured and imprisoned for years. McCain refused early release, unwilling to break the military code of honor; Cheng and Valladares also refused release, unwilling to deny their religious beliefs. Subjects profiled in other stories may be much easier to relate to—the single parent who simply had no money and a family to support; the alcohol or drug-abuser; the business failure. They started with a simple, common problem but came up with some amazing solutions.

We write about people from all over the world; many ended up in America, but started life someplace else. Rebiya Kadeer had to leave her home in China but continued to fight for Uighur rights. Joseph Brodsky left the Soviet Union but still celebrated Russian culture as an American citizen. Tenzin Gyatso, better known as the Dalai Lama, was born in Nepal but was forced to move to India. We also cover Africans like Nelson Mandela; a number of British citizens—including Richard Branson, Douglas Bader, and J. K. Rowling; Corazon Acquino from the Philippines; Azim Premji from India; and Diego Maradona from Argentina, among others.

Many of those we write about are still living; most of the rest have died only recently. But we also include some who have had special historical impacts showing the history of resilience in America and Great Britain. Abraham Lincoln, Ulysses Grant, Thomas Paine, Charles Darwin, and Winston Churchill all prove that the amazing comeback has a great lineage.

We examine the lives of politicians, writers, artists, soldiers, entrepreneurs, civil rights activists, scientists, athletes, inventors, investment advisers, political prisoners, actors, and singers. Entrepreneur is the most frequent category of occupation, but that covers everyone from billionaire media king (and New York City mayor) Michael Bloomberg to Soapworks founder Amilya Antonetti. Singers include rapper Mary K. Blige and The *Sound of Music*'s Julie Andrews. The physically disabled includes those who are deaf and/or blind, or without arms and/or legs—and one man who was completely paralyzed, with the ability only to blink one eyelid, which he used to amazing effect.

The political spectrum is wide; both the Republican and Democratic candidates for U.S. president in 2008 are included, as are liberals, conservatives, socialists, and libertarians. If there is a common political theme, it is the fight against totalitarianism in all its forms. Our profiles include blacks, whites, Hispanics, Asians, Africans, and a few we didn't know how to classify. Of the more modern subjects, about half are women.

Despite their wide variety of backgrounds, all of the individuals profiled here have one thing in common: an amazing and inspiring comeback story.

ANDRE AGASSI (B. 1970)

American Tennis Player

At the bottom:

1997—Andre Agassi stared at the small mound of crystal meth powder his friend "Slim" had just poured on the coffee table. He leaned over and snorted, then slipped back into his chair and felt "a moment of regret, followed by a vast sadness." Just two years earlier, Agassi had been the top tennis player in the world, reaching the rank of number one after a decade as a professional, during which time he had won Wimbledon, the U.S. Open, and the Australian Open as well as numerous lesser tournaments. During the early 1990s, he helped the United States win three Davis Cup titles, and he took the gold medal in men's singles at the 1996 Olympics, held in Atlanta. In addition to his success on the court, Agassi was the closest thing his sport had to a rock star; he stood out to fans—and advertisers—with his flashy, charismatic personality, his colorful outfits, and his long, flowing hair. By the end of 1996, however, Agassi's success began to wane. He suffered early-round losses in the U.S. and Australian Opens, and an old wrist injury resurfaced, limiting the number of matches he would play in 1997. He continued to use crystal meth throughout the year and eventually failed a drug test, but he evaded punishment by claiming that he had accidentally consumed a spiked soda. His world ranking slipped to number 141, and he no longer felt a love for the game. It seemed as though Agassi's once-bright career was fading fast.

At the top:

1999—Andre Agassi could barely keep his composure as he addressed the crowd in Paris, where he had just won his first French Open title. "I never dreamed I'd ever be back here after so many years, I'm so proud," said Agassi, his voice shaking. "I'll never forget this, I'll never forget this. I'm very blessed." Agassi began the tournament ranked thirteenth in the world and had made a surprising run to the final match, where he defeated Andre Medvedev—a victory that was itself a remarkable comeback, as Agassi had been down two sets to none in the five-set match before storming back to take the title. With the win, Agassi completed one of the most remarkable comebacks in tennis history, and he became only the second men's player ever to have won all four of the major tournaments (Wimbledon, the U.S. Open, the French Open, and the Australian Open) since Rod Laver did so in 1969. Agassi went on to win Wimbledon once more and take another two Australian Open titles, returning several times to the number-one spot in the next few years while remaining in the Top 10 for the rest of his career.

The comeback:

Years later, Agassi described the failed drug test as a wake-up call. He realized that "My name, my career, everything [was] now on the line. Whatever [I had] achieved, whatever [I had] worked for, might soon mean nothing." He stopped using crystal meth shortly afterwards and put himself on an intense training regimen. With his ranking so low, Agassi was unable to play in some of the major tournaments and had to work his way back up by appearing in the so-called "Challenger Series," which is to professional tennis what the minor leagues are to professional baseball. He carried his own bags and no longer received VIP treatment at tournaments. Along with younger, unknown hopefuls, the former top player in the world had to struggle up from square one. Agassi took it all in stride, however, and did not allow himself to think he deserved an easier path because he had already won the top prizes in his sport. He was no longer a superstar, but the humbling experience taught him to appreciate what he'd achieved—and what he'd lost—and it stoked his competitive fire. He focused on improving himself one day at a time, and before long he was back, better than ever.

JULIE ANDREWS (B. 1935)
English Singer and Actress

At the bottom:

1997—For the past year and a half, Julie Andrews—one of the most accomplished stage and screen actresses of the late twentieth century—had been starring in the Broadway version of *Victor/Victoria*, the musical film Andrews had starred in fourteen years earlier. Audiences flocked to hear the voice from such memorable classics as *Mary Poppins* and *The Sound of Music*—the voice that had helped her win an Academy Award, two Emmy Awards, and five Golden Globes over the past three decades. During the last few months of the stage show, however, Andrews had missed over thirty performances. Sidelined with bronchitis and pneumonia, Andrews was having trouble with her beautiful singing voice, which had taken a beating over her career. By the time *Victor/Victoria* ended its Broadway run, Andrews had developed a noncancerous cyst on the left side of her throat. Doctors removed the cyst, promising her that her voice would return within six weeks. It didn't. She later described her voice as having a "fried sound," with "certain notes that just don't appear." Her husband, the filmmaker Blake Edwards, told a reporter a year after the operation that he didn't think she'd ever sing again. "It's an absolute tragedy," he said. "If you heard [her voice], you'd weep."

At the top:

2004—Seven years after her failed throat surgery, Julie Andrews sang again for the first time on screen. The film was *The Princess Diaries 2*, a lighthearted sequel to one of the surprise hits of 2001; in the two films, Andrews plays the queen of a fictional country called "Genovia." Marketed to pre- and early-teen girls, both films did quite well at the box office, generating $300 million in combined revenues and introducing Andrews to a new generation of filmgoers. Although her singing performance in the sequel was brief (and pitched lower than her usual soprano), anyone who had followed Andrews' career would have appreciated what that performance meant to her. By 2004, Andrews had also pursued a new avenue for her creative talents, as she and her daughter Emma had begun writing a series of children's books that told stories about characters who triumph over adversity. The books—especially the "Dumpy the Dump-truck" series—were well received and earned high marks from educators and librarians. For Andrews, the messages in the books were drawn from her own experiences, and she drew inspiration from the idea that she might be able to help guide young readers to see the silver lining during difficult times. As she explained to a group of educators, "If you think about it, the books I write for children are really an extension of my singing voice."

The comeback:
Andrews describes herself as an extremely private person, and so for several years after her surgery she quietly focused on recovering from the trauma of the surgery and its aftermath. To friends, she admitted that it was unlikely that her voice would return to its previous level, but she was confident that "a certain part of it" would return with time. Even so, with the loss of her "stock-in-trade," she found herself asking, "Who am I? What do I do?" She kept busy with a string of nonmusical roles in plays and films and tried not to dwell on the fact that her singing voice was not improving. She kept a stiff upper lip and refused to brood about her condition in public; she recognized that she had enjoyed a remarkable career and that she still had much to offer to her audience. She also realized that she could develop a new audience and even venture into new areas of creativity with her writing—something she'd always hoped to do more of but had never had the time to pursue.

AMILYA ANTONETTI (B. 1967)
American Entrepreneur and Author

At the bottom:

1993—Just an ordinary suburban mother from San Leandro, California, Amilya Antonetti couldn't figure out why her new baby boy, David, was suffering so terribly. He cried constantly, keeping his parents awake at all hours of the night. His breathing was often short and marked by a dry, hacking cough; he developed horrible skin problems, with bumpy rashes covering his body. At times when she changed his diaper the skin on his legs and bottom would simply peel away in sheets. David's eyes seemed glassy, and he had a chronic runny nose. A variety of doctors and specialists were baffled by the baby's condition. They took X-rays, drew blood, checked him for allergies—and yet they were unable to explain what might be wrong. Some chalked it up to colic; others suggested she was overreacting. Meanwhile, Antonetti's heart was breaking. "The euphoria of David's arrival was replaced with a tidal wave of fear," she wrote in 2003. "All I knew was that my son, the most precious gift I had ever received, was in agony, and nothing I did seemed to ease his suffering."

At the top:

2003—Amilya Antonetti looked at her company books for the previous year and was astonished to see that Soapworks, the company she'd founded in 1995, had more than $10 million in sales. Dubbed "the better choice mom" by Oprah Winfrey, Antonetti had just finished her first book, *Why David Hated Tuesdays*, a guide for parents looking to make their homes less toxic and safer. Soapworks had grown out of Antonetti's discovery that ordinary household chemicals were making her son sick; each year, the company's sales had doubled as Antonetti and her growing stable of employees (she had more than fifty by 2003) developed new products. Her bar soaps, laundry soaps, body washes, non-chlorine bleaches, and all-purpose cleaners were sold at stores like Trader Joe's, Linens 'n Things, and Hudson Bay Companies. Her success had been covered on Winfrey's show as well as on *The Early Show* on CBS, and she was a much-sought speaker for business conventions and parenting groups. And most importantly, her son David had lived the past seven years without discomfort.

The comeback:

For two years, Antonetti watched as her son's condition remained unchanged. She listened to his doctors and hoped he would somehow improve. At last, she'd had enough and took matters into her own hands. She began to keep a detailed journal of her son's life, trying to discover some sort of pattern or trigger that might explain his condition. Soon, she noticed that her son was always worse on the days of the week that she cleaned the house. For the first time in her life, she read the labels on her cleaning products and began to research some of the chemicals they contained. In the course of her reading, she found cases of other children who experienced adverse reactions to common household cleaning supplies. Immediately, she stopped cleaning the house. Dishes piled up and the laundry stayed dirty, but for the first time in his life, David was sleeping peacefully through the night and was noticeably less ill.

Unable to find soaps or cleaning products that were free of the chemicals that seemed to provoke her son, Amilya Antonetti began experimenting in her own kitchen sink. She collected soap recipes from the nineteenth century and, before long, had developed a line of homemade products—hand, dish, and laundry soaps—that did not make her son sick. She began to meet other mothers facing similar problems, and she realized the products she was making might have a wider application. And so, in November of 1995, Antonetti launched Soapworks, a small company that produced nontoxic soaps.

When grocery stores elected not to stock her products, she took out ads in local newspapers and sold directly to mothers who were concerned about their kids' allergies. When an advertising executive at a local radio station saw Antonetti's newspaper ads, he offered her airtime to promote her products. With a good radio voice, Antonetti was soon offered a guest slot on a weekly talk show, and with two hundred fifty thousand listeners, she quickly found herself swamped with orders. None of this would have happened if Antonetti hadn't taken charge of the situation and realized that *she* was the best expert on her child's well-being. "We are taught to look to 'experts' for our answers," she writes, "only to find out that they often have no real-life experience on the subject. When all is said and done, change begins with you. Strength, willpower, responsibility, commitment and integrity grow from within and blossom only under your direction."

CORAZON AQUINO (1933–2009)
Filipino Politician

At the bottom:

1983—On August 25, a grieving, fifty-year-old woman sat quietly in her Manila home, looking down at the body of her husband, trying to ignore the bullet wound that had disfigured the lower half of his face. Benigno Aquino, a leading opponent of Philippine dictator Ferdinand Marcos, had been living safely in exile with his family for the past three years in Boston, Massachusetts. Just four days earlier he had returned to Manila to plead with the government to restore democratic government before the political situation in the Philippines descended into chaos. Both Aquino and his wife Corazon knew he was a marked man and that it was entirely possible he would not survive the trip.

During the 1970s, the former Philippine senator had been imprisoned for seven years by the Marcos government for his political activities, and he was viewed as a clear threat to the regime. Shortly after Benigno Aquino stepped off his plane, a single assassin shot him in the back of the head, killing him instantly. Once notified, Corazon Aquino and her five children immediately flew from Boston to Manila, where the heartbroken widow became the last of more than one hundred thousand mourners to pay their respects to their fallen hero. Aquino and his wife had suffered through his imprisonment and their joint exile, and now she was a widow: "Just when I was getting used to having him to myself—indeed, just when our youngest, who was a year-old when he was detained, was basking in the special affection he lavished on her to make up for the time he had lost—I lost him again."

At the top:

1986—Two and a half years after her husband's death, Corazon Aquino received word that Ferdinand Marcos—the man who had ordered the assassination—was leaving the country forever. Millions of Filipinos immediately filled the streets in cities and towns across the nation, celebrating the end of Marcos' twenty-year dictatorship and cheering the new, undisputed president of the Republic of the Philippines: Corazon Aquino. The previous day, she had been inaugurated by two justices from the nation's

Supreme Court in a quiet ceremony in Quezon City, while Marcos himself stubbornly clung to power. According to the vote count maintained by an independent election-monitoring organization, Aquino had defeated President Marcos in a razor-thin election marked by extraordinary degrees of fraud and voter intimidation from the dictator's supporters. After three weeks of intense public and international pressure, Aquino prevailed, and the democracy her husband had always dreamed of at last came into being.

Over the next six years, Aquino transformed her country for the better. She oversaw the drafting of a new constitution, returned power to local governments, established a land reform policy that allowed poor farmers to acquire property, and instituted other reforms that moved the nation away from its unpleasant past. For her efforts, she received numerous human rights and humanitarian awards and honors, including a nomination for the 1986 Nobel Peace Prize. When former President Aquino died of cancer in 2009, Philippine president Gloria Macapagal-Arroyo remembered her as a "national treasure."

The comeback:
Before her husband's assassination, no one could have imagined Corazon Aquino as a national leader. She always described herself as "just a housewife," and though she supported her husband's political career, she devoted most of her time to raising their five children and did not play a prominent role in Philippine politics. During campaign events, she remained off stage and listened to her husband's speeches rather than appearing directly at his side. Though she eventually made a few political speeches on her husband's behalf while he was in prison, she was happy to learn that one of her daughters—who was six years old at the time—was willing to speak instead.

Nevertheless, when her husband died, Aquino realized that she needed to carry on his work with the same fearlessness he had shown. She participated in pro-democracy demonstrations during the next two years, and although she was reluctant to seek political office, she agreed to run for the presidency when opponents of the Marcos government explained to her that she was the only person who could unite the opposition. Unlike most political leaders, Corazon Aquino did not seek power but found it thrust upon her. She was determined to carry on her husband's memory and to restore the democracy for which he had given his life.

MARY KAY ASH (1918–2001)
American Entrepreneur

At the bottom:

1963—Mary Kay Ash had spent more than two decades building a career in a business dominated by men. She was a tough woman, having endured a heartbreaking divorce after World War II, when her husband returned from the war and left her with three young children to raise. After the divorce, she entered the world of sales and became quite good at it—so good that she was eventually hired as a trainer. For the previous ten years, she had been working as a training director for a Dallas-based company and had grown increasingly frustrated by the treatment she received from her bosses. For years, she watched as new male employees—men she'd trained herself—vaulted over her in the company hierarchy, where they were offered salaries that were nearly twice what she earned. "What really angered me," she wrote later, "was when I was told that these men earned more because they had families to support. I had a family to support, too."

Even worse than the lack of equal pay was the lack of respect she received for her ideas. On numerous occasions, Ash presented new marketing plans that were dismissed with the explanation that she was "thinking just like a woman." When she was passed over once again for a promotion in favor of a man she'd trained, Mary Kay Ash could no longer stifle her frustration. She resigned. She didn't know how she'd earn a living, but she was determined not to give her best effort for a company that didn't value it.

At the top:

1987—By the time Mary Kay Ash retired from the cosmetics company she'd founded in 1963, she had become one of the great entrepreneurs in American history. Her company, Mary Kay Cosmetics, had grown into a business that sold more than $400 million worth of wholesale beauty products annually and had more than two hundred thousand sales consultants who marketed the company's cosmetics to customers in the United States, Canada, Australia, Germany, and a handful of other countries. By 2008, Mary Kay had expanded to more than fifty nations, with annual sales worldwide of roughly $2.6 billion. Ash herself was a respected entrepreneur who earned numerous honors in her lifetime, including the Horatio

Alger Award as well as an induction to the U.S. Business Hall of Fame. Her charitable foundation raised money to support women suffering from domestic violence as well as to provide support for cancer research.

The comeback:

Though Mary Kay Ash was bitter about the treatment she'd received as a corporate employee, she knew she'd get nowhere if she dwelled on the negative. To turn her attitude around, she sat down and made a list of all the good things that had taken place over the twenty-five years she'd been working in business. As she wrote in one of her numerous books, "Forcing myself to think positively did wonders for my spirit." She composed the list partly as a therapeutic exercise, but also because she had a notion of writing a book for women in the business world. When she finished, she wondered if she might not just go ahead and launch a business of her own.

Using the five thousand dollars she'd managed to save over the years, she financed the purchase of a skin-care products company and opened a store of her own in Dallas. "I was middle-aged, had varicose veins, and had no time to fool around," she wrote later in her life. She quickly recruited more than three hundred "sales consultants" and developed a business that utilized all the lessons she'd learned from her early experiences. She insisted that her employees work hard and set high standards for success, but she also believed that people were motivated to succeed when their accomplishments and ideas were recognized and valued. She tried to treat her employees as she wished she had been treated by her former employer.

DOUGLAS BADER (1910–1982)
English Pilot

At the bottom:

1931—Douglas Bader, pilot in the Royal Air Force, lay in a hospital bed, his face pale and covered in a mist of sweat. The morphine only barely numbed the pain as his eyes darted around the room. He drifted in and out of consciousness as members of his family drifted in and out of the room. Before long, he felt a strange but pleasant sense of relaxation, telling himself, "I've only got to shut my eyes now and lean back and everything's all right." Bader had lost both of his legs—they had been crushed in an accident that took place as Bader was performing aerial stunts for friends—and he was in fact dying. His promising career as a pilot for the RAF was over, and it seemed as though his life would soon follow. When he learned of a fellow pilot who'd died in an accident, Bader grumbled that his friend was the fortunate one. "I'd rather be killed outright," he said, "than left like this."

At the top:

1945—The skies over London were filled with planes, as more than two dozen air squadrons skimmed at a low altitude over the city. The sound of the motors was astonishing to witnesses, who watched the latest Spitfires, Typhoons, Mustangs, and Tempests flying together in tight formation just above the city skyline. Leading the fly-past was Douglas Bader, the legless pilot who—having been allowed to return to the RAF when the force suffered from a lack of experienced pilots—had scored more than twenty kills during World War II before he was shot down and captured behind German lines.

His skill and heroism during the war had earned him the respect of his nation and had turned him into one of the great aerial legends of the twentieth century. He had served as commander of several squadrons and downed eleven planes during the crucial Battle of Britain. His exploits as a prisoner of war had only added to his legendary status—he caused so much trouble for his German captors that they eventually threatened to take away his prosthetic legs. When U.S. forces liberated his prison in April of 1945, Bader immediately asked for a Spitfire so he could rejoin the fight. In subsequent years, Bader's story was retold numerous times in books and depicted in film. He worked with fellow amputees for the rest of his life and was eventually honored with knighthood in 1976. He had married for the first time in 1935, 4 years after losing his legs. After 37 years of marriage, his first wife died, and he remarried.

The comeback:

It would be an understatement to describe Douglas Bader as "tenacious." Not only did he recover from an accident from which most men would not have survived, but he also returned to the cockpit, despite warnings from doctors and his own superior officers that he would never be able to fly again. Quietly dismissed by the RAF in 1932, Bader vowed that he would fly again, even if no one else seemed to share his optimism. He was determined not to wait out the rest of his years behind a desk. Putting himself through an accelerated program of physical therapy, Bader constantly challenged himself in ways that no one else would. He clawed his way back, rejoining the RAF in 1939 after the war broke out and at last fulfilling the vow he'd made after losing his legs nearly ten years before. Bader proved a lot of people wrong along the way, but he never doubted himself and refused to let his injury keep him from the skies.

JEAN-DOMINIQUE BAUBY (1952–1997)
French Editor and Author

At the bottom:

1996—Until a massive stroke destroyed his brain stem in late 1995, French journalist Jean-Dominique Bauby was known as a brilliant, witty writer and great lover of life. Since 1991, he had served as editor-in-chief of the magazine *Elle*, the largest fashion magazine in the world; he was only forty-four and yet was one of the most important voices in French culture. On December 8, 1995, Bauby finished a day of work at his office and hopped in his car to meet his son for dinner. On the way, he was overcome with exhaustion and began seeing double. He felt as though he'd been drugged. After pulling his car over at an intersection, he collapsed and slipped into a deep coma.

When he regained full consciousness in late January, he was in a naval hospital at Breck-sur-Mer on the coast of the French Channel. Immediately, he realized that he was immobile. The stroke had left him with a terrifying condition known as "locked-in syndrome," which meant that, while he could not move and could not breathe without a respirator, he was fully conscious of his condition. He could hear, smell, and feel; the only muscle in his body that he could control was his left eyelid. Bauby felt as though he were trapped in "a giant invisible diving bell [that] holds my body hostage."

At the top:

1997—Jean-Dominique Bauby's memoir, *The Diving Bell and the Butterfly*, was published a little over a year after he'd emerged from his coma. "Dictated" using his only working muscle—his left eyelid—the book was a remarkable achievement and its initial press run of twenty-five thousand copies sold out in a single day. Released to overwhelmingly positive reviews, the book describes his condition with what one reviewer described as a "sweet, even humorous, lyricism." In it, Bauby reflects on his life and the people he loves—his children, father, girlfriend—and he reveals a spirit that refused to die, even as his own body escaped his control. If his body had somehow been submerged in a "diving bell," his mind could take flight, he explained, "like a butterfly." With his imagination intact, "There is so much to do. You can wander off in space or in time, set out for Tierra del Fuego or for King Midas' court. You can visit the woman you love, slide down beside her and stroke her still-sleeping face. You can build castles in Spain, steal the Golden Fleece, discover Atlantis, realize your childhood dreams and adult ambitions." He gazed at the beach and ocean and imagined that he was directing famous French films. Though he was fed through a tube, he dreamed of cooking elaborate meals and in the book describes the enormous banquets he would host as he lay in his bed. Though Bauby himself died only two days after the book's release, his story touched readers across the world. In 1998, *The Diving Bell and the Butterfly* was turned into a critically acclaimed film.

The comeback:

As one review of Bauby's memoir explained, his condition redefined the word "unbearable." Most people could not imagine how someone in Bauby's condition could muster the will to live, much less communicate their story with such grace. However, Bauby's speech therapist developed a novel way to allow him to reach out beyond the "diving bell." She arranged the alphabet into a sequence based on the frequency of each letter's use in the French language. She—and later on, a writer named Claude Mendibil—would recite the list of letters slowly until reaching the letter Bauby wanted, at which point he would blink once. Through this painstaking process, Bauby was able to communicate with those around him.

Over the course of two months, he dictated a 130-page manuscript to Mendebil, blinking more than two hundred thousand times along the way. Bauby plotted out the entire book—from word to sentence to paragraph—in his mind the night before each session of dictation. Though he knew the prospects for recovery were slim, Bauby produced a book that reflects the overwhelming optimism he maintained while writing it—that he might someday wiggle his toes or swallow food on his own. With the help of patient and dedicated caregivers, Bauby was able to put his dreams and hopes into words that would outlive him.

BILLY BEANE (B. 1962)
American Baseball Executive

At the bottom:

1990—When the 1989 regular season ended, Billy Beane had been one of the least productive players on the best team in baseball. His Oakland Athletics would go on to win the World Series that year, but Beane had to watch it all on television, since he was left off the post-season roster. A decade before, Beane was among the top young prospects in the nation. He had a remarkable throwing arm, great speed, and an overall athleticism that made him a multi-sport star at his San Diego high school. The quarterback of the football team and the high scorer on the basketball team, Beane was a standout pitcher who could knock the stuffing out of a baseball.

Everything came easy to Billy Beane, and major league scouts pegged him as one of the top picks in the 1980 draft. Selected by the New York Mets in the first round, Beane fizzled as a major leaguer. After several seasons in the minor leagues, he bounced around between four teams from 1984 to 1989, batting a meager .219 in only 148 games—not even a full season's worth of work over the course of six years. By the spring of 1990, it was clear that Billy Beane was finished as a major league player—just another fading prospect who never lived up to his potential on the field.

At the top:

2002—Few baseball experts expected the Oakland Athletics to hold on to their American League Western Division title in 2002. Billy Beane had just watched his biggest star—slugger Jason Giambi—leave the team as a free agent and sign with the deep pocketed New York Yankees, whose overall payroll was more than double that of the Athletics. Beane's club had been a pleasant surprise in 2001, winning the division and nearly defeating the Yankees in the first round of the playoffs. But with less cash to sign the best players, the Athletics seemed unlikely to duplicate their quirky success from the year before. By early September, however, the team was on fire, winning twenty consecutive games, a league record, and on their way to a season in which they tied the Yankees for the most regular season wins. Although Billy Beane's Athletics lost to the Minnesota Twins in the playoffs that year, his reputation as a successful general manager, who could win without a huge payroll, was secure. He and his team's success were the subject of the best-selling book, *Moneyball: The Art of Winning an Unfair Game*, by Michael Lewis.

The comeback:

Truth be told, Billy Beane had never felt comfortable as a baseball player. After high school, he had really wanted to attend Stanford University and sit out the major league draft, but he went through with the draft and, under significant pressure from his parents, eventually signed a contract with the New York Mets. He loved the game, however, and wanted to remain a part of it even after his playing career tailed off. When he finally hung up his cleats, he asked the Oakland Athletics for a job as a scout—a highly unusual career change for a former player, but one that satisfied the analytical side of Beane's personality.

In 1993, he was promoted to assistant general manager, where he and the general manager began developing unusual statistical models to determine which players to draft and which players to sign on the free agent market. With a smaller payroll than teams like the New York Yankees or the Boston Red Sox, the Oakland Athletics could not afford to sign the big-name stars. Instead, they used their scientific principles to locate players who were "undervalued" and could be signed to smaller, more affordable contracts.

When Beane was appointed to the position of general manager in 1998, his methods brought the team in a positive direction. Beginning in 1999, the team began posting winning records, and in 2000 the Athletics made the playoffs for the first time since 1992, and they did it with one of the smallest payrolls in the entire league. The success that had eluded Beane as a player was now in his grasp as a general manager. Although he never truly enjoyed being a player, he realized that he could be useful in—and that he could be excited by—other aspects of a game he still loved. As a player, he had been trying to fulfill the expectations of others; as a general manager, he was pursuing goals on his own terms. And by rejecting the conventional wisdom that insists that championships can only be won with big-name talent, Beane discovered a different way to find value in players, and in himself.

TONY BENNETT (B. 1926)
American Singer

At the bottom:

1979—Tony Bennett's career was in a shambles. Throughout the 1950s and '60s, he had been one of the most popular recording artists in the United States, with a string of jazz hits that sold millions of records and kept him at the top of the charts. With the rise of rock and roll, however, Bennett's musical style seemed less relevant by the early 1970s, and his career began to falter. To his horror, Bennett's record label had asked him to record versions of contemporary pop songs as a way of connecting with younger listeners. The idea literally made Bennett sick to his stomach—he was so disgusted with himself for agreeing to the project that he threw up before recording it. (Not surprisingly, the album bombed.)

By the end of the decade, he had lost his record label, he and his manager had parted ways, and seemingly no one outside Las Vegas was interested in paying to see him perform on stage. Even worse, he had acquired an accelerating drug habit, which neither his wallet nor his body could tolerate—and had squandered his marriage. Buried under a mountain of debt and facing an IRS investigation, Tony Bennett hit rock bottom in 1979 when he nearly overdosed on cocaine while soaking in a bathtub.

At the top:

2006—At the age of eighty, Tony Bennett was on top of the world again. His album, *Duets*—which consisted of songs he performed with artists like Barbara Streisand, Sting, the Dixie Chicks, and Elton John among others—had been released to great critical acclaim and popular appeal, winning two Grammy Awards, including Best Traditional Pop Vocal Album (an award he had accepted four times in the previous five years.) Altogether, Bennett has received to date a total of thirteen Grammys since his comeback, along with two Emmy Awards for live televised concerts in 1996 and 2007. His album sales have topped fifty million worldwide, and he has been rewarded with an endless list of honors, including induction into the Big Band and Jazz Hall of Fame; a Grammy Lifetime Achievement Award; and a lifetime award from the American Society of Composers, Authors, and Publishers. Reflecting on his astounding later-life success, Bennett wrote, "I felt like I had been to the moon and back."

The comeback:

In his time of need, Tony Bennett came to rely on those closest to him for support. As Bennett described in his autobiography, his near-lethal overdose "jolted" him out of the haze into which his life had sunk. As he was being rushed to the hospital, he realized that he was throwing away everything. "I knew I had to make major changes in my life," he wrote. He called up his son Danny—also a musician—and explained that he had lost his way and needed some help desperately.

Bennett's son helped him take control over the areas of his life that had gone off track. Indeed, Danny became his father's manager, putting Bennett on a tight budget and moving him from Las Vegas back to New York City. He put his father in a one-bedroom Manhattan apartment and began booking shows at small theaters and colleges. Together, Bennett and his son began reinventing his career with a deliberate effort to appeal to younger audiences. His 1986 comeback album, *The Art of Excellence*, was a surprise hit and put Bennett back on the charts for the first time in fourteen years. Subsequent albums achieved gold status and won him his first Grammy since 1962. He appeared on *The Simpsons* and on MTV, recording an unlikely episode of *Unplugged*—a program in which artists perform without electric instruments—that eventually won Bennett a Grammy Award in 1994.

Bennett rediscovered success not by completely molding himself to the tastes of a new audience; instead, Bennett found ways to make the music of *his* generation appealing to younger listeners. As he explained, "What meant the most to me was that I had accomplished all of this without compromising my music."

ROBERT "ROCKY" BLEIER (B. 1946)
American Football Player

At the bottom:

1969—The bullet tore through Rocky Bleier's left thigh, and he collapsed in a heap just before a grenade blast ripped into him. Writhing in agony in a Vietnamese rice paddy, Bleier could barely comprehend the damage he'd sustained to the bones, tendons, and muscles of his right foot. After he was rescued and evacuated to Thailand, the doctors who treated him were unsure if he'd ever be able to walk normally. One thing was certain: The rookie running back for the Pittsburgh Steelers was finished as a professional football player.

He'd been drafted with less than two months to go in his first season in the American Football League, and though he would only rush for 39 yards on 6 carries that year, Bleier expected to play a bigger role on the team the next year. During his college years at Notre Dame, he had been a team leader and helped lead the Fighting Irish to a National Championship in 1966. Along the way, the gritty son of a Wisconsin tavern owner had come back from knee surgery to serve as captain during his senior season. Now, however, his playing days were over—there would be no coming back from this.

At the top:

1979—With seconds remaining in the Super Bowl, Rocky Bleier lunged at the bouncing ball and clutched it tightly in his arms as he dropped to the ground. By recovering the kickoff, Bleier assured that the Pittsburgh Steelers would win the game, 35–31 over the Dallas Cowboys. It was the third time in five years that Bleier and the Steelers had won the championship, and the sturdy fullback had played an important role in each victory, either blocking for the team's star running back Franco Harris or by rushing for yards himself. In the 1979 Super Bowl, Bleier caught the touchdown pass that gave his team a lead it would never relinquish. Over the course of his career with the Steelers, Bleier would earn four Super Bowl rings while rushing for nearly 4000 yards and scoring 23 touchdowns. A favorite among Steelers fans, Bleier was also highly respected by his teammates, who knew him as the sort of player who never sought the limelight but always did whatever his team needed to win. When he retired in 1980, he was the fourth-leading rusher in team history.

The comeback:

"I'm a breathing example of what you can do if you want to," Bleier told a writer in 1986. He had been written off many times before his war injuries. At 5 feet 9 inches tall and 210 pounds, he was thought by many pro scouts to be too small and too slow to play at Notre Dame, much less in the NFL. But what Bleier lacked in size he made up for with hard work and stubborn determination. "I didn't want to face the truth," Bleier wrote in his autobiography. "I have a certain self-discipline, an ability to persuade myself that reality is not what it seems." Somehow, Bleier persuaded himself that a shattered and shredded foot did not mean the end of his football career.

Less than a year after his injury, Bleier arrived at the Steelers' training camp, thirty pounds lighter and still recovering from the surgeries that had reconstructed his foot. Though walking and running caused him severe pain, he nearly made the team in 1970. The following year, Bleier was back and made the Steelers' practice squad. By 1972, he earned a spot on the roster, and two years later had become the starting fullback for a team that would dominate the league during the second half of the decade.

MARY J. BLIGE (B. 1971)

American Singer

At the bottom:

1995—By the usual measures, Mary J. Blige had already proven herself to be a rags-to-riches success. A high school dropout, Blige had grown up in New York during the 1970s and early 1980s, an era when there were few worse places to be black and poor. Economic opportunities were minimal and the city's infrastructure was crumbling. Drugs and alcohol blighted neighborhoods like Blige's, where the violence of everyday life trickled down to the smallest and weakest in the community. She suffered physical abuse from her father, who abandoned the family when she was four, and a family friend later molested Blige.

Her childhood was miserable, yet she managed to escape her upbringing through the power of her voice. In 1988, a record company executive heard a recording Blige had made at a White Plains shopping mall karaoke machine. The next year, she became the youngest artist and the first woman to sign with Uptown Records. It took several years for her career to take off, but when it did she became one of the most popular artists of the early 1990s. Her debut album, *What's the 411*, sold three million copies in the second half of 1992 alone.

Her second album, *My Life*, made an equally strong showing in 1994, but by then Blige's actual life was heading off the rails. She was drinking heavily, smoking tremendous amounts of marijuana, and snorting cocaine as often as she could get it—which, given the amount of money she was earning, was as often as she wanted it. It seemed as if she were trying to derail her young career. She missed interviews, canceled concerts, blew her money, and soon gained a reputation as someone who was difficult to work with. Recording industry insiders soon began to predict that her star would fade. "She won't last," they said. "She'll self destruct." Blige, however, didn't seem to care.

At the top:

2007—With her Grammy Awards for Best R&B Performer, Best R&B Song, and Best R&B Album, Mary Blige completed a sweep of all the major music awards—the American Music Awards, the Billboard Music Awards, and the Grammy Awards. Her album, titled *The Breakthrough*, captured Blige at the peak of her career. It was her seventh multi-platinum album (she now has eight), with more than seven million copies sold throughout the world. The album earned her a raft of awards and remained in the top spot of the Billboard R&B chart for nearly four consecutive months. Her previous album had not sold as well as earlier efforts, but *The Breakthrough* indicated that Blige wasn't finished. "I could have accepted all the talk of 'Oh, she's finished, she's washed up, she's 35.'" But when I did [this album] I went into it like, 'Uh, uh, I ain't finished yet.' My people are not finished with me and I could feel it in my heart."

The comeback:
In the midst of her self-destructive spiral, Blige caught a glimpse one day of a picture of herself that wasn't at all flattering. "I said to myself, 'Gosh, I look bad,'" she explained to a reporter several years later. When she began to evaluate her behavior, she realized that she was no longer a kid and needed to take responsibility for her own actions, starting with the seemingly little things. By appearing for interviews on time, for example, she demonstrated that she cared about her relationship, with reporters, who were an important link between herself and her fans.

She also realized that she needed to surround herself with people who were genuinely concerned about her as a person, not just as a source of profit for the record company. To that end, she hired her sister as her business manager, a decision that put her career in the care of someone who loved her but was willing to let her know when she was making bad decisions in her life. By the time her third album was released in 1997, Blige had quit using drugs, experienced a religious awakening, and begun a new relationship with a man she would later marry. That album was the creation of someone who had brought her personal life back from the brink of disaster.

MICHAEL BLOOMBERG (B. 1942)
American Entrepreneur and Politician

At the bottom:

1981—Michael Bloomberg had given fifteen years of his young life to Salomon Brothers, the only employer he had ever really had after finishing his MBA at Harvard. He had enjoyed a meteoric career with the financial services company, making partner at the age of thirty-one after proving himself to be one of the best equity block traders in the company. But in 1979, Salomon Brothers suddenly moved him from the trading floor—where all the action was—to systems development, where he found himself tucked away behind the scenes with computer nerds. He wondered why anyone would put him in charge of the office computers, since he knew absolutely nothing about them. But Bloomberg knew the answer to that question—he was being nudged into oblivion. Sure enough, when Salomon was acquired by Philbro two years later, Bloomberg was squeezed out of his job along with six other partners who were cut loose. He received $10 million for his partnership interest from the company as he was shown the door, but he was unwanted and out of work nevertheless, having crash-landed in the midst of a huge recession that only added more fog to the road ahead.

At the top:

2010—With a net worth of more than $18 billion, Michael Bloomberg ranked as the eighth wealthiest American and was the richest and most powerful person in New York City, where he has served as mayor since his election in 2001. His company, Bloomberg L.P., had become not merely a dominant presence on Wall Street—having developed computer information systems for trading firms—but had also become a major news provider, with a wire service as well as cable television and news radio channels devoted to coverage of the marketplace. The company also owns a popular market news Web site as well as a variety of other multimedia information platforms that have a global reach. Bloomberg himself owns 88% of the company, so he bears most of the risks and rewards for each of his ventures. He also has emerged as one of the most generous philanthropists of his generation. Over the years, Bloomberg has given more than $300 million to Johns Hopkins University (his alma mater) and routinely gives away $150–$200 million a year to a variety of foundations and causes, including efforts to control tobacco consumption in developing countries. As a three-term mayor, Bloomberg has generally had high approval ratings, and New York has been ranked as one of America's safest major cities, as well as one of the most economically vibrant.

The comeback:
It goes without saying that $10 million is a lot of money. With his partner's share from the sale of Salomon Brothers, Michael Bloomberg could have sat back and eased into a life of comfort, far from the hectic pace of Wall Street. Instead, he went out and bought his wife a sable coat, telling her that "Job or no job, we are still players." The next morning, he sat down at seven o'clock and began drawing up plans for a new business venture. Years later, Bloomberg explained that "nobody offered me a job and I was too pig-headed to go look for one, so starting a business was a relatively simple idea."

Though he had known nothing about computers when he was shoved into the systems department at Salomon, he drew on his experiences there to imagine a new computer system for traders, one that would provide real-time data about the market and provide information about publicly traded securities, particularly bonds, in a way that allowed brokers to compare them. With some former colleagues from Salomon Brothers, Bloomberg put together a team and began working on a project to build just such a machine. He approached Merrill Lynch and offered them the opportunity to invest in the project and become its first customer. When Merrill Lynch purchased 30 percent of his new company, Bloomberg had more than enough capital to get up and running. Within six months, the new trading computer system was complete, and orders for "The Bloomberg" began pouring in.

JOHN BOGLE (B. 1929)
American Mutual Fund Manager

At the bottom:

1974—For the first time in his career, John Bogle felt the sting of failure. He was heartbroken, and his career was in a shambles. At the age of forty-four, the former executive vice president was unemployed. Bogle had spent more than two decades ascending the ranks of Wellington Management Company, which managed some of the most successful and respected investment funds in the country. At the tail end of a long bull market, Bogle had developed a new high performance fund and orchestrated a merger between Wellington and a Boston-based investment firm whose managers had enjoyed great success in the flourishing market of the early 1960s.

Unfortunately, the merger worked out badly for everyone, especially Bogle. The stock market soured in the early 1970s, and the funds under Bogle's control lost millions for their investors. Meantime, the company's stock lost 80 percent of its value. In the midst of an emerging bear market, Bogle did not get along with the Boston group, and he rammed heads with other executives at Wellington, who blamed the company's ills on Bogle's merger. When the Wellington board asked for his resignation, he stubbornly refused, daring them to fire him. They did just that, turning him out on January 23, 1974.

At the top:

2004—Thirty years after the Wellington catastrophe, John Bogle could look back with satisfaction on his accomplishments. By now one of the most successful mutual fund managers in the world, Bogle was acknowledged as one of the world's "Most Powerful and Influential People" by *Time* magazine. That same year, *Institutional Investor* gave Bogle a Lifetime Achievement Award, a recognition he earned for developing the Vanguard Group, an immensely successful investment management company that he'd started in the wake of his firing. The author of seven books on investing and mutual funds, Bogle has attracted a popular following among investors who—trusting his approach to money management—loyally refer to themselves as "Bogleheads." His most important and lasting contribution has been the creation of "index funds," mutual funds that try to match the rise and fall of market indexes like the Dow or the S&P 500. Prior to Bogle, few people in the financial services industry believed investors would settle for "average" returns, but Bogle recognized that most mutual funds charge high fees and yet don't beat the market averages with any consistency, and he suspected, correctly, that many ordinary Americans would appreciate the simplicity and low cost of index funds.

The comeback:
John Bogle's comeback began within hours of his firing in 1974. As he told *Investor's Business Daily* in the summer of 2009, "Probably my most dominating characteristic is determination." Unwilling to accept defeat, Bogle hopped a train to New York and convinced the directors of two Wellington funds to give him independent control of its assets. From these humble origins, Vanguard eventually controlled nearly a trillion dollars in assets held by nearly twenty million investors. Its funds were consistently rated among the best in the United States. Learning from his previous failures, Bogle's unique approach allowed Vanguard to offer extremely low fees. Over time, passively managed index funds have grown enormously in popularity, and research has shown that, over the long term, they usually outperform actively managed funds.

SUSAN BOYLE (B. 1961)
Scottish Singer

At the bottom:

2007—When her mother died at the age of ninety-one, forty-six-year-old Susan Boyle from Blackburn, Scotland, fell into a deep depression and secluded herself in her home for days at a time. She had been caring for her mother since her father passed away in the early 1990s, and now she was alone in the world for the first time in her life. Her eight siblings had all moved away, and the eccentric Boyle was now supposed to fend for herself despite having a minimal education, almost no work experience, and a personality that could best be described as kind but odd.

Singled out as a child for being "slow"—she did in fact suffer from learning disabilities and never performed well in school—the young Boyle had been called "Susie Simple," a nickname that followed her into her adult life. She did not have many friends, but she did attend church and sang in the choir, something her mother had introduced her to when Susan was a girl. Boyle's mother had indeed been her greatest musical fan and believed her daughter had an exceptional voice. Now, however, with her mother's passing, Boyle didn't have the same enthusiasm as before. For the next two years, she barely sang a note.

At the top:

2009—By the time Susan Boyle had finished singing "I Dreamed a Dream," one of the best-known songs from *Les Miserables*, the studio audience for the television show *Britain's Got Talent* had erupted into a prolonged, deafening roar. The show, which features ordinary Britons performing before a live audience and a panel of judges, usually included a performance or two that was so horrid as to be unwatchable; the audience that evening clearly had expected Boyle to be one of those performers. When she stepped out onto the stage, the awkward, plain-looking woman elicited chuckles and rolling eyes as she explained that she hoped to be the next Elaine Page, referring to one of England's best-known musical actresses. When the music began and Boyle started to sing, looks of amusement turned to stunned amazement as she delivered a nearly perfect performance that left at least one of the judges wiping tears from her eyes. Boyle's remarkable performance was broadcast throughout the world on television, and video clips were viewed millions of times on sites like YouTube. A little more than six months later, Boyle's first studio album came out and became the world's biggest selling album of 2009, even though it had been released the last week of November.

The comeback:

Boyle's mother had always encouraged her to audition for a program like *Britain's Got Talent*, but Boyle had a hard time imagining herself in a televised talent show. Almost two years after her mother's death, Boyle was still grieving, but the idea of making her mother proud gave her the incentive she needed to audition. "I realized I wanted to make my mum proud of me," she explained, "and the only way to do that was to take the risk and enter the show." In the weeks prior to the audition, Boyle practiced in her bedroom—the same one she'd grown up in—by holding a hairbrush in front of the mirror.

After several weeks of practice, the day of her performance arrived. She knew she didn't look like an aspiring star, but that didn't matter to Boyle. "I expected people to be a wee bit cynical," she says. "But I decided to win them round. That is what you do. They didn't know what to expect. Before *Britain's Got Talent*, I had never had a proper chance. It's as simple as that. You just have to keep going and take one step at a time and one day you will make it. You just don't give up."

RICHARD BRANSON (B. 1950)
English Entrepreneur

At the bottom:

1971—Richard Branson, an ambitious, twenty-one-year-old entrepreneur, sat in a London jail cell, humiliated and filled with remorse. Branson, founder and publisher of a student magazine known simply as *Student*, had recently decided to branch out into music sales when he realized that he could undercut record stores by offering discounted music through the mail. Calling the business Virgin Mail Order Records, Branson and his business partner, Nik Powell, were soon overwhelmed with orders. Before long, the pair opened a shop of their own, and Branson even began looking for a house to convert into a music studio.

In spite of his apparent success, however, Branson was losing money and found himself in debt. At this point, he hatched an ill-advised—and illegal—scheme to sell records that he told authorities were being shipped to Belgium. Because the records were supposedly for export, he did not have to pay the sales tax; when he sold them to English customers, he was thus able to increase his profit margin by a sizable amount. After Branson had sold several large batches of records this way, customs officials detected his debt-relief scheme, and he was arrested. He was spared a prison sentence by accepting a large fine, which his parents paid by taking out a second mortgage on their home.

At the top:

2006—Thirty-five years after narrowly avoiding a prison sentence, Richard Branson presided over a bewildering array of business holdings and was almost universally recognized as one of the most adventurous entrepreneurs on the planet. In 2006, *The Sunday Times* estimated that he was the ninth wealthiest person in the world, with an astonishing fortune valued at well over $3 billion. After returning to his record shop in 1971, Branson had worked overtime to repay his debts, using every spare bit of available cash to open one store after another. The music label he created in 1972, Virgin Records, signed some of the most innovative rock performers of the 1970s and '80s (including the Sex Pistols, Warren Zevon, and XTC) and broadened Branson's reach into international markets. From there, Richard Branson's Virgin brand expanded into every imaginable industry; he launched several airlines, a line of soft drinks, a brand of vodka, a publishing house, a bridal goods chain, a cosmetics company, a life insurance company, a rail venture, and a company known as Virgin Galactic that plans to offer space flights to the public. By 2006, more than three hundred separate companies made up Branson's Virgin empire, and he remains ever watchful for the next opportunity.

The comeback:
In his 1993 memoir, Losing My Virginity, Branson explained that "avoiding prison was the most persuasive incentive I've ever had." Determined to pay down his debts and not suffer another humiliation stemming from illegalities, Branson threw himself into his work. Though he continued to take risks, Branson stuck to the legal variety. For Branson, "work" and "fun" have never been separate, and his ability to choose business projects that excite him is one of the reasons his business universe has continued to expand.

A renowned risk-taker, Branson has raced speedboats and taken long-distance hot air balloon journeys, including several that established world records for distance, speed, and balloon size. During an unsuccessful world record attempt across the Atlantic, Branson's balloon crashed, and he nearly drowned before being rescued by the Royal Air Force. His business philosophy has been equally adventurous, though arguably less life threatening. Rejecting the conventional wisdom that business owners should stick to what they know, Branson has always been eager to undertake new projects, no matter how far-fetched. Though Branson failed plenty of times along the way, he has always seen business—and life—as an opportunity to put big, bold ideas into play.

JOSEPH BRODSKY (1940–1996)
Russian Poet

At the bottom:

1964—At the age of twenty-four, a young, barely published poet named Joseph Brodsky learned a brutal lesson about the willingness of the Soviet Union to tolerate artistic independence. Brodsky had not been widely published and, even worse from the perspective of the authorities, he shirked "useful work" in the pursuit of his art. Born into a Jewish family in Leningrad at a time when anti-Semitism was rife throughout Soviet society, Brodsky lived with his poor family in a cramped one-room apartment. Brodsky left school at the age of fifteen and embarked on a decade of completely unsuccessful efforts to find work he enjoyed. He took jobs as a milling machine operator, a morgue attendant, a boilerman on a Soviet ship, and a hospital orderly.

He began writing poems as a teenager and taught himself what he wished to learn. He read widely in philosophy, religion, and poetry, getting books wherever he could find them (including garbage dumpsters). He began publishing poems in *samizdat* journals—underground, typewritten publications that usually expressed ideas not permitted in state-run media. His poetry had just begun to receive some critical attention when the Soviet authorities intervened and charged him with "having a worldview damaging to the state, decadence and modernism, failure to finish school, and social parasitism." At his trial, the judge asked him where he had received permission to become a poet. Brodsky replied that his calling had come "from God." He was convicted of "social parasitism" and sentenced to five years of hard labor.

At the top:

1987—As he accepted the 1987 Nobel Prize for Literature, Joseph Brodsky took a moment to reflect on the writer's need to be alert to dangers posed by government censorship of the arts. With his own ordeal in mind, Brodsky explained to the audience that "as long as the state permits itself to interfere with the affairs of literature, literature has the right to interfere with the affairs of the state." By 1987, Brodsky had not only become one of the great poets of his generation, but he was also a symbol and example of the relationship between artistic expression and political freedom, arguing on many occasions that Western literature in particular had helped the world both recover from and make sense of the horrors of Nazism, Communism, and world war. (Moreover, his best work was written in English, a language he had taught himself during his teenage years.) A professor at Mount Holyoke College in South Hadley, Massachusetts, Brodsky had received some of the most prestigious awards in American letters. In the 1980s alone, he received a MacArthur "Genius" grant, a Guggenheim Fellowship, an honorary doctorate in literature from Oxford, and the National Book Award for a collection of essays titled *Less Than One*.

The comeback:

Brodsky's trial and sentence had received a great deal of international attention from artists and writers, and the trial marked a turning point in the emerging dissident movement within the Soviet Union. International pressure helped lead to Brodsky's early release, but Soviet authorities continued to hound him; as his work received greater attention from literary critics in Western Europe and the United States, the Soviet Union at last expelled him in 1972. With the help of Carl Proffer, a Slavic language specialist at the University of Michigan, Brodsky came to the United States to teach and write.

Though Soviet officials likely assumed he would be less interesting and relevant as an exile from his homeland, Brodsky entered into the most creative period of his life. He published several volumes of poetry as well as several plays and books of essays that earned him a growing array of honors. In spite of his obvious grievance against the Soviet state, Brodsky never relinquished his pride in Russian culture and history. Like many Communist dissidents, Brodsky was able to distinguish between the Russian people and the government that had censored and harassed him. He was also grateful for the opportunities he'd received as an "exile" in the West, and he was (along with his literary allies) able to make the best possible use of the hand he'd been dealt. After receiving word of his Nobel Prize in 1987, he said "I'm the happiest combination you can think of. I'm a Russian poet, an English essayist, and an American citizen!"

CAROL BURNETT (B. 1933)
American Actress

At the bottom:

1954—Carol Burnett was an aspiring actress with big teeth, a gawky figure, and seemingly no opportunities to break into the theatrical world of New York City. She had recently moved there with her boyfriend after their junior year at the University of California at Los Angeles. Though she'd performed in a number of musicals and comedies while at UCLA, Burnett had been a theater major for only a little over a year, and her resumé was awfully thin for someone looking to make a career on stage. When she began approaching agents, they either turned her away or assumed that she would only be able to find work in a chorus here and there. When she expressed an interest in leading roles, they rolled their eyes or stared back in disbelief.

To get by from week to week, Burnett took a job as a hatcheck girl at a restaurant on 49th Street, where she earned enough to pay the rent at the boardinghouse where she lived. Recent family trauma had only added to the challenges Burnett faced that year. Her father, Joseph Burnett, had just died, having abused alcohol over the course of many years before finally drinking himself to death; her mother, also an alcoholic, would succumb three years later. Though Burnett's parents loved her and had never mistreated her, alcohol had always disrupted their lives, and they had never been able to provide a stable home life for her. Burnett had been raised for the most part by her grandmother, who did not approve of Burnett's move to New York and asked her to come home by Christmas if she had not become a star.

At the top:

1978—Carol Burnett smiled, thanked her audience and, for the last time, sang, "I'm So Glad We Had This Time Together," the theme song from one of the most successful television programs of the previous decade. After eleven seasons and dozens of Emmy Award nominations (including three actual awards), *The Carol Burnett Show* was ending its run on CBS. Burnett herself had become one of the most respected comedians of her generation. The show relied on a classic vaudeville format featuring short comic skits and musical numbers, combined with celebrity guest appearances and question-and-answer sessions with her audience. The show allowed Burnett to display her own wide-ranging talents as a singer, actress, and comic—including her famous "Tarzan" yell—but was also a showcase for Burnett's colleagues, Harvey Korman, Tim Conway, and Vicki Lawrence, each of whom became a star in their own right. After *The Carol Burnett Show* ended, it continued to run in syndication and Burnett continued to appear on stage and screen, earning a variety of Emmy and Golden Globe nominations for her work. In 2003, Burnett was a recipient of the Kennedy Center Honors, and in 2005 she was awarded the Presidential Medal of Freedom, with President George W. Bush praising her "goodness of heart, her sincerity, and the wonderful spirit that comes through" in her performances.

The comeback:

Burnett had been caught in a classic dilemma facing many aspiring performers: She could not expect to get work until she had more experience, but she would not gain any experience until she found more work. Instead of waiting around for an opportunity to find her, Burnett created one for herself. With the other young women living at her boarding house, she organized variety shows that soon enough caught the attention of some television agents and producers, who booked her for several brief stints on a children's television show and cast her as Buddy Hackett's girlfriend on a short-lived comedy called *Stanley*. She also began performing at a nightclub called the Blue Angel, where she performed and sang for appreciative audiences.

Finally, in 1959, she caught her big break—a starring role in a Broadway musical, *Once Upon a Mattress*, which earned her glowing reviews from *The New York Times* and *The New Yorker*. When the show closed after almost two years, Burnett moved on to *The Garry Moore Show* and a weekly nationwide audience. When her own weekly show went on the air in September of 1967, few were surprised when it became an immediate hit.

ALBERT CAMUS (1913–1960)
French Philosopher and Novelist

At the bottom:

1930—Albert Camus, a seventeen-year-old French boy, coughed violently and looked down, horrified at the splatter of blood in his hand. He knew what this likely meant: He had tuberculosis, a chronic lung disease for which there was still no effective treatment and which killed tens of thousands of people every year worldwide. His youthful fantasies of a career in soccer were over, and there was a very real chance he would not be well enough to finish his studies at the University of Algiers. Tuberculosis was simply the latest blow in a young life already plagued with difficulties.

Born into a peasant family in Algeria, Camus never knew his father, who died at the Battle of the Marne, which took place in 1914, during the first awful months of The Great War. His mother, an illiterate domestic worker, struggled from then on to keep her two sons fed, clothed, and housed; though Camus loved her dearly, he wrote later of the "coldness" she exhibited toward her children. Now, due to his illness, Camus' future was suddenly more limited, despite having gained admission to university. He would not be able to teach for a living, nor would he be permitted to join the military—two paths that a healthy, intelligent young man might pursue to rise from his poor background. How would young Albert make his way in the world?

At the top:

1957—Albert Camus rose to the podium at Stockholm's City Hall, where he had been summoned to receive the Nobel Prize for Literature, and gave a brief speech. At age 44, He became the second-youngest person, after Rudyard Kipling, to receive the award, and he was the first African-born recipient. A novelist, essayist, and playwright, Camus had become one of his era's most important voices against the "instinct of death" that he believed underlay the rise of fascism and totalitarianism during the first half of the century. During World War II, Camus participated in the French Resistance against Germany's occupation, writing for an underground newspaper; after the fighting ended, he spoke out against the suppression of freedom in the Soviet Bloc countries of Eastern Europe as well as against the arms race that came to dominate the Cold War. As part of his broad focus on human rights after the war, he worked to end the conflict between the French government and Algerians who wanted independence from French colonialism. As a writer, Camus explored the problems of individual freedom and moral responsibility, and novels like *The Stranger* and *The Plague* received enormous critical attention.

The comeback:

Though Camus' tuberculosis would flare up throughout the remainder of his life, he maintained (in the words of one contemporary critic) "a flair for being happy." As the narrator in Camus' last novel *The Fall* declares, "Let's not beat around the bush; I love life — that's my real weakness. I love it so much that I am incapable of imagining what is not life." Though his dreams of being a professional soccer player died with his illness, Camus' spirit did not. He always had an interest in writing, and as a young man he began to experiment with different forms of fiction, non-fiction, and drama.

For Camus, however, writing was not merely a source of pleasure but, as he saw it, a means of changing the world. Because he'd grown up in a poor community in a European colony, Camus was keenly attuned to questions of inequality and freedom, and he viewed art as something that must work in "the service of truth and the service of liberty." By using his artistic talent to focus on some of the most important issues of his generation, Camus transcended his own physical infirmity and achieved rare greatness.

CHESTER CARLSON (1906-1968)
American Inventor

At the bottom:

1930—Chester Carlson's early life was almost too horrible to be believed. The son of a barber, Carlson was born in Seattle but lived an uprooted life as his father moved the family from one new place to another along the west coast, seeking work from Washington to Mexico before eventually landing in San Bernardino. Both of his parents suffered chronic health problems. Both had tuberculosis, while his father was afflicted with spinal arthritis as well. Carlson's mother died of tuberculosis when he was a junior in high school, a loss that he never truly overcame. His mother's death meant that he would have to care for his father full time.

Carlson found a job working at the San Bernardino County poor farm, where he and his father lived in an old chicken coop—a single-room with a concrete floor that reverberated with the constant sound of his father's coughing. Carlson, afraid of catching the disease that had killed his mother, lived outside the coop, in a hut he built from scrap lumber. In high school, he earned good grades in science and fancied himself a future inventor. After high school, he worked his way through three years of junior college before transferring and earning a degree in physics from the California Institute of Technology. Carlson graduated in 1930, just as the Great Depression began to choke the life out of the U.S. economy, timing that worsened his already poor luck. After sending out more than eighty letters to companies around the United States, Carlson landed a job with Bell Labs in New York city for a mere thirty-five dollars a week. After only a few weeks at Bell, Chester received the news that he was being laid off.

At the top:

1965—On May 7, 1965, Chester Carlson was presented with a gold key by the Patent, Trademark and Copyright Institute, which was honoring him as "Inventor of the Year." Carlson had just received word that his thirty-seventh patent had been accepted by the U.S. Patent Office in Washington, D.C. Carlson's most famous invention, electrostatic photocopying, had earned him over $150 million and made Xerox—the company that developed Carlson's ideas—one of the most important names in business.

Before his untimely death of a heart attack in 1968, Carlson anonymously gave away about two-thirds of his earnings (about $700 million in today's dollars) to the NAACP and other civil rights organizations, as well as to the American Civil Liberties Union. In 1981, Carlson was inducted into the National Inventors Hall of Fame.

The comeback:
After being laid off from Bell Labs, Carlson realized he would probably have to look for work outside his field of training and expertise. After a while, he was fortunate to find a job in the patent department at P. R. Mallory, an electronics company best known for producing batteries (Mallory eventually became Duracell). Carlson's job was boring, but it gave him an income and time to think about a problem that he had taken an interest in: how to produce copies of documents without relying on the inefficient and expensive processes currently in use. As a physicist, Carlson had the mindset to solve complex problems, and he'd always wanted to invent something useful. So he set up a lab in his kitchen, to the annoyance of his wife (who eventually left him).

By 1937, he had figured out how to reproduce images by projecting them onto a sulfur-coated zinc plate, which he then sprinkled with fungal spores, enabling the image to be transferred to waxed paper, resulting in a copy. It was a cumbersome process, but it worked. After patenting the process, Carlson shopped the idea to nearly two dozen large corporations—including IBM, Kodak, General Electric, and RCA—all of whom took a pass. Finally, in 1947, Carlson signed an agreement with a small company in Rochester, New York, called Haloid. After improving the process and naming it "xerography," Carlson's invention was introduced to the world as the Xerox copier. By 1959, Haloid had introduced the first automated copier; by 1965, the company had changed its name to Xerox and was raking in more than $500 million a year in revenue.

DALE CARNEGIE (1888–1955)
American Author

At the bottom:

1912—Dale Carnegie not only hated selling cars, but he was broke and living in a run-down apartment. The scores of cockroaches who lived with him were the closest things he had to friends—what's more, they likely ate better than he did. The son of a Missouri farmer who had struggled every day to keep his land, Carnegie was used to the feeling of humiliation. During his first year at Missouri State Teacher's College in 1906, he was certain that all the other students were laughing at him—mocking him for his failures or for his shabby clothes, which fit him badly, or for the fact that he couldn't afford to live in town. Now, six years later, Carnegie couldn't help wondering if he was doomed to a life of failure. He wanted to write for a living, but standing around in the showroom every day, selling Packards, or not selling them, as the case happened to be, left him too exhausted to think, much less compose the Great American Novel.

At the top:

1937—One year after the initial release of his most famous book, *How to Win Friends and Influence People*, Dale Carnegie had sold well over half a million copies and earned a staggering $150,000 in royalties (the equivalent of more than $2 million today). His publisher, Simon and Schuster, had raced through seventeen printings in less than six months, making Carnegie one of the most famous people in the country. Everyone wanted his insights, and leaders from the worlds of business and politics beat down his door for the opportunity to share a few moments with him. Based on the self-improvement course he'd been teaching for the past twenty-five years, Carnegie's book sold more than five million copies in his lifetime and was translated into nearly three dozen languages. The training institute he founded in 1912 had graduated more than 450,000 people who used his principles—his "Drivers of Success"—to improve their leadership, communications, and problem-solving skills.

The comeback:

As he labored away in a career he hated, Carnegie reflected back on the only major success he'd enjoyed in his young life. During college, he had turned himself into an expert debater, which he hoped would win him the respect and friendship of his peers. Though he failed miserably in his first dozen debates, Carnegie continued to practice—rehearsing speeches aloud to his father's cows as he milked them each night—and eventually won school-wide forensic and debating competitions.

Drawing on his collegiate experience, Carnegie set out in 1912 to change his life by coaching others on how to succeed in public speaking. After being turned down by Columbia University and New York University, Carnegie brought his course to the YMCA in Harlem. A few years later, Carnegie's course had become so popular that he was earning thirty dollars a night (the equivalent of $650 today). By reaching back to his past and reacquainting himself with a period of success and satisfaction, Carnegie discovered that he could help himself by helping others.

NIEN CHENG (1915–2009)
Chinese Political Dissident

At the bottom:

1966—In the middle of an August night, Nien Cheng was awakened by more than three dozen Red Guard officers at her home in Shanghai. It was the first year of the Chinese Cultural Revolution, and the Communist regime had just initiated a campaign known as "The Destruction of the Four Olds," which aimed to eradicate old customs, culture, habits, and ideas. In Shanghai, hundreds of "bourgeois" defenders of the old order were being murdered, and hundreds more would take their own lives.

In the midst of all this, Nien Cheng demanded to know why the Red Guard was at her home, and she insisted on seeing their search warrant. The Red Guard brushed her aside, insisting that the constitution—one of the "old" things—was irrelevant and that "only the teachings of our great leader Chairman Mao" would be recognized. After vandalizing her home by smashing furniture, shredding and burning books, and destroying paintings, the Guard arrested her and took her to a prison. For the next six years, she was subjected to solitary confinement, a sparse diet, interrogation, and even torture. All this was because the Chinese government erroneously believed that Cheng—a manager at the Shell Oil Company office in Shanghai—was a British spy.

At the top:

1988—With the Statue of Liberty towering overhead and a giant American flag waving in the late summer breeze, Nien Cheng raised her right arm and took the United States Oath of Citizenship. As she did, her sleeve fell a bit, displaying the scars on her arm caused by the special handcuffs used throughout the Chinese prison system during the worst years of the Cultural Revolution. It had been twenty-two years since her arrest in Shanghai; her memoir, *Life and Death in Shanghai*, had been published to great praise in 1987 and quickly became a best seller. Chang was invited to a White House banquet at which she sat next to President Ronald Reagan. *Time* magazine published extensive excerpts of her book. Stanley Karnow, an American journalist best known for his great history of the Vietnam War, wrote at the time that "her narrative deserves to rank with the foremost prison diaries of our time." From then until her death in November of 2009, Cheng was recognized around the world as a powerful voice for democracy in China and elsewhere.

The comeback:

The Chinese Communists took away so much from Nien Cheng. They robbed her of more than six years of her life. They murdered her daughter, who became one of the hundreds of thousands of people who lost their lives in the Cultural Revolution. Yet Cheng triumphed over her Communist oppressors by turning to her Christian faith and by turning Chairman Mao Zedong's own words against her captors. She reminded her interrogators that Mao's *Little Red Book* advised the Chinese people to fear neither hardship nor death. She refused to be helpless. In spite of the physical brutality she routinely faced, she did not give in, did not admit guilt where none existed, and withstood torture that would have broken people half her age and twice her size.

"I've always been a fighter," she recalled years later. "When I'm confronted with a difficult situation, my first reaction is not to get frightened, it's 'Oh, wonderful, here's a situation that really calls on me to do something.'" At one point during her ordeal, when her captors realized they were not going to extract a confession from her, Cheng was offered the opportunity to leave prison and resume her life. She refused, insisting that she would remain in prison until the government apologized publicly. In the end, the officials who dragged her into prison in the first place were forced to drag her out. After her release, Cheng came to North America, first to Canada in 1983, and then to the United States, where she settled and became a citizen in 1988.

DALE CHIHULY (B. 1941)
American Artist

At the bottom:

1976—On a rainy night in England, a relatively unknown American glass artist named Dale Chihuly flew through the windshield of the car he was driving when it collided head-on with another vehicle. Not wearing a seatbelt, Chihuly was the only person harmed in the accident; he nearly died from blood loss, and lacerations to his face cut deeply into his left eye. When Chihuly regained consciousness, doctors informed him that he would never be able to see properly. Without both eyes, Chihuly's depth perception would be permanently altered, making it difficult for him to produce symmetrical glasswork—and symmetry had been one of the most important aspects of glasswork since the Venetians revitalized the craft of glassblowing seven hundred years ago. Dale Chihuly was fortunate to survive the wreck, but his career faced a steep road ahead.

At the top:

1996—Dale Chihuly arrived in Venice, the birthplace of modern glass-blowing, with fourteen chandeliers. The chandeliers had been produced in collaboration with scores of master glassblowers in Finland, Ireland, and Mexico and consisted of thousands of individual parts. Chihuly and his team placed the finished chandeliers throughout Venice, and the film of the project turned Chihuly into one of the most well-known American artists of the era. His work can now be found in virtually every significant art museum in the United States as well as abroad, and various pieces of his work are owned by patrons such as Queen Elizabeth II, Bill Gates, Elton John, and Bill Clinton among others. His traveling exhibitions draw audiences to museums who might never have visited otherwise, and he is credited with bringing glasswork from the world of crafts into the realm of high art. One journalist has described Chihuly as the general of a "Napoleonic marketing campaign" that has produced a luxury market for glass.

The comeback:

Chihuly returned to his art as quickly as he possibly could after the accident, covering his eye with a black eye patch that would become one of his defining features. Like most patients who suffer from eye injuries, Chihuly's brain compensated for the loss of depth perception, which he was able to partially regain over time. His work was altered by the loss of his eye—but in a way that few would have predicted. Rather than attempt to produce symmetrical glasswork, Chihuly embraced asymmetrical forms and began producing wildly creative new pieces that looked, in the words of one author, "like dinosaur eggs that had hatched and mutated into some organic form that seemed almost alive."

Chihuly's accident allowed him the chance to see the world and his art differently and to imagine new possibilities for his work. In 1978, he earned his big break when the Renwick Gallery—part of the Smithsonian Institution—selected Chihuly for a solo show. Over the next decade, Chihuly developed a reputation as a relentless promoter of his own work, building up his small glassblowing shop into an immensely profitable conglomerate that produces, warehouses, and ships thousands of pieces each year to museums and art collectors around the world. Though additional physical problems forced Chihuly to stop blowing glass in the late 1970s, he hired apprentices to put his vision into form and maintained control over the artistic process, likening himself to a film director or a dance choreographer.

WINSTON CHURCHILL (1874–1965)
English Politician

At the bottom:

1894—Winston Churchill, the twenty-year-old son of a distinguished English family, opened the letter he'd just received from a father he barely knew. In it, Lord Randolph Churchill, 7th Duke of Marlborough, expressed grave disappointment in his eldest child, who had been up to that point a complete "washout." A failure at school in most subjects, Churchill was likewise an inept sportsman, detesting cricket and football with as much energy as he hated math and classical languages. His family offered him little support—he longed for his parents' approval but never received it—and they shook their heads when young Winston flunked his army officer's examination twice before passing with the lowest possible marks. His father was dying, and both he and Winston were sure the young man's life would come to nothing.

At the top:

1945—Prime Minister Winston Churchill appeared before a massive crowd on the balcony of the Ministry of Health building on May 8, 1945. Germany had just surrendered to the allied forces led by England, the United States, and the Soviet Union. Churchill spoke to the nation and in one of his most memorable speeches proclaimed, "This is your victory! It is the victory of the cause of freedom in every land. In all our long history we have never seen a greater day than this. Everyone, man or woman, has done their best. Everyone has tried. Neither the long years, nor the dangers, nor the fierce attacks of the enemy, have in any way weakened the independent resolve of the British nation." When Churchill declared, "This is your victory," many in the crowd interrupted him, shouting back, "No! It is yours!"

The comeback:

With his father's death, Churchill realized that he was now "the master of my fortunes." By the time he was twenty-five, Churchill had become a lieutenant and participated in five military campaigns in Cuba, India, the Sudan, Pakistan, and South Africa. As a war correspondent during the Boer War, he'd been captured and spent his twenty-fifth birthday in a South African prison before plotting an escape that made him a national hero. Elected to Parliament for the first time in 1900, Churchill had a career that was filled with many ups and downs. During World War I, for instance, he planned the disastrous invasion of Gallipoli; during the 1920s, as Chancellor of the Exchequer, he made numerous policy mistakes that helped lead his Conservative Party to defeat in 1929. But even during his most difficult political phase—his "Wilderness Years" during the 1930s, when he found himself isolated and ignored within his own party—Churchill never wavered from his convictions. During those years, he continued to speak out on issues he regarded as vital, especially the dangers posed by Nazi Germany, even though it seemed that no one was listening.

Churchill was best known during the war for his soaring and inspiring speeches, especially the three he delivered in May and June of 1940, when he urged the English people to remain steadfast even as German forces swallowed up much of Europe. If necessary, he declared, "We shall go on to the end... We shall fight on the beaches, we shall fight on the landing grounds, we shall fight in the fields and in the streets, we shall fight in the hills; we shall never surrender."

JAMES H. CLARK (B. 1944)
American Entrepreneur

At the bottom:

1961—Trouble seemed to find Jim Clark wherever he happened to be; when it didn't, Clark sought it out on his own. He had grown up in a poor family in Plainview, Texas. Abandoned by his father at a young age, Clark had a chip on his shoulder and gained a reputation as a troublemaker. At times, his misbehavior was relatively harmless, as when he smuggled a skunk into a school dance. At other times, his misadventures were more dangerous. Once, for example, he set off a small bomb on a school bus; another time, he set of a string of firecrackers inside another student's locker, a prank that nearly caused a fire.

When he was a junior, he swore at a teacher in class, telling her to "go to hell" after she upbraided him for dodging his assignment for the day. He received an out-of-school suspension; rather than come back, he decided he'd had enough, and dropped out to enlist in the navy. At training camp, Clark continued to act out. Given an aptitude test for math, he filled in all the optical scan bubbles for every question and was reprimanded. Shipped off to sea for nine months, he faced constant bullying and humiliation from his shipmates and superiors, who spared few opportunities to let him know how stupid he was. Clark seethed, vowing to avenge his treatment somehow.

At the top:

1999—It's not often that someone has enough spare change lying around to donate $150 million to a university to found a department and erect a new building, but that's precisely what Jim Clark did in October of 1999 when he offered a huge endowment to Stanford, where he had once taught computer science. By the late 1990s, Clark was a billionaire who had founded numerous successful hi-tech start-ups, including Netscape, Shutterfly, MYCFO.com, and Healtheon. A "serial entrepreneur," Clark was known as a hotheaded, restless seeker, someone who—in the words of one author—was always trying to identify the "new, new thing" before everyone else. His success with Netscape was arguably his most notable achievement, as the Web browser launched him onto the *Forbes* list of the four hundred wealthiest Americans by the mid-1990s (when Netscape stock rose from $6 to $171 per share). His gift to Stanford was an acknowledgement that genius and innovation are not simply the result of individuals like Clark, but are fostered by educational institutions that can help change the world by giving creative men and women a direction for the future.

The comeback:

After his first nine-month voyage as a navy enlistee, Clark retook the aptitude test he had deliberately botched the previous year. This time, he did well, and—encouraged by a senior officer—he began taking classes in math and science at Tulane University in New Orleans. "I became excited by the challenge of understanding how things work, understanding the world," he told a journalist in 1994. By his thirtieth birthday, Clark had acquired a PhD in computer science from the University of Utah.

He admitted years later that part of his motivation stemmed from wanting to prove his doubters wrong. Regardless, after earning his doctorate he spent most of the 1970s in academia, teaching at the New York Institute of Technology, the University of California at Santa Cruz, and Stanford University. In 1982 he left the academic world and cofounded Silicon Graphics, a company that produced hardware and software for graphic design and visual effects in film. Clark invented a new type of computer chip that allowed designers to produce three-dimensional graphics—an innovation that transformed Hollywood animation, auto and aircraft design, and video games, among other things. A little over a decade later, Clark lost control of the company and left. With Marc Andreesen—who had designed Mosaic, the original Internet browser—Clark founded a company called Netscape, which kicked off the great Internet gold rush.

MAX CLELAND (B. 1942)
American Politician

At the bottom:

1968—Captain Max Cleland, a twenty-five-year-old soldier from Atlanta, woke up five hours after a grenade shredded both his legs and one of his arms. He had been looking forward to leaving Vietnam and had only a month left of his tour when he was asked to set up a radio relay station during the battle of Khe Sanh. After being dropped off by a helicopter, Cleland stooped to the ground to pick up a grenade that one of his soldiers had dropped. It exploded. By the time Cleland regained consciousness, he had lost a tremendous amount of blood and was lucky to be alive, but as he drifted in and out of a haze of morphine and despair, he wondered how he could possibly live out the rest of his life. Over the next weeks and months, Cleland endured extraordinary physical and psychological pain. "Inevitably," he wrote in 2009, "I was left feeling like I had fumbled the ball. Game over, and I lost. No one had shot me. No one had thrown the grenade at me. I had blown myself up and ruined my life. It was all my fault."

At the top:

1997—After Max Cleland was sworn in as Georgia's newest United States senator, he choked up and cried while speaking to a group of supporters following the ceremony. As he explained to a journalist a few weeks later, he had found himself overcome by "the incredible feeling that dreams can come true, that our deepest heartfelt desires, believe it or not, sometimes can be met by the grace of God and the help of good friends." He saw his election as "the completion of a thirty-year journey, an odyssey." The 1996 election had been close—with the difference of only thirty thousand votes between the candidates—and Cleland would only serve one term in office, losing a similarly close election in 2002. But during his six years in the Senate, he worked on important veterans' issues and has continued to be an advocate for veterans even after his defeat.

The comeback:

After his terrible injuries, Max Cleland spent the next two years acclimating himself to a very different life. It was a difficult transition, and when he set out to live on his own in 1969, he fell into some unhealthy habits, including spending far too much time drinking heavily and partying with a group of fellow injured veterans he'd met while at Walter Reed Hospital in Maryland. Eventually, Cleland realized that he needed to move forward with his life and be productive; he realized that it was his choice to live or die, to waste the rest of his life or to make something of the situation he'd been handed.

He had recently testified before the Senate regarding the difficulties Vietnam veterans were facing after returning to civilian life, and the experience renewed his interest in politics. Imagining that he might be able to do more for fellow veterans, Cleland decided to run for public office. In 1970, he won a seat in the Georgia state senate, becoming the first Vietnam veteran and—at only twenty-eight years old—the youngest to serve in that legislative body.

He happened to win his first election the year Jimmy Carter was elected governor of Georgia, and when Carter ascended to the White House in 1976, he brought Cleland on board to head up the Veterans Administration. During his early years in public office, Cleland was a strong advocate for veterans as well as the physically handicapped. When he returned to Georgia politics in the early 1980s, he served more than a decade as secretary of state and led the way in establishing new ethical guidelines for state officials. His reputation for honesty as well as his long record of fighting for others positioned him well to make a run for the United States Senate when longtime Georgia Senator Sam Nunn retired in 1996.

FRANCIS FORD COPPOLA (B. 1939)

American Film Director

At the bottom:

1966—As a film student at UCLA, Francis Ford Coppola had been known as a promising screenwriter. After winning the Samuel Goldwyn Award, a prize awarded by the Goldwyn Foundation for the best screenplays produced by students in the University of California system, Coppola was hired by Roger Corman, the king of 1960s low-budget schlock films. During the years he spent with Corman's production company, Coppola served as screenwriter, production assistant, second unit director, and even did sound work on occasion—anything to keep himself productive. From there, Coppola moved on to work as a contract writer for Seven Arts, a production company owned by Warner Brothers.

His three years with Seven Arts were severely disappointing. Though he made a good salary, his screenplays were ignored and he was not given the opportunity to direct films of his own. He worked on more than a dozen screenplays for Seven Arts, but few of them ever entered production. The ones that *did* make it to screen were complete flops. By 1966, Coppola was badly in debt and, for good measure, had blown all his savings—twenty thousand dollars—on a stock market gamble gone awry. "I was broke," Coppola remembered. "I'd lost all my money. I owed the bank $10,000. And I had two kids and a wife to support. . . . I was very depressed." The promising screenwriter had apparently joined the swollen ranks of Hollywood failures.

At the top:

1975—Francis Ford Coppola sounded a bit sheepish as he accepted his Academy Award for *The Godfather, Part II*, which had just been selected as Best Picture of the year. "We tried to make a film that would be a really good film," said Coppola, "and—well, thank you very much." Earlier in the evening, Coppola had accepted the Oscar for Best Director (also for *The Godfather, Part II*). He added these honors to those he'd received over the past five years, including Best Adapted Screenplay for *The Godfather* (1973) and Best Screenplay for *Patton* (1971). In addition to his Oscar wins, several other films written or directed by Coppola had been nominated for Academy Awards, including *The Conversation* (1975) and *American Graffiti* (1974). In the space of a few years, Coppola had emerged as one of the great directing talents in American cinema. His films during that decade—especially the *Godfather* saga and *Apocalypse Now* (1980)—were among the most memorable of their era. In addition to his storied career as a director, Coppola has also successfully developed numerous other business ventures, including a winery in Sonoma County, California, as well as several restaurants and resorts in the United States and abroad.

The comeback:

The turning point in Coppola's career came with *The Rain People*, a 1969 film written and directed by Coppola and based on a screenplay he'd written nearly a decade before while he was at UCLA. After his contract with Seven Arts expired, the young filmmaker began working on his own. He remembered the years of stifled creativity, and he wanted to make sure that nothing interfered with his vision. In a trick of self-promotional deception, he received a contract for the film from Warner Brothers after spreading a rumor that he was working on a "secret project" in New York. Hearing the rumors, and worried that another studio might offer the talented young filmmaker the money and authority he craved, Warner offered Coppola a deal that gave him total control over the project—the writing, directing, and editing would adhere to his vision.

Coppola also sunk a lot of his own money into the production, buying equipment that he would later use to found his own mini-studio. As he explained at the time, "If you're not willing to risk some money when you're young, you're certainly not ever going to risk anything in the years that follow." *The Rain People* was not an enormous critical success, but it was a solid film that allowed Coppola to showcase his talents as a writer and director—something he'd never been given an opportunity to do while he was under contract with Seven Arts. By working independently, taking risks, and finding a way to create films on his own terms, Coppola took charge of his own career and began to fulfill the promise he'd shown as a younger man.

CHARLES DARWIN (1809–1882)
English Naturalist

At the bottom:

1827—As a child growing up in Shrewsbury, England, Charles Darwin was curious about science and the natural world, but he did not apply himself very well to his studies. His hobbies included collecting plants and dead insects, as well as bird watching and the esoteric science of crystallography. But formal education did not interest him, and his work disappointed his headmasters as well as his own father, who once warned the young Darwin that he would be a "disgrace to yourself and all your family." Darwin's father, Robert, was a doctor who expected his son to follow in his own footsteps. He sent the young Charles to the University of Edinburgh in 1825 to study medicine, but lectures bored him and he found himself to be squeamish at the sight of blood. He attended lectures in zoology and geology and pursued studies of marine invertebrates, but he could not overcome his hatred for medicine. In 1827, to his father's dismay, he left the university without completing a degree.

At the top:

1864—In November of 1864, Charles Darwin received the prestigious Copley Medal, an award given by the Royal Society of London to honor great scientific achievements. After leaving Edinburgh, Darwin enrolled at, and went on to graduate from, Cambridge. Though it was widely expected he would enter the Anglican ministry, Darwin instead took a job on the HMS *Beagle*, serving as a naturalist on the ship during its five-year voyage around the world from 1831 to 1836. Darwin's observations during the journey provided him with the basis for his theory of "natural selection," which he spent the next several decades perfecting.

His most famous book, *On the Origin of Species*, was released in 1859 to great scientific and popular acclaim. The first edition (more than twelve hundred copies) sold out before the book was even on the shelves of bookstores, and although his theories proved controversial, most scientific thinkers recognized his work as a tremendous contribution. By the end of the century, "Darwinian" ideas had migrated beyond the biological sciences and into other fields, including geology, sociology, psychology, political science, history, and even literature. More than being one of the world's great biologists, Darwin helped change the very nature of how people look at the world around them.

The comeback:

Charles Darwin withstood a great deal of family and social pressure to become one of the greatest naturalists in history. Like many great thinkers, Darwin preferred to discover and study the world on his own and did not perform well in a formal educational setting. Although he was troubled by his father's career expectations and did not want to disappoint him, Darwin also recognized that his father's expectations were not the sort he would be able to fulfill.

Darwin charted his own career path and pursued studies that interested him. He seized opportunities—like the job aboard the *Beagle*—in spite of his father's disapproval. Darwin also pursued his studies even though he knew his theories about evolution would upset religious thinkers and prominent members of English society. He was a perfectionist who spent decades refining his ideas and adding further layers of evidence to them. The stress of his work even made him physically ill, but he knew his ideas and observations needed to be published, and so he never abandoned them.

PAULA DEEN (B. 1947)
American Cook and Entertainer

At the bottom:

1978—Thirty-one years old and terrified of stepping outside her Albany, Georgia, home, Paula Deen had been at home almost all of the time during the last eight years, and the problem was getting worse each day. She was raising two boys, and yet she couldn't muster the courage to take them to baseball practice. "Almost every time I had to go outside by myself," she wrote, "that panic would start in and drop me to my knees. Couldn't breathe, couldn't stop trembling." The nausea and weakness convinced her she was in fact slowly dying. Even the *thought* of leaving her house caused her to sweat and lose feeling in her arms. She had no name for her sickness, but she knew how to combat its symptoms. By staying indoors— and by never entertaining the thought of leaving—Paula Deen knew she would be able to breathe easily.

At the top:

2007—Reflecting back on where she'd been three decades earlier, Paula Deen was as amazed as anyone in her place would have been to be receiving two daytime Emmy Awards. Her show—*Paula's Home Cooking,* a Southern-themed cooking show she hosted on the popular Food Network—received the award for Outstanding Lifestyle Program, while Deen herself was named Outstanding Lifestyle Host. Viewers of her show could hardly have guessed that she was once too scared to venture out in public. Her energetic, bubbly charm had turned "The Queen of Southern Cooking" into one of the most popular food personalities of the decade, and her fans purchased her books, her cooking and decorating magazine *Cooking with Paula Deen*, and her line of baking mixes and seasonings as fast as they could.

The comeback:

Paula Deen's illness cost her years of social contact and ruined her first marriage. Remarkably, though, she recovered from her severe, two-decade-long bout with agoraphobia without therapy of any kind. For twenty years, she devoted herself to cooking meals for her kids, because cooking was something she could do without leaving the house. "I could concentrate on what was in my pots and block out what was in my head," she explained. Though she had no formal culinary training, she became skilled at cooking traditional Southern fare—fried chicken, pickled green beats and okra, sour cream pound cake, and more.

For Deen, cooking was her therapy; in those days, she notes, good Georgia housewives didn't seek out the help of a psychiatrist. And so she lived with her condition, year in and year out until finally (in 1989) she decided she'd had enough and took a part-time job as a bank teller in Savannah, Georgia. While working in Savannah, she began making and selling boxed lunches to downtown office workers. After building up a base of customers, she decided to open a small restaurant and watched it grow into a local attraction. In 1996, she opened a second restaurant and appeared on an episode of *The Oprah Winfrey Show* devoted to the topic of entrepreneurial women. The success of her two restaurants led to a cook-book deal with the QVC network, which sold seventy thousand copies of *The Lady & Sons Savannah Country Cooking* on the first day alone. By 2002, she had secured a television deal with the Food Network, where she proved to be an instant hit.

WALT DISNEY (1901–1966)
American Filmmaker

At the bottom:

1923—Walt Disney was not only bankrupt and heartbroken, but he was surviving on the bare minimum; a diet of cold, canned beans and a shower once a week at a train station. Friends were worried about his weight, wondering if the twenty-two-year-old artist had tuberculosis. He hadn't expected things to go so wrong so quickly. While working as an advertising artist, Disney had begun producing short, animated pieces that he sold to a Kansas City theater owner beginning in 1921. Known as "Laugh-O-Grams," Disney's cartoons proved popular and earned him recognition and minor celebrity status.

Using nearly all of his modest savings and eventually quitting his day job as an advertising artist, Disney purchased a Universal camera for three hundred dollars and began hiring young animators for his new studio, which he imagined would produce longer animated films, including parodies of well-known fairy tales like "Little Red Riding Hood." Unfortunately, Disney overestimated the market for cartoons; theaters used them as add-ons to regular features, but no one was willing to pay much for them. To compound the problem, no one—including Disney himself—really knew much about animation to begin with, and the Laugh-O-Gram company failed to turn anything close to a profit. Before long, Disney could no longer afford to pay his artists, and in early 1923 he pulled the plug on his studio.

At the top:

1959—Walt Disney sipped a V8 and leaned back in his chair, his office filled with tokens of his achievements—a bookcase filled with children's books, color posters from his studio's films, a portrait of Mickey Mouse, and an enormous aerial photograph of Disneyland, the amusement park that Disney had opened four years earlier in Anaheim, California. "We have a business here we built from scratch," he told a reporter from *Think* magazine, "and boy, we had to scratch plenty." The previous year, Disney Productions had earned $50 million from its three television series, books, toys, and related merchandise. The Disney Company was responsible for full-length animated classics like *Fantasia, Snow White,* and *Peter Pan* as well as live-action films including *20,000 Leagues under the Sea, Old Yeller,* and *Swiss Family Robinson.* Millions of children watched *The Mickey Mouse Club* five days a week, while families everywhere enjoyed the studio's weekend show, *The Wonderful World of Disney.* Disney's stock value had leapt nearly 700 percent since 1952, and there seemed to be no end to the company's growth. As Roy Disney, Walt's partner and younger brother put it, "our product is practically eternal."

The comeback:

For someone who was indeed gravely disappointed by his first failure, Walt Disney never let on to others the depth of his humiliation, and he remained consistently upbeat. "I never once heard Walt say anything that would sound like defeat," one of his friends remembered. "He was always optimistic . . . about his ability and about the value of his ideas and about the possibilities of cartoons in the entertainment field. Never once did I hear him express anything except determination to go ahead." Disney himself admitted later in his life that the bankruptcy of Laugh-O-Gram Films had toughened him up, leaving him more determined and able to withstand failure if it came along again. Rather than brood over failure, Disney picked himself up and moved to California, where he quickly opened a new studio and found a distributor for his new work.

Disney would suffer more setbacks in his career—he lost control over one of his first major cartoon characters, Oswald the Rabbit, in 1928—but Disney bounced back quickly, creating a new character that he based on a pet mouse he'd adopted in his younger days. He decided to name the new character "Mortimer," though he soon changed the name—at his wife's suggestion—to "Mickey." Over the years, Walt's tireless imagination and relentless marketing turned "Disney" into a symbol of American culture throughout the world.

JOE DUDLEY (B. 1937)

American Entrepreneur

At the bottom:

1953—Born into a poor African American farming family in Aurora, North Carolina, Joe Dudley not only grew up in perilous economic circumstances, but he had the additional burden of having a terrible speech impediment that led most people to assume he was stupid. Labeled a "slow learner" at school, he was held back in the first grade and again several years later. Though his mother encouraged him to believe he could do anything he wanted, Joe Dudley instead accepted the impressions of others. He slacked off in his classes and exhibited a bad attitude toward his teachers. By the time he was a junior in high school, most people—including Dudley himself—believed he was heading toward a bleak future.

At the top:

2003—From his eighty-thousand-square-foot corporate office, a sixty-six-year-old Joe Dudley reflected on the mission of his company, Dudley Products, which took in $30 million annually with its line of cosmetics marketed to black consumers. In addition to overseeing his line of hair and beauty products, Dudley also ran a chain of cosmetology schools that operated throughout the world, including campuses in Japan, Korea, and Brazil, as well as two in Zimbabwe. Even with large conglomerates like L'Oreal and Alberto-Culver competing with his business, Dudley remained a powerful, independent presence in the market. And he was determined to retain his independence and not sell out to a larger corporation. "I don't have anything against people who sell their company," he explained. "But I didn't build my company to sell it. I built my company as an example of what you can do with difficulties in life. . . . I want to show young African Americans that they can run a business too."

The comeback:

During his junior year of high school, Joe Dudley was dumped by a girl who explained that she was leaving him for another boy. "He is smart," she said "and you are dumb." Humiliated by the rejection, Dudley was for the first time in his life determined to show everyone that he wasn't "slow" or "dumb" after all. His motivation led him back to the education he'd taken lightly for so many years. Beginning with his elementary school textbooks, Dudley started over and taught himself everything he had refused to learn up to that point. He graduated the following year and enrolled at North Carolina A&T, the state's historically black university in Greensboro.

While pursuing his degree in Business Management, he financed his tuition by selling Fuller hair care products door-to-door. (Fuller Products had been founded by a Louisiana sharecropper named Samuel Fuller, who was by the 1950s the wealthiest African American man in the United States.) Dudley continued to sell Fuller products until 1967, when he and his wife struck out on their own, creating a line of hair care products that sold well throughout North Carolina. In 1976, Samuel Fuller hired Dudley to take over the operations of Fuller Products; by then, Dudley had become so successful that he was able to merge the two companies under his own name. Only six years after its founding, Dudley Products had just absorbed the largest black hair products company in the nation.

ALBERT EINSTEIN (1879–1955)
Swiss Physicist

At the bottom:

1901—After graduating with a math and physics degree from the Swiss Federal Institute of Technology in Zurich, Albert Einstein was unable to secure a teaching position anywhere for the next several years. His parents continued to support him financially but insisted that, if he could not find a job, he leave Switzerland and live with them in Milan, Italy. By April 1901—a year after he earned his degree—Einstein had sent letters of inquiry to nearly every physics department in Europe, pleading for the opportunity to join their faculty. Many of his letters went completely unanswered. In 1903, Einstein at last returned to Switzerland and took a job in a patent office, where he earned a tolerable income but enjoyed almost no contact with other physicists.

At the top:

1922—Albert Einstein received the Nobel Prize in Physics in 1922. Over the previous two decades, Einstein had completely revolutionized the field of physics and had received a string of prestigious academic appointments at universities in Switzerland, Czechoslovakia, and Germany. His published work on photoelectricity, atomic theory, electrodynamics, and other subjects had sealed his reputation as one of the most brilliant thinkers in the history of science. For the rest of his life, Einstein continued to produce great insights into physics, but he also spoke out passionately on political and humanitarian issues.

The comeback:

Even as he suffered from a lack of job opportunities, Albert Einstein refused to give up his dream of making important contributions to the science he loved. As he told his friend Marcel Grossman, "I leave no stone unturned and do not give up my sense of humor." He compared himself to a donkey and noted that God had given them both thick skins. When he finally received the patent office job, Einstein continued to conduct experiments and research, even though he was isolated from his peers. In 1905, he published four separate articles in the most prestigious German physics journal. Although these articles did not immediately bring him renown, they would eventually be seen as Einstein's most original and ingenious work. From his quiet job in a patent office, Einstein was on his way to becoming one of the most important thinkers in human history.

LARRY ELLISON (B. 1944)
American Entrepreneur

At the bottom:

1991—Larry Ellison was never the sort of person to shy away from danger, but on Christmas Day, 1991, the forty-seven-year-old software executive took a risk that nearly killed him. While bodysurfing in Hawaii, Ellison was caught by a fast-moving, thirteen-foot wave that heaved him onto the beach. Later, he described the sound of his own bones breaking as resembling the sound of shredded wheat being crushed. He heard his ribs snapping and felt a piece of his surfboard—shattered by the impact—slam into his neck, breaking it at the sixteenth vertebra.

Before he had managed to recover fully from his surfing mishap, Ellison ventured out on a mountain bike ride that led to a second accident, leaving one of his arms being shattered, requiring extensive surgery. Although Ellison survived these accidents with no permanent damage, his physical rehabilitation was made more challenging by the adversity that had come to surround his professional life. Oracle—the database software company he had cofounded in 1977 with fourteen hundred dollars of his own money—was on the brink of destruction.

After doubling its sales almost every year since 1979, the company nearly imploded when it revealed that dubious accounting practices had overstated corporate earnings for many years. In 1990, Oracle's profits were practically nonexistent; in early 1991, it posted its first-ever loss, and later that year it was forced to revise previous years' earnings statements. Compounding the company's problem, Oracle had released a software package that performed badly and became the subject of jokes throughout the software industry. Oracle laid off four hundred workers—the largest cuts in its history. Oracle stock lost 80 percent of its value, tumbling from twenty-five dollars a share to five dollars a share. Many observers wondered if the company could survive.

At the top:

2000—In late April of 2000, Larry Ellison went to bed as the richest man in the world, barely surpassing Bill Gates, with a fortune topping $53 billion. More importantly, by this time Oracle had returned to its position of dominance within the database segment of the software industry. Ellison had driven Oracle to launch a series of innovative products, including a database with a built-in Web server and the first Internet file system. Throughout the first decade of the twenty-first century, Oracle acquired one software company after another and became the third-largest revenue producer in the software industry, trailing only IBM and Microsoft. Ellison's success with Oracle guaranteed that he would be remembered as one of his generation's greatest technology entrepreneurs.

The comeback:

Ellison's return to the top began with a frank admission: He had been an ineffective leader. The risk-taking attitude that had nearly killed him in Hawaii had also nearly killed his company. Like everyone in business, he needed to figure out how to be aggressive without sabotaging his chances at success. He had allowed quality control to slide and placed the wrong people in charge of accounting. He had put unreasonable demands on his sales staff, creating an incentive system that encouraged them to dump as much product on the market as they could, as quickly as they could, regardless of whether clients could actually pay for it.

His body—like his company—was badly injured, but it could recover, and similar accidents could be avoided with the right amount of caution and foresight. Ellison admitted that he needed help managing his own company, so he brought in a new CFO and even took the surprising step of replacing himself as chairman for a period of time; in the end, half of the executives at Oracle were replaced with more experienced officers. As Ellison nursed his physical wounds, his company charted a course for recovery. He never lost his aggressive edge—he continued to believe that his own success required others to fail—but he and Oracle did not repeat the recklessness of earlier years.

Over the next decade, the company regained the trust of investors and customers; it broadened its reach by acquiring smaller software companies that specialized in health care, banking, retail, and insurance among other niches. Betting on the growth of the Internet, Ellison focused on acquiring and developing products that could run via Web browsers. Ellison maintained his active lifestyle—especially through yacht racing, including several appearances in the America's Cup—but he remembered a few lessons about taking risks. When a storm killed six sailors (none from his ship) during a 1998 race in Australia, Ellison decided to leave ocean racing to the professionals.

RUTH FERTEL (1927–2002)
American Entrepreneur

At the bottom:

1965—Ruth Fertel never expected to be a thirty-seven-year-old divorced mother of two, living paycheck to paycheck, and wondering how she would ever be able to afford college tuition for her teenage sons. But that's where she found herself in 1965. Fertel was a brilliant woman who had graduated from Louisiana State University at the age of nineteen with a dual major in physics and chemistry. For two semesters, she taught science at McNeese Junior College in Lake Charles, Louisiana, before leaving the work force when she decided to get married in 1948.

When she and her husband parted ways eleven years later, Fertel tried to put her education to good use by accepting a job as a lab technician at Tulane University Medical School in New Orleans. The income from her job provided enough to get by, but with her ex-husband more or less out of the picture, Fertel needed to think about her sons' future and realized that her income would not be enough.

At the top:

1995—After three decades in the restaurant business, Ruth Fertel presided over a successful empire of upscale steak houses that stretched across the United States, and even crossed the Pacific Ocean, with franchises in nearly fifty locations around the world—including New York City, Cancun, and Taipei. "Ruth's Chris Steak House" generated roughly $160 million in annual sales. Fertel was awarded the "Entrepreneur of the Year" award by the Horatio Alger Association in 1995 at the age of sixty-eight.

Though she had decided in 1992 to enter "semi-retirement," Fertel had continued to work between seven and eight hours a day and to play a central role in the corporation. "I don't think I'll ever really retire," she told a reporter in 1992. "It's too much fun watching what's going on and watching things grow. That's the fun part of it. I just like to win. When you're growing and the stores start making money, to me that's fun. I'm helping all of these [franchisees] make money, and it's very gratifying." By the time Fertel died of cancer in 2002, her business had expanded even more, with nearly one hundred restaurants and sales approaching $250 million a year.

The comeback:

Though Ruth Fertel had no experience running a business and had never shown much of an entrepreneurial streak, she was naïve enough to believe that she might do well enough to provide a better life for her sons. Combing through the classified ads, she decided to take a chance on a seventeen-table, sixty-seat steak restaurant on the outskirts of New Orleans. Originally founded on February 5, 1927, the very day Ruth Fertel was born, Chris' Steak House served good food and had a good reputation, and the owner was willing to sell it for eighteen thousand dollars. Though Fertel believed she could maintain the restaurant's success, her attorney strongly advised her against the purchase; even the bank president warned her that she could be making a huge mistake.

Using her house as collateral, however, she secured a loan and became a restaurant owner a few months after her thirty-eighth birthday. With seemingly everyone expecting her to fail, Fertel plunged herself into the job; she butchered her own meat and did a huge portion of the food preparation, all while maintaining a demeanor of Southern hospitality that kept her customers returning for more. "I've always had a lot of confidence in my ability to do anything that I set my mind to," Fertel explained years later. "I'm not a restaurateur; I'm a business person who owned a restaurant. I just had confidence and never once thought that I couldn't do it or would fail."

Though she had agreed to keep the restaurant's original name, it was not long before Chris' Steak House was firmly identified with Ruth Fertel. She earned a lot of goodwill in the community after Hurricane Betsy, which hit the city a few months after she bought the restaurant. With electricity out all over the city, Fertel turned on the gas stoves and cooked nearly everything she had on hand, then had it delivered to needy communities around the area. The good publicity—combined with the high quality of the restaurant's food—helped Fertel grow her customer base.

After a few years, the steak house was doing such phenomenal business that Fertel opened a second restaurant, and then a third. When a fire damaged the original building, Fertel reopened in a new, larger space and filled it with hungry diners. One of them, a fellow named Tom Moran, had been encouraging Fertel for several years to expand her vision even farther. In 1976, Fertel agreed to begin franchising her restaurant, which now went by the memorable (if somewhat awkward) name of "Ruth's Chris Steak House."

DEBBI FIELDS (B. 1956)

American Entrepreneur

At the bottom:

1976—Debbi Fields was starting to hate being around other married couples. A native of Oakland, Fields had recently married a Stanford graduate, and she felt self-conscious about the fact that she—unlike most of the women she met through her husband—had never gone to college and did not have a career or much of a life outside her home. As a kid, she never had many hobbies (aside from baking cookies), and she was never a strong student in school.

As Fields recalled in 2004, "I was young, had no college credentials, and came from little means. I was blonde, and people figured I had no brains. Growing up, my sisters nicknamed me 'Stupid.'" Now, Debbi Fields was young and married and eager to prove that she could make something more of herself. "When people asked me what I did, I'd say, 'I'm a house-wife' and they'd walk away. I decided right then that I never wanted to feel that way again." She wanted to open a small shop and sell cookies, but everyone in her life warned her that her lack of education and business experience would lead to quick failure.

At the top:

1993—After sixteen years in the cookie business, Debbi Fields was successful beyond anyone's wildest imagination. Fields, Inc. had become an international franchise, with hundreds of stores in seven countries and annual revenue of almost $90 million. Harvard Business School had made a case study out of Fields' use of computer technology to streamline her operations, and her cookbooks (most notably her first, *Mrs. Fields Cookie Book*) had sold millions of copies. By the early 1990s, Fields was ready to scale back her involvement in the company's day-to-day operations, and in 1993 she relinquished controlling interest to private investors. Since then, the company she founded has grown even larger, with close to two thousand franchises that have made "Mrs. Fields" synonymous with cookies.

The comeback:

Debbi Fields had learned from her father that life was about doing what you loved—and if there was one thing that Debbi loved to do, it was making cookies. She convinced her husband, Randy, to help her get a small business loan, but even he wondered if she'd last more than a month or two. He even bet her that she'd fail to sell fifty dollars worth of cookies the first day. When her first shop opened in August of 1977 in Palo Alto, California, it seemed at first that Randy was right—no one even bothered to enter her shop before noon.

At last, Debbi decided to stand outside the front door and hand her cookies to anyone who passed by. At the end of the day, she'd sold seventy-five dollars worth of cookies. From there, Debbi Fields developed a management approach that involved setting small, incremental goals and striving to improve her product. Her motto became "Good enough never is." Though she always kept one eye on the larger goal—making the best possible cookie—Fields focused on the little things. "If goals are within reach," she told a reporter in 1999, "they don't look so daunting."

HENRY FORD (1863–1947)
American Auto Manufacturer

At the bottom:

1901—There was little reason for anyone to believe that Henry Ford would make a name for himself in the new world of automobile manufacturing. A farm boy from Dearborn, Michigan, Ford left home as a teenager and took up work as a machinist for the Westinghouse company before moving on to the Edison company, where he was employed as an engineer. Fascinated by steam power, Ford developed several designs for a "quadricycle" between 1894 and 1896, before founding his own company—the Detroit Automobile Company—in August of 1899. Within eighteen months, it had failed. Product quality was not to Ford's satisfaction, and the price for the consumer was higher than he hoped. Like so many other failed businessmen, Ford went back to the drawing board. Between 1900 and 1908, there were more than five hundred companies established to manufacture automobiles, and Ford's initial failure was simply one of hundreds of similar stories.

At the top:

1924—With his remarkable and simply named "Model T," Henry Ford controlled half the national market for automobiles. After founding the Ford Motor Company in 1903, Henry developed several models that were light and inexpensive, the sort of vehicle that would allow a man to "enjoy with his family the blessings of hours of pleasure in God's open spaces." The Model T served that purpose well. By 1910, the company was unable to keep up with demand.

In order to produce vehicles as fast as they were being purchased, Ford completely altered the nature of assembly-line production. In 1914, Ford's highly paid workers—who earned an unheard-of wage of five dollars per day—could build a car in ninety-three minutes. A decade later, Ford's massive factories churned out a car every ten seconds. Henry Ford had not only revolutionized the auto industry, but he had also revolutionized manufacturing in general. Companies all over the world imitated his approach to business, and his chief product—the automobile—transformed the way that people lived.

The comeback:

Henry Ford was devoted to the idea that automobiles should be within the reach of ordinary families, and that the people who made the cars should be able to afford to buy them. His two great innovations—a speedy production process that reduced costs and a wage scale that paid workers well—were the keys to Ford's success at a time when many of his competitors were aiming for a wealthier market. While striving relentlessly to perfect the design of the Model T, Ford also thought constantly about how to make the production process more efficient and inexpensive. Ford's genius lay in his ability to balance a variety of goals: to make a product that was sturdy and reliable, while within the reach of everyday consumers, and to provide his workforce a decent standard of living.

VIKTOR FRANKL (1905–1997)
Austrian Psychiatrist

At the bottom:
1944—Viktor Frankl, a thirty-nine-year-old psychiatrist from Vienna, was one of fifteen hundred people—mostly Jews like himself—being transported by train to an unknown destination. Each car was packed with prisoners, stuffed so full that the grey dawn was visible only through the tops of the windows. No one knew where the train was heading. Most expected it would carry them to a German munitions factory, where they would be employed as slave laborers for Adolf Hitler's war machine. The whistle of the engine, Frankl recalled, sounded "like a cry for help in commiseration for the unhappy load which it was destined to lead into perdition." At last, the train slowed, and someone in the car spied a sign that caused hearts to stop beating. The train had arrived at Auschwitz.

Prior to the war, Viktor Frankl had been a successful psychiatrist in Vienna, where he treated patients with severe depression and suicidal tendencies. Now, however, he was simply a number, just one of millions of Jews herded into a concentration camp. At Auschwitz, the odds of surviving the first few hours were small, as the vast majority of prisoners were immediately sent to the gas chambers. Those who were not killed on the first day could expect to become slave laborers, enduring starvation and disease as long as their bodies could sustain them.

At the top:
1991—In the thirty-five years since the publication of *Man's Search for Meaning*, Viktor Frankl's first book had been published in twenty-two languages and had sold more than three million copies in English alone. Frankl's specific contribution came in the form of what he called "logotherapy," a term derived from *logos*, the Greek word for "meaning." As Frankl argued for more than a half century, humans are driven not by a search for power or pleasure (as Nietzsche or Freud would have insisted) but instead by a quest for meaning. Individuals, Frankl believed, have the inherent freedom to find meaning in our lives, no matter how much suffering they may face. Suffering represents one way that humans discover meaning in life; they may also, he wrote, discover meaning through doing positive

deeds as well as by experiencing something that has value (such as love, nature, or art). In 1991, the Library of Congress listed Frankl's book, which details his experiences at Auschwitz and lays the basis for his approach to psychotherapy, as one of the ten most influential books published in the United States during recent decades. Along with more than thirty other books Frankl wrote before his death in 1997, *Man's Search for Meaning* put Viktor Frankl in high demand as a lecturer, and he traveled the world for the rest of his life, contributing to the development of humanistic psychology and inspiring several generations of psychiatrists.

The comeback:

During his seven months at Auschwitz, Viktor Frankl learned more about human psychology than all of his education and experience had taught him up to that point. In the midst of one of the worst experiences any human has ever had to endure, Frankl saw men and women refusing to succumb, despite the horror that surrounded them; he watched them escape into their minds, where they were able to find "a way out" from the reality of the camp. They prayed, they daydreamed, they thought of friends and loved ones and happier times from the past. Their spiritual lives, he wrote later, helped them adapt, strengthened them, and improved their chances of surviving the ordeal. Their thoughts, memories, and hopes gave them something to live for and provided them with something positive they could communicate to others.

The key, Frankl observed, was that these survivors chose not to give up everything to their captors. "They may have been few in number," he wrote in *Man's Search for Meaning*, "but they offer sufficient proof that everything can be taken from a man but one thing: the last of his freedoms—to choose one's attitude in any given set of circumstances, to choose one's own way." Frankl himself had lost nearly everything in the Holocaust—his mother, father, brother and wife were all killed during the war—but he never surrendered his search for meaning in life.

BUCKMINSTER FULLER (1895–1983)
American Designer and Inventor

At the bottom:

1933—In October, a teardrop-shaped, experimental three-wheeled car—a prototype that resembled a racing boat more than an automobile—rolled over during a test drive, killing its driver and seriously injuring two potential investors. The "Dymaxion," as it was called, was the brainchild of a man named Richard Buckminster Fuller, who was not an engineer but rather saw himself as a philosopher who put his ideas into physical form. In this case, the Dymaxion was supposed to be a lighter-weight and more energy-efficient vehicle than conventional cars. Indeed, it wasn't even supposed to be a "car" at all. Instead, Fuller hoped that he might eventually be able to add wings that allowed the Dymaxion to fly as well as cruise along the ground. But the wreck of the Dymaxion prototype discouraged investors, and Fuller was, not for the first time, broke and without any viable economic prospects.

It was only the latest of numerous failures in Fuller's young life. He had been expelled from Harvard—twice—and had cycled from one job to another after serving a two-year stint in the United States Navy during World War I. He and his father had founded a housing design company that had gone bankrupt in 1927, and—adding personal tragedy to failure—his youngest daughter had died from complications of polio and spinal meningitis. At a relatively young age, Fuller was, in his own words, a "throwaway," a man who had become "discredited and penniless."

At the top:

1983—On February 23, 1983, Buckminster Fuller received the Presidential Medal of Freedom from Ronald Reagan in the East Room of the White House. Reagan described Fuller as "a true Renaissance Man, and one of the greatest minds of our times." He added that "Fuller's contributions as a geometrician, educator, and architect-designer are benchmarks of accomplishment in their fields. . . . Mr. Fuller reminds us all that America is a land of pioneers, a haven for innovative thinking and the free expression of ideas." In the half-century since the crash of his experimental car, Fuller had emerged as a leading figure in American architecture and design. He was best known for developing the geodesic dome—a spherical structure comprised of equilateral triangles—and other design structures that were aimed at "doing more with less." Long before most Americans were thinking of issues like energy conservation and energy efficiency, Fuller was working on ways to harmonize the "built" environment with the natural world. His geodesic dome structure became the model for buildings around the world (including Disney's EPCOT center), and his influence could be seen among subsequent generations of architects. During his career, Fuller taught at several colleges and universities, including Southern Illinois University and Washington University in St. Louis. He held twenty-eight patents during his life, wrote several dozen books, received nearly fifty honorary degrees, and circled the world numerous times giving speeches and introducing others to his ideas.

The comeback:
Though Fuller experienced numerous disappointments and, with his daughter's death, suffered from a terrible personal loss, his unique philosophy and worldview helped him to move beyond tragedy and setback. In short, Fuller believed that humans could use science and reason to better understand how people fit into the universe and natural world, but he also understood that these efforts were bound to hit roadblocks along the way; in other words, he saw his work as being helpful to the progress of humanity, even when it seemed he was hopelessly unsuccessful. He was part of an evolutionary process. To Fuller, everything was an experiment and, because experiments sometimes failed to bring results, the proper response to failure was to keep experimenting, to keep thinking and moving toward solutions.

After his personal and professional struggles in the 1920s and early 1930s, Fuller continued to experiment with designs for vehicles as well as for homes and other buildings. He worked for a while as science correspondent for *Fortune* magazine during the late 1930s, and after World War II he took a position at the progressive Black Mountain College in North Carolina. There—given the time and resources and intellectual community to bring his work to maturity—he developed the design for his famous geodesic dome and showed how its stable but lightweight structure could provide the basis for more efficient architectural designs. Although the dome was not widely used (as Fuller had hoped it would be) to solve the postwar housing crisis in the United States, it was soon adopted widely for industrial use and was introduced to a wider audience at the 1964 World's Fair in New York City.

GUY GABALDON (1926–2006)
American Soldier

At the bottom:

1938—Guy Louis Gabaldon was on a fast track to a misspent life. Born into a poor Chicano family in a barrio of East Los Angeles, Gabaldon was a rebellious youth who spent most of his early years defying his parents and running wild in the streets. He hung out with older kids who hung around the sleazier points of interest in East L.A; he stole beer and liquor from local saloons; he ran with a multiracial band of ruffians known as the "Moe gang," who stole cars, ripped off grocers, and hopped rides on trains. For a young Mexican American boy growing up in the midst of the Great Depression, opportunities for a decent future were tough enough even for kids who stuck to the straight and narrow. For a kid like Guy Gabaldon, there seemed to be nothing but rough times ahead. His parents were exasperated—nothing they said or did seemed to make an impression on their headstrong son.

At the top:

1944—As the war in the Pacific ground onward, an eighteen-year-old private in the U.S. Marines named Guy Gabaldon had a peculiar plan. One night in June, he snuck out of camp on the Japanese island of Saipan and returned several hours later with two prisoners. His commanding officers were outraged and warned him against pulling a similar stunt again. The next night, however, he slipped away again; this time, he came back with several dozen Japanese soldiers, all of whom had come voluntarily, without a shot being fired. Gabaldon's method was simple. After crawling within earshot of an enemy bunker, he would call out in Japanese, warning the soldiers that U.S. Marines were poised to strike with overwhelming power the next morning. He would explain, however, that the soldiers could save their lives by surrendering and coming with him. The Japanese fighters on Saipan were exhausted, and their supplies were low.

Though they had been trained to fight to the death and never to surrender to the Americans, Gabaldon was able to convince about fifteen hundred Japanese soldiers to follow him back to American lines. In one night alone, Gabaldon brought back more than eight hundred enemy fighters. The struggle for Saipan cost more than three thousand American lives, and ten times as many Japanese. For his astonishing bravery—and for saving so many lives (Japanese as well as American)—"The Pied Piper of Saipan" was awarded a Silver Star, one of the highest military honors given by the United States. In 1960, Gabaldon's Silver Star was upgraded to a Navy Cross; that same year, Gabaldon's exploits were portrayed on the silver screen in a film called "Hell to Eternity." In an interesting twist, Gabaldon returned to Saipan in 1970 and opened a successful seafood business.

The comeback:

At the height of his youthful unruliness, Guy Gabaldon befriended a couple of Japanese American kids named Lyle and Lane Nakano. Their parents had been born in Japan, but the boys were American citizens. Gabaldon spent most of his time with kids who had no respect for tradition and authority, who regarded their parents and other elders as fools. But with the Nakano brothers, Gabaldon saw a different way of life. They were honest and studious in school, and they respected the law as well as their parents and grandparents. Gabaldon was fascinated by Japanese culture and began spending time with the Nakano family, who taught him a great deal about their language and customs. Eventually, Gabaldon moved into their home and lived with them for seven years. His parents supported his decision, because they recognized the positive effect the Nakanos were having on their son.

When the United States entered World War II in 1941, the Nakanos—along with 120,000 other Americans of Japanese ancestry—were sent to an internment camp. In 1943, the government began offering Japanese American men like Lyle and Lane Nakano the opportunity to enlist in the armed services; when Gabaldon learned that his friends had joined the fight, he decided to enlist as well. Drawing on the language skills he'd picked up from his friends, and following their example of patriotism and service, Gabaldon put himself in a position to become one of the war's most interesting heroes.

CHRIS GARDNER (B. 1954)

American Investment Advisor

At the bottom:

1981—Chris Gardner had just watched his big break in life evaporate before him, and now he was sitting in a San Francisco jail, humiliated over unpaid parking tickets totaling twelve hundred dollars. Gardner had endured a difficult, impoverished Louisiana childhood that included abandonment by his biological father as well as physical abuse at the hands of his stepfather. To make matters worse, when he was eight years old his mother was imprisoned for trying to murder his stepfather, and he and his three sisters spent much of their childhood being bounced around the foster care system.

Gardner managed to escape the horror by joining the navy, where he developed an interest in medicine and made plans to become a doctor after receiving his discharge. He abandoned those plans but remained within the medical industry, working as a lab assistant and medical equipment salesman. His earnings were meager—the equivalent of about thirty thousand dollars a year in today's dollars—and were not enough to support his girlfriend and newborn son.

A chance encounter with a well-dressed stockbroker driving a Ferrari inspired Gardner to abruptly shift focus. Now, he suddenly believed, he was destined to be a millionaire. His girlfriend thought he was insane; the parking tickets he racked up while futilely seeking jobs at brokerages seemed to confirm her judgment. At last, it seemed he had landed a trainee position with E. F. Hutton, but the job disappeared when the man who hired him was fired. Gardner's girlfriend was furious, especially since he'd quit his sales job to accept the job that no longer existed. When a loud argument between the couple brought the police to their apartment one night, Gardner was taken into custody. Though he was not charged as a result of the domestic dispute, his outstanding parking tickets led to a ten-day jail sentence. When he was released, the unemployed Gardner came home to find his apartment empty and his girlfriend and son gone.

At the top:

2006—Chris Gardner's bestselling memoir, *The Pursuit of Happyness*, told the remarkable story of a rags-to-riches journey that eventually led to a life as a multimillionaire stockbroker. His book was also made into a major motion picture, starring Will Smith as Gardner. The founder of Gardner Rich, LLC, Chris Gardner sold his stake in the company in 2006, earning millions that he parlayed into the creation of another company, Christopher Gardner International Holdings, which has offices in New York, Chicago, and San Francisco. In addition to his financial success, Gardner has become a powerful role model, earning a Father of the Year Award in 2002 from the National Fatherhood Initiative. He is also highly active in a variety of educational foundations and has sponsored numerous initiatives to improve the lives of the poor and homeless throughout the United States.

The comeback:

Gardner was unemployed and abandoned, but he was not willing to give up on his dream of success. The road from the bottom was long for Gardner. He managed to earn a spot with Dean Witter Reynolds shortly after getting out of jail, but he was entering a highly competitive field with no experience or education that would be relevant to the industry. His monthly income was significantly less than what he had earned in medical sales, and he found it impossible to meet his living expenses. His responsibilities were compounded several months later when his girlfriend returned and handed Gardner full custody of their son.

Even though he was employed in a white-collar job, Gardner and his son were homeless for an entire year, sometimes sleeping in a public transit restroom, before he could afford to rent an apartment of their own. Through it all, Gardner was fiercely committed to raising his son and offering him the love and stability he had lacked himself as a child. He worked harder than ever, placing literally hundreds of calls a day to potential clients. "Every time I picked up the phone," he recalls, "I knew I was getting closer to digging myself out of the hole." He migrated to Bear Stearns and eventually became a top earner, successful and confident enough that, by 1987, he could launch his own brokerage.

EVELYN GLENNIE (B. 1965)
Scottish Musician

At the bottom
1977—Since the age of eight, Evelyn Glennie had been aware that she was having difficulty with her hearing. Over the next few years, the sounds of the world faded so gradually that she often did not notice the progression of her deafness. When her rural, Scottish primary school replaced its old bell with an electronic signal, for example, she suddenly realized that she had been responding to the vibrations of the bell rather than the sound itself. Doctors eventually diagnosed her with gradual, irreversible nerve damage, but they could never pinpoint the cause. For a while, hearing aids helped young Glennie, who feared that the loss of her hearing would interfere with her efforts to learn to play the piano and the clarinet, as well as a variety of other musical instruments in which she'd taken a great interest.

Her teachers recognized her extraordinary young talent, and at the age of nine she received the highest mark in the United Kingdom on the Grade One exam for the Trinity College of Music. In recognition of her performance, she was invited to perform at Cowdray Hall in Aberdeen; by then, however, her auditory nerves had degenerated so badly that she could not hear her own name being called when it was time to perform. She was fitted for more powerful hearing aids, but she grew increasingly frustrated. As she wrote in her autobiography, "I was looking at the prospect of being classified for life as disabled, and cut off from the music that was beginning to seem vital to my own happiness." By the age of twelve, Glennie was almost completely deaf.

At the top:
2000—By her thirty-fifth birthday, Evelyn Glennie was arguably the greatest percussionist in the world. It was unusual enough that Glennie was a percussionist with a severe hearing impairment, but the fact that she was a solo artist as well was remarkable by any standard. Audiences around the world sought out her performances and purchased her music. She had received a mountain of major awards, including a Grammy Award in 1989 for Best Chamber Music Performance of the Year; the Royal Philharmonic Society's Soloist of the Year award; honorary degrees from numerous

universities; and recognition as a fellow at the Royal Academy of Music and the Royal College of Music.

The comeback:

Glennie credited several factors for her musical accomplishments. For starters, her parents continued to support her musical interest even after her hearing faded for good; they carted her from one rehearsal to another and were remarkably patient when she focused her efforts on percussion instruments. She was also fortunate to have music teachers who worked closely with her and helped her *listen* to music that she could not in fact *hear*. This involved hours of drilling, during which she used her hands and feet—placed on walls or the floor—to "feel" specific notes that her instructor would play. She learned to identify vibrations with notes, and in effect taught herself an entirely new way of experiencing music. She attended musical concerts and brought sheet music with her, following the score and paying attention to what the conductor and other performers did as they moved through the performance.

At the bottom of it all, Glennie had an inner desire for musical expression that she refused to let go when her hearing disappeared. When others—doctors, fellow musicians—advised her to think of music as a hobby and not as a potential career, Glennie refused to listen and only practiced harder. Glennie's deafness often causes people to wonder why she would be interested in continuing to play music. She explains that, although she is profoundly deaf, she can still hear low frequency vibrations and has trained herself to "hear" sounds based on visual and sensory cues. (This is one reason she plays barefoot—to feel the music and, in a sense, "hear" it with her feet.)

As Glennie has written, "Music represents life. A particular piece of music may describe a real, fictional, or abstract scene from almost any area of human experience or imagination. It is the musician's job to paint a picture which communicates to the audience the scene the composer is trying to describe. I hope that the audience will be stimulated by what I have to say (through the language of music) and will therefore leave the concert hall feeling entertained. If the audience is instead only wondering how a deaf musician can play percussion then I have failed as a musician."

WHOOPI GOLDBERG (B. 1955)
American Actress

At the bottom:

1974—Caryn Elaine Johnson stared at her tiny baby and wondered how she would ever be able to support her. She wondered how her own mother had done it—raising her and her brother alone in a New York City housing project after their father left the family when the children were young. Though Caryn had been married to her baby's father, and she was fortunate that he was a drug counselor who'd helped her kick the habit she'd picked up since dropping out of high school two years earlier, their marriage turned out to be a disaster. They had just separated after a difficult year of marriage, a marriage that collapsed for good a few months after their daughter was born. Now, at the age of nineteen, Johnson was divorced and broke, with minimal job prospects and an infant to care for. She'd never really had a job, and without a high school diploma there were few options, and none of them good.

At the top:

1991—Only the second African American woman to win an Academy Award, Whoopi Goldberg accepted her Oscar statue and reflected on her childhood. "As a little kid, I lived in the projects," she told the audience, "and you're the people I watched. You're the people who made me want to be an actor. I'm so proud to be here." Goldberg's award—for Best Supporting Actress in the 1990 film *Ghost*—vaulted her into the top tier of Hollywood performers, and she was soon able to command some of the highest fees in the business. Before her award, she had received high marks (and an Oscar nomination) for her leading role in the 1986 film *The Color Purple*, but she had demonstrated her wide-ranging talent in comic and action roles as well.

Following her success with *Ghost*, Goldberg continued to show her versatility with memorable roles in films like *Sister Act, Ghosts of Mississippi*, and *Boys on the Side*. She became the first black woman to host the Academy Awards in 1994 and has since hosted the ceremonies three other times. In addition to her outstanding work in film, Goldberg has also found success in television, most recently as one of the hosts on the popular daytime talk show *The View*, which attracts nearly four million viewers a day. "I am the epitome of what the American Dream basically says," Goldberg explained recently. "It says you could come from anywhere and be anything you want in this country. That's exactly what I've done."

The comeback:

The only thing Caryn Johnson knew how to do was perform. As a child, she had grown up watching Abbott and Costello films, the Three Stooges, and old Hollywood films; like many American kids, she dreamed of a day when she might appear on screen. Although she had performed in children's theater in New York and even managed to appear in the choruses of a few Broadway productions, she did not possess any formal training and had never been seen as a budding star. Still, with nothing left to lose, she packed up her daughter shortly after her marriage ended and moved across the country to southern California.

Living in San Diego, she took the stage name "Whoopi Goldberg" and began searching for acting jobs. While working as a bricklayer, she also took cosmetology courses and soon found work doing makeup at a mortuary. None of her jobs lasted long, however, and Goldberg spent periods of time over five years on public assistance while she cared for her daughter and pursued her dream of acting. Having set out on her own, though, Goldberg wanted to be self-reliant and was delighted when she was actually able to make a living from her work. "The greatest thing I ever was able to do," she said once, "was give a welfare check back. I brought it back to the welfare department and said, 'Here, I don't need this anymore.'" Eventually, she helped found the San Diego Repertory Theater and began building a reputation for her solo performances.

With a talent for comedy as well as drama, and drawing on her own background, Goldberg created an array of characters that served as the basis for her first touring show in 1983. Her work received attention and encouragement from the film and stage director Mike Nichols, who brought her show to New York. There, Goldberg caught the eye of Steven Spielberg, who cast her two years later in the leading role for the film *The Color Purple*. Her performance earned her an Oscar Nomination and quickly established her as a rising star.

JAMI GOLDMAN (B. 1968)
American Sprinter

At the bottom:
1988—As she struggled through a snowdrift, nineteen-year-old Jami Goldman didn't realize these were the last steps she'd ever take. While driving
home from a ski trip to spend the holidays with her family, Goldman
and her friend Lisa Barzano had skidded off a deserted road in northern
Arizona. Stranded inside a Chevy Blazer, the pair had no food or water, no
source of heat, and no way to contact the outside world. After three days
inside the vehicle, they tried to make an escape; unable to move more
than a few feet from the car, Goldman and Barzano retreated. But those
few minutes in the snow would prove devastating, as frostbite began to
set in. When the young women were finally discovered by a snowmobiler,
after a maddening eleven days of being trapped, they were dehydrated and
near death. Goldman's legs were in terrible shape and later, despite three
weeks of futile therapy, both legs were amputated below the knee.

At the top:
2000—It was July 14, and Jami Goldman looked up into the crowd of
twenty-five thousand people in Sacramento, all buzzing with excitement
as they watched the field of Olympic hopefuls prepare for their qualifying
heats. At thirty-two years old, Goldman was there with other physically
disabled athletes, readying for an exhibition race at her best distance, the
100-meter dash. Jami had hoped to secure a slot in the Paralympics, to be
held in Sydney later that year, but she was not among those who quali-
fied; though she was a double amputee, she competed against athletes who
might have lost only one leg or part of a leg. Even so, Goldman was an
elite runner in her sport, setting a world record for a double-BK ("below
the knee") amputee in both the 100-meter and 200-meter events. She
had also appeared in a commercial for Adidas and would eventually go on
to appear in two Steven Spielberg films. But on this day, Jami Goldman
turned in the race of her life, shattering her own world record by more
than half a second.

The comeback:

Nine years after losing her legs, Goldman had learned to use artificial limbs but was still adjusting, physically and mentally, to her status as a double amputee. She moved to Southern California and earned a degree at Cal State Long Beach. Then, in 1996, her prosthetics fitter urged her to try running. Wearing newly designed, J-shaped prosthetics known as "Cheetahs," Goldman—who had never enjoyed running before her accident—suddenly found her calling. "Running has changed my life," Goldman recalls. "It was hard work and it still is, but a lot of wonderful things have happened to me because of my running. It's helped me become more accepting of myself as an amputee." Not only did Goldman learn to enjoy running, but she also became exceptionally good at it and began entering competitions. Within a few years, she had caught the eye of Barbara Edmonson, a former Olympic medalist and former world record holder in the 100-meter dash. Goldman began training alongside able-bodied Olympic hopefuls, pushing herself to be faster each day.

TEMPLE GRANDIN (B. 1947)
American Psychologist and Author

At the bottom:

1949—Temple Grandin's parents were terribly worried about their young daughter. At the age of two, she was not yet speaking and showed evidence of having either emotional or neurological problems. After seeing several doctors, young Temple was diagnosed with autism, a neurological disorder that affects social interaction and communication and often results in repetitive behaviors. At a very young age, Temple seemed overly sensitive to loud noises and would howl madly at sounds (like a popping balloon) that are a normal part of everyday life; decades later, she explained that loud noises made her ears feel as if they were being pierced with a dentist's drill. Unlike most young children, she seemed averse to being touched and would recoil or even cry when her parents held her, as if physical contact with others was painful to her. (In reality, Grandin wanted to feel the comfort of being hugged, but the stimulation was so intense that it overwhelmed her "like a tidal wave.")

These problems did not lessen in intensity as Grandin moved through her childhood. Though she eventually learned to speak, she still had difficulty getting the words out and often resorted to screaming because it was the only way she could communicate. Her hearing problems also continued; in response to her oversensitivity to noise, her brain often seemed to shut out sounds entirely. She was unable to speak on the telephone and often missed her favorite songs on the radio because her hearing simply cut off.

At the top:

2010—Temple Grandin's reputation within the animal science and autism advocacy communities was already well established, but the depiction of her life in an HBO film starring Claire Daines brought her unlikely story to the attention of millions of viewers. Since receiving her PhD in animal science in the late 1980s, Grandin has worked as a professor at Colorado State University and has become known internationally for her widely used livestock facility designs. By drawing on her experiences with autism—especially her overpowering feelings of anxiety in certain situations—Grandin designed slaughterhouse corrals that reduce stress in cows and pigs. In addition to writing and editing several books about animal psychology, animal welfare, and the humane handling of livestock, Grandin has also written extensively about autism, including a collection of essays about her own life called *Thinking in Pictures*.

The comeback:

Grandin acknowledges that she was fortunate to have two parents who believed their daughter could be helped and could learn to function on her own. They refused to have her institutionalized and placed her in a nursery school where teachers had experience with autistic children; they sought out speech therapists who knew of strategies for helping someone like Temple; and they taught her how to know the difference between "good" and "bad" behavior, even though these concepts were too abstract for their daughter, whose thought patterns were of a highly visual nature. (They told her, for example, that "good" meant delivering flowers to a neighbor. Grandin learned that if something she was doing brought to mind that sort of pleasant image, she was behaving well.)

In spite of her difficulties as a youth dealing with her autistic condition, Grandin benefited from strong mentors who encouraged her to take control of her behavior. When she was goofing off and not doing well in high school, her science teacher motivated her to take an interest in various science projects, then explained that if she wanted to go to college and be a scientist, she would have to buckle down and study. Mentors like this "forced me to realize that I had to change my behavior. People on the [autism] spectrum can't just be sitting around complaining about things. They have to actively try to change things." Grandin did just that. She went on to earn degrees in psychology and animal science from Franklin Pierce College and Arizona State University before receiving her PhD in animal science from the University of Illinois.

ULYSSES S. GRANT (1822–1885)
American General and President

At the bottom:

1859—By the end of the year, Ulysses S. Grant faced extraordinary difficulties that would have driven many of his peers to despair. Grant had been in the United States Army in one position or another from the age of 17. Although he had not been an especially strong student at West Point, he gained a reputation for bravery and fearlessness during the Mexican-American War and expected to spend the rest of his life in the service of his country. In 1854, however, his career as a soldier came to an abrupt end. Rumor had it that Grant had been discovered drunk by a superior officer, and was forced to resign. Whatever the cause of his resignation, Grant had few options and a family to support. To make matters worse, he suffered from chronic fevers. He failed as a farmer and as a bill collector, before at last begging his father for a job in his leather shop, in 1860, only a few months before the election of Abraham Lincoln as President.

At the top:

1865—Less than six years later, Ulysses S. Grant had achieved historic greatness on the field of battle. After leading Union forces in terrific fights across Tennessee, Arkansas, and Mississippi, Grant led his nation's army to ultimate victory by forcing the Confederate General Robert E. Lee to surrender at Appomattox, Virginia. After years of brutal fighting between his and Lee's men, Grant's Army of the Potomac had prevailed at last, bringing an end to the bloodiest conflict in American history. Tremendously popular in the North, Grant was elected president in 1868, and despite scandals in his first term, reelected in 1872, becoming the first two-term president since Andrew Jackson, forty years earlier. Shortly before his death, he wrote his memoirs, published by Mark Twain, which sold 300,000 copies, providing his family with financial security after his death.

The comeback:

Grant was able to turn around his career — and his country's history — by working his way up from the very bottom and by never backing down from his mission. When eleven states protested Lincoln's election by attempting to leave the Union, Grant left his father's leather shop and resumed his life as a soldier, helping recruit militia volunteers in Illinois. Before long, his hard work was rewarded with a series of promotions of increasing responsibility, and finally to command of all the Union armies. Grant always seized the opportunity for victory, which endeared him to President Lincoln, who thought his other generals were often too timid. Despite his widely rumored drinking problems, his determination to fight impressed President Lincoln, who asked him to become the highest ranking general in the US Army. Grant proved worthy of the job, defeating his enemies all across the state of Virginia, before defeating them for good in April 1865. When Lee was finally forced to surrender, Grant offered relatively generous terms, which did much to allow the healing process between the North and South to begin. Three years later, never having previously held elective office, Grant was elected President of the United States. At age 46, he became the youngest president elected up to that time.

ANDREW GROVE (B. 1936)
Hungarian Entrepreneur

At the bottom:

1956—On November 4, 1956, two days after his twentieth birthday, Andrew Grove awoke in his home in Budapest, Hungary, to the sound of artillery fire, which sounded like "wooden planks being dropped." Having lived through the Second World War, Grove knew immediately what he was hearing. "My heart started pounding," he wrote many years later. "I jumped out of bed and ran into the big room. It was still dark outside, but my parents were already up and wrapped in their bathrobes. My father was intently fiddling with the radio. No one said anything. We all knew what was going on."

Soviet forces, already stationed inside Hungary, had just driven to the edge of Budapest to suppress an anti-Communist uprising that had toppled the pro-Soviet government the previous week. The Soviets were unwilling to allow one of their Warsaw Pact satellites to go its own way, and they were prepared to brutalize the Hungarian people in order to regain authority. Several shells struck Grove's house that night, damaging the roof and courtyard. The next day, Soviet troops arrived and demanded lodging in his family's home. The Hungarian Revolution was over, and Grove—a young university student at the time—despaired for his country's future under even tighter Soviet control.

At the top:

1997—Forty years after his arrival in the United States, Andy Grove was named "Man of the Year" by *Time* magazine. As CEO of Intel Corporation, Grove headed a company that absolutely dominated the world's microprocessor market. Intel produced 90 percent of the semiconductor chips that powered personal computers, and the company had grown over the past three decades from a small Silicon Valley start-up into a company worth $115 billion. Intel was at the time the seventh most profitable company in the world, with profits of more than $5 billion a year and earning its stockholders annual returns of 44 percent for the past ten years. In an increasingly digital world, Andy Grove had become an essential figure. The chips his company produced had helped enable the so-called "Information Age" and an economic boom during the 1990s that would create millions of jobs and lift the U.S. economy to its best position in decades. When Grove was a young Hungarian boy dreaming of a better life, America had "a mystique of wealth and modern technology; it was a place with lots of cars and plenty of Hershey bars." By 1997, it had also become a place with plenty of computers, nearly all of them containing microprocessors produced by Andy Grove's company.

The comeback:
In the immediate wake of the failed revolt, Grove's family made a decision: their son Andy would flee the country, joining the hundreds of thousands of Hungarians to do so after the restoration of Communist rule. In the course of crushing the revolution, nearly three thousand rebels and civilians were killed, along with seven hundred Soviet soldiers, in the worst fighting that Europe had seen since 1945. Though Grove's family did not actively support the revolt, they had been delighted by the possibility of a non-Communist government and knew that they did not want their son to remain in Hungary under Communist rule. Though he did not want to say goodbye to his parents, Andy longed for the life of opportunity he believed was available in the United States.

After a harrowing and dangerous escape through the woods and villages of western Hungary, Grove made his way to Austria and then to New York City. In America, he quickly learned English while also working toward his college degree. An outstanding science student, he would soon earn a Ph.D. in chemical engineering from Berkeley. He joined the rush of young, ambitious science and technology wizards making their way to Silicon Valley, where in 1968 Grove joined two associates in founding a semiconductor start-up by the name of Integrated Electronics Corporation—"Intel" for short.

TENZIN GYATSO (B. 1935)
Tibetan Spiritual Leader

At the bottom:

1959—Tenzin Gyatso, the twenty-four-year-old Buddhist leader of the Tibetan people, had watched with horror for the past several years as the Chinese brutalized his people. Gyatso was known to Tibetans as the fourteenth Dalai Lama—a hereditary title given to the leaders of the Gelug sect, who were also the leaders of the Tibetan state. He had been formally enthroned as Tibetan ruler in November of 1950, a few weeks after the Chinese invaded and occupied his country. The Chinese claimed sovereignty over Tibet and soon forced the Dalai Lama to accept an agreement that handed over control of his country to the Communist government in Beijing. Though the Dalai Lama was allowed to retain his title, he was a mere figurehead, without any real authority; as a Buddhist, he resolved to try and maintain peace in his country, believing that violence could only be counterproductive.

Over the next decade, however, the Chinese waged a brutal campaign against Tibetan resistance fighters. They bombed towns and villages, killing thousands and causing many more to flee into overcrowded refugee camps near larger cities like Lhasa. Political dissidents were tortured, disemboweled, hacked to pieces, and dragged to their deaths behind horses. In 1959, the Tibetan resistance became an open rebellion. When it was rumored that Chinese military officials were going to take the Dalai Lama into custody in their quest to suppress the revolt, tens of thousands of his followers surrounded his residence at Norbulingka Palace.

After several tense days in which the Tibetan people faced down the Chinese army, army officials informed the Dalai Lama that they would soon begin firing on the crowd. Realizing that escape would be the only means of preventing massive bloodshed, Gyatso disguised himself as a Tibetan soldier and slipped out of the palace. Three weeks later—after a difficult, mountainous trek through rainstorms and blizzards—the exhausted young man crossed the border into India, not knowing if he would ever see his homeland again.

At the top:

1989—Only months after watching as the Chinese government carried out another devastating political assault on dissenters—this time at Tiananmen Square—the Dalai Lama accepted the Nobel Peace Prize, which was awarded for his ongoing struggle to find a peaceful means to the liberation of Tibet. In his acceptance speech, Tenzin Gyatso explained that "he would accept the honor on behalf of the six million Tibetan people, my brave countrymen and women inside Tibet, who have suffered and continue to suffer so much. They confront a calculated and systematic strategy aimed at the destruction of their national and cultural identities. The prize reaffirms our conviction that with truth, courage, and determination as our weapons, Tibet will be liberated."

In the three decades since his flight to India, the Dalai Lama had become a symbol for nonviolence and peaceful resistance to people all over the world, joining figures like Gandhi and Martin Luther King, Jr. Although Tibet remains under occupation—with the Chinese government steadfastly refusing to negotiate—the Dalai Lama has helped preserve the very Tibetan culture that China sought to eradicate. Because of the Dalai Lama's efforts, the issue of Tibetan independence has remained in the international public eye for more than a half century.

The comeback:

Though he has received personal awards—including numerous human rights awards, the Congressional Gold Medal in the United States, as well as honorary citizenship in Canada, Italy, and the Ukraine—the Dalai Lama has never sought personal aggrandizement but has instead placed the peaceful liberation of his people above all other goals. Though he longed to return to a free and independent Tibet, Tenzin Gyatso never despaired; his profound religious faith and his belief in the possibility of non-violent change sustained him over the years.

In exile, he continued to struggle for the Tibetan people, including the tens of thousands who followed him into India. He created educational and cultural programs to help maintain Tibetan language, religion, and history; he helped found hundreds of Buddhist monasteries and nunneries; he worked through the United Nations to try and find a peaceful international solution to the Tibetan occupation.

BETHANY HAMILTON (B. 1990)
American Surfer

At the bottom:
2003—Bethany Hamilton never saw the shark that ripped off her left arm. The young Hawaiian girl was perched atop her surfboard early in the morning on October 31, 2003, taking a few morning runs at Tunnels Beach, Kauai. Her father, her brother, and a friend had joined Hamilton, who at the age of thirteen was well on her way to becoming a world-class professional surfer. She'd been winning national championships since she was ten and had recently signed an endorsement deal with a surf apparel company, Rip Curl, which funded her training and gave her a boost toward her goal of becoming one of the best surfers in the world.

When a fourteen-foot tiger shark tore into her arm just below the shoulder, however, Hamilton's aspirations as well as her life were suddenly in grave danger. Although she remained calm throughout the aftermath, she lost a tremendous amount of blood and could easily have died during the forty-five-minute trip to the hospital. Surgeons were able to clean and suture the wound and, using skin from her armpit, were able to cover the stump. When she regained consciousness, her doctors explained that she would be able to live a normal life with only one arm; Hamilton wondered, however, if she'd ever be able to surf again.

At the top:
2009—Bethany Hamilton smiled and reflected on her second-place finish. "I'm really happy with my performance," she told the reporter. "I think my nerves got the better of me in the Final. I should've made a couple of turns where I fell. I'm kind of bummed about that last wave, but I guess that's surfing." A little more than five years after losing her arm, Hamilton had just surprised the surfing world by taking second place at the Billabong Association of Surfing Professionals World Junior Championships, held in North Narrabeen, Australia. On her way to the finals, she knocked off two heavily favored surfers and nearly defeated Pauline Ado of France before settling for the runner-up's trophy. To get even this far had been a remarkable testimony to Hamilton's strength and skill. Fulfilling the dream that had been interrupted by the shark attack, Hamilton had joined the

women's professional circuit the previous year and placed well throughout the season, finishing 2008 ranked fourteenth in the world. Experts on the sport expected that this was merely the beginning of a long and successful career.

The comeback:

Bethany Hamilton didn't know what her accident might mean for the career she longed to have, but she was determined to be optimistic. Hamilton, a devout Christian, has always credited her religious faith as well as her family with giving her the strength she needed to return to the surf. "It never crossed my mind that I might never get on a surfboard again," she explained recently. Before I even left the hospital, I decided that I was going to surf."

Indeed, only a few weeks after her accident, Bethany and her friend Alana—herself a world-class surfer who was with Hamilton the morning of the attack—stepped into the water at a beach on Kauai's North Shore and paddled into the surf on a longboard. "It was like coming back after a long, long trip," she wrote in *Soul Surfer*, her account of the accident and her recovery. Before long, she had figured out how to stand up on the board—a difficult task in itself, since surfing requires great balance and strength—and within a few days she was beginning to feel comfortable doing the sorts of maneuvers that made her a rising star. By this point, Hamilton's story was known to people all over the world—even to those who previously had known nothing about surfing—and she would have countless opportunities over the next few years to inspire people with her words as well as her performances.

STEPHEN HAWKING (B. 1942)
English Physicist

At the bottom:

1963—Stephen Hawking, a recent graduate of Oxford, was a twenty-one-year-old Cambridge graduate student in theoretical astronomy and cosmology when he began to exhibit unusually clumsy behavior. He fell down a flight of stairs and seemed to be stumbling more frequently as he walked. Hawking felt a growing numbness in his limbs. While visiting his family during holiday break, he fell down during an ice skating session with his mother and was unable to pick himself up. His parents urged him to visit the family doctor, who referred him to a specialist.

After two weeks of grueling medical tests, Hawking received terrible news. He was suffering from Motor Neuron Disease (known in the United States as Amyotrophic Lateral Sclerosis or, more commonly, Lou Gehrig's disease.) Over time, doctors explained, the nerve cells in Hawking's spine and brain would gradually crumble, causing his muscles to cease functioning. He would soon enough be confined to a wheelchair, and as he neared death he would find it nearly impossible to swallow or breathe. There seemed to be no hope that Hawking would live to complete his degree; indeed, the doctors prepared him for the likelihood that he would suffer an agonizing death within two years, or sooner.

At the top:

2006—Stephen Hawking, now almost completely paralyzed and unable to speak since the mid-1980s, received the Copley Medal from the Royal Society, which recognized his decades of contributions to theoretical physics and theoretical cosmology. The Copley Medal predates the Nobel Prize by almost two full centuries and is in fact the world's oldest award for scientific accomplishment. Hawking's theoretical work on subjects such as black holes, the shape of the universe, quantum gravity, and wormholes, among other contemporary issues in physics, had assured him a role as one of the most important scientific thinkers of the twentieth century. His numerous popular books—especially the best-selling *A Brief History of Time*—had made him a household name as well, even among people who knew almost nothing about physics. While serving as an ambassador for science, he has also proven to be a role model for people facing physical challenges. He often jokes about the limitations his disease has placed upon him, observing that while "there are some things I can't do, they are mostly things I don't particularly want to do anyway."

The comeback:
While he was in the hospital, having just received his grim diagnosis, Stephen Hawking watched a young boy succumb to leukemia. He realized that despite his unfortunate situation, he had already enjoyed a longer and more fortunate life than this poor child, whom he thought of often over the years whenever he felt a twinge of self-pity. Hawking found that his disease gave him a renewed sense of purpose and urgency. He began dreaming that he had been given a reprieve from an execution, and he realized that he still had worthwhile goals to accomplish.

Struggling against pessimism, Hawking returned to Cambridge and threw himself into his studies; he developed a romantic relationship with the woman who would later become his first wife. And though his physical condition deteriorated rapidly, his mind was sharper than ever. He lived to complete his thesis, by which time his contributions to theoretical physics were already creating a buzz within the scholarly community.

LAURA HILLENBRAND (B. 1967)
American Author

At the bottom:

1987—Laura Hillenbrand was finishing her junior year at Kenyon College in Ohio, driving back to school with her boyfriend and another friend when she suddenly felt nauseated. By the time she reached home a half hour later, she was doubled over with chills and a burning sensation in her abdomen. Over the next few days, her condition worsened. She could barely hold down any food, and her muscles ached terribly. Finally, she woke up one morning to discover that she could not get out of bed. Doctors ran test after test but were unable to discover the cause of her distress.

She took a leave from college and returned to her mother's house in Maryland. She had lost twenty pounds, and her lymph nodes were swollen. "During the day," she recalled, "I rattled with chills, but at night I soaked my clothes with sweat. I felt unsteady, as if the ground were swaying. My throat was inflamed and raw. A walk to the mailbox on the corner left me so tired that I had to lie down." She had difficulty reading words on a page and seemed incapable of focusing on a conversation long enough to understand it. As her condition worsened, "My world narrowed down to my bed and my window. I could no longer walk the length of my street." Her hair began to fall out, and her throat and mouth burned with a severe and seemingly incurable strep infection. As her body deteriorated, she sank into a deep depression, all made worse because no one could tell her what was happening.

At the top:

2001—Laura Hillenbrand's first book, *Seabiscuit: An American Legend*, was released in March of 2001, almost exactly fourteen years after she first began exhibiting the symptoms of chronic fatigue syndrome. The subject of the book was appropriate enough for someone in Hillenbrand's condition. It told the true story of a gimpy, underdog horse and his misfit jockey who somehow managed to become champions during the Great Depression, capturing the attention of the entire nation and helping to make horse racing one of the most popular sports of the era. Two weeks after the book's release, Hillenbrand's editor and agent called to deliver extraordinary news. "You're number one!" they shouted into the phone, explaining that *Seabiscuit* had topped the *New York Times* best-seller list. A year later the book had sold 800,000 copies, and a film was in the first stages of production. (It would eventually be released in 2003 to similar acclaim.) More importantly for her, it proved she could overcome—if only temporarily—a disease from which she will likely never recover. "The illness got me used to accepting that I couldn't do or have very much. All possibility disappeared from my life," she told a reporter in 2002. "Now, with all this love coming in and people believing in me, I can believe in myself. So in a way, Seabiscuit is to me what he was to people in the Depression. He is possibility."

The comeback:

For almost a decade, Hillenbrand slogged through each day as the symptoms of her illness ebbed and flowed. At times she had more energy and could take walks and live a moderately active lifestyle; at other times, she could barely muster the energy to leave her bed. Nevertheless, she was determined not to live a life of total confinement and began to do some freelance writing for what she described as "an obscure [horse] racing magazine." She wrote a few short articles from her bed, earning fifty dollars per story. By the mid-1990s, she was suffering from periodic bouts of vertigo and could write only a paragraph or two per day, but she persisted.

In 1996 she stumbled across a story about Seabiscuit; she was familiar with the tale, having owned an old children's book about the horse, but she became interested in the story of Red Pollard, Seabiscuit's jockey. The more she read about the unlikely pair, the more she wrote. What began as a short piece for the magazine *American Heritage* soon became Hillenbrand's obsession. With the aid of her boyfriend—who stuck with her throughout her illness—Hillenbrand spent the next two years researching and writing. "When I was too tired to sit at my desk," she wrote, "I set the laptop up on my bed. When I was too dizzy to read, I lay down and wrote with my eyes closed." By throwing herself into a story of renewal and resilience, she was able to give herself the gift of hope.

JAMES EARL JONES (B. 1931)
American Actor

At the bottom:

1936—Five-year-old James Earl was humiliated, unable to get the sound of his Sunday school classmates' laughter out of his head. He had recently moved from rural Michigan with his maternal grandparents, "Mama" and "Papa," who had basically raised him since shortly after his birth in Akabutla, Mississippi. His father and mother had split up before Jones was born, and his mother was frequently away from the family, searching for work wherever she could find it in the midst of the Great Depression.

When it no longer became possible to get by on the farm in Mississippi, Jones' grandparents brought the whole family—including aunts, uncles, and cousins—northward to a Michigan farm they'd never seen. The move traumatized Jones, as he'd left the only life he'd ever known and entered a strange world. Suddenly, the young boy with a beautiful singing voice developed a stutter. When the kids at church laughed at his deep southern accent, the stutter worsened. Before long, Jones refused to attend Sunday services; not long after that, he refused even to speak. For the next eight years, he was virtually mute.

At the top:

1969—Broadway theater critics who watched James Earl Jones in *The Great White Hope* had nothing but praise for his performance as the controversial early-twentieth-century boxer Jack Johnson. One reviewer praised Jones' "uncanny evocation" of Johnson's boxing style, while another described Jones' performance as being "like a whirlwind." *Newsweek*'s review praised his ability to "expand before your eyes from a flare point of inarticulate feeling to a storm system of emotion," presented "with a style so clear and confident." Jones had been acting on stage, in film, and on television for over a decade, but *The Great White Hope* gave him his big break. For his Broadway performance he received a Tony Award for Best Leading Actor; when the play was turned into a film, he received a Golden Globe Award for Best New Star (1971) and an Academy Award nomination for Best Actor in a Leading Role. In the subsequent four decades, Jones has assured himself a place as one of the great actors and vocal talents in American culture. In addition to his most famous vocal performance, as Darth Vader in the *Star Wars* series, Jones has been honored for his work in the August Wilson play *Fences* (1987), the television series *Roots*, and the film *Cry, the Beloved Country* (1996). He has been nominated for nine Emmys (with two wins), five Golden Globes (with one win), and numerous other awards, including a Life Achievement Award in 2009 from the Screen Actors Guild. He is known, above all, for his clear and sonorous voice.

The comeback:

After eight years of near-total silence, Jones was noticed by one of his teachers, a man named Donald Crouch, who discovered that Jones was a skilled young poet. Although Crouch knew of Jones' intense fear of speaking, he insisted that he recite one of his verses. Jones, while terrified, nevertheless wanted to break out of his silence and responded to his teacher's request by standing up one day and reciting his poem. He stuttered but managed to get through the exercise. The next day, the teacher called upon him again; again, Jones rose to the challenge. Gradually, his impediment disappeared, and the beautiful voice his family remembered came back.

When he entered the University of Michigan several years later, Jones pushed himself even farther by auditioning for plays and eventually choosing drama as a major. He didn't necessarily think he could pursue acting as a career, however, and looked instead toward a possible career in the army. At Michigan, he was enrolled in ROTC and in the early 1950s received his lieutenant's commission before being assigned to an infantry-training unit in Colorado. There, his acting dreams received further encouragement from an unexpected source—his commanding officer, who surprised Jones by urging him to give it a shot. "Why don't you go out and try it," he said. "You can always come back. March. Go climb that mountain." And so he did, moving to New York and slowly climbing his way toward the top.

REBIYA KADEER (B. 1947)
Uighuran Entrepreneur and Human Rights Advocate

At the bottom:
1997—The fifty-year-old mother of eleven looked around the fifty-square-foot room. "The toilet," she wrote later, "was nothing more than a hole with a little hose next to it to flush away the waste. The light bulb in the ceiling fixture had been removed. The walls were damp, green, and crumbly." Certainly, Rebiya Kadeer was no stranger to adversity. Born into poverty, she was also a Uighur, a member of a Turkic ethnic group who for decades have resisted their subordination within the People's Republic of China. Kadeer's family was forcefully removed from their small farm during the "Great Leap Forward" of the late 1950s, when millions of Chinese died of starvation and malnutrition resulting from rapid agricultural collectivization and massive pushes for rapid industrial growth. Yet Kadeer had persevered.

After starting out as the owner of a laundry business in the 1970s, she had leveraged her success and opened a department store in the 1980s. Eventually, she founded a large trading company, becoming a "millionairess" by the mid-1990s with assets that ranked her as one of the wealthiest people in China. Throughout her business career, she had been a philanthropist and an advocate for Uighur economic development and political rights. She was even appointed to be a representative in the National People's Assembly, the highest (but largely powerless) legislative body in China. By the late 1990s, her growing activism landed her in trouble with the authorities. After the Chinese government executed several dozen Uighur independence activists in 1997, Kadeer denounced the government's conduct on the floor of the Assembly. In August 1997, she was arrested and received an eight-year sentence.

At the top:
2009—Four years after her release from prison, Rebiya Kadeer was the world's most visible activist for Uighur rights. Condemned as a "terrorist" by the Chinese government, Kadeer has nevertheless always insisted that progress for her people must come nonviolently. Known as the "spiritual mother" of the Uighur people, she was elected in 2007 as president of

the World Uighur Congress as well as the Uighur American Association. Without Kadeer's soft-spoken but fierce advocacy, the plight of the Uighur would certainly not have received the same degree of worldwide attention that it has. In addition to alerting the world to China's oppressive policies, Kadeer has also helped inspire the Uighur to continue their protests inside China itself. By 2009, she had become the symbol of her people, much as the Dalai Lama symbolized the struggle of Tibet.

The comeback:
While she was in prison, Rebiya Kadeer's case received the attention of groups like Amnesty International and Human Rights Watch, and governments around the world (including the United States) urged the Chinese government to release her. Based on her political work prior to imprisonment as well as her status as a prisoner of conscience, she received the 2004 Rafto Prize for human rights, which is awarded by the Rafto Foundation to bring greater attention to individual voices silenced by oppressive or corrupt governments. The following year, Kadeer was released into the custody of the United States, where she resettled and continued her advocacy for Uighur rights.

While outsiders might have helped win Kadeer's release, her success as an advocate for Uighur rights has stemmed directly from her refusal to be silenced and her steadfast faith in democracy. As one American official explained, "The difference between Rebiya Kadeer and other dissidents is that she hasn't disappeared since leaving jail, and that is the real problem China has with her—she's not following the script." Although the Chinese government has imprisoned three of her sons for "security" crimes, Kadeer has not softened her criticism and has not taken her new freedom for granted. "The tactics I use are to make the most of living in a free democracy," Kadeer explained in testimony before Congress in April of 2009. "Simply telling the truth about what is happening to my family and my people. And I have faith in the power of democracy and truth."

HELEN KELLER (1880–1968)
American Writer and Activist

At the bottom:
1882—At the age of nineteen months, Helen Keller contracted a brief illness (most likely scarlet fever or meningitis) that left her without either sight or hearing—a severe and extremely rare double handicap. Over the next few years, Keller and her family were able to communicate through a series of crude signs that she developed with the young daughter of her family's cook. Although Keller was able to understand some of what was happening around her, she was "vexed" (as she explained in her autobiography) and sometimes grew so angry that she "kicked and screamed" until she became exhausted. Her parents feared they would be unable to manage her when she grew older; her mother worried that she might someday be raped. No one knew what to do.

At the top:
1964—An eighty-four-year-old Helen Keller was awarded the Presidential Medal of Freedom by President Lyndon Johnson. This award represents the highest civilian honor an American can receive, and it was given to Keller in recognition for her decades of public service. Over the course of her life, she had worked on behalf of women's rights, argued passionately against war, and advocated for civil liberties and the dignity of working people. She helped found the American Civil Liberties Union and Helen Keller International—which supports projects to combat blindness and malnutrition—and wrote numerous books, including her famous autobiography, *The Story of My Life*. Most importantly, plays, books, and films have been made about her life, which serve as an inspiration to millions of people around the world.

The comeback:
"The most important day I remember in all my life," Helen Keller wrote in 1902, "is the one on which my teacher, Anne Mansfield Sullivan, came to me. I am filled with wonder when I consider the immeasurable contrasts between the two lives which it connects." Sullivan, a young teacher from Boston, traveled to Tuscumbia, Alabama, in 1887 to live at the Keller

estate and try to help young Helen connect with the world around her. Kate Adams Keller, Helen's mother, had sought the advice of specialists around the country. Her efforts eventually led her to Alexander Graham Bell, who put her in touch with the Perkins Institute in Boston, where Anne Sullivan had once been a student. Sullivan's work with Keller was "a brilliantly successful experiment," as Bell himself described it. (Alexander Graham Bell and Keller remained close friends for the rest of his life and corresponded often.) Sullivan helped her pupil learn to read Braille (in five languages) and even taught her to speak.

Without Sullivan's guidance—and without the efforts of her parents, who possessed the money and necessary patience to help their daughter—Helen Keller could not have become the person known to the rest of the world. Keller herself possessed a remarkable fighting spirit and a determination to see justice done on behalf of the weakest and neediest in the world. For the rest of her life, she fought for others as vigorously as others had fought for her. "You can do anything you think you can," Bell once wrote to Helen. "Remember that many will be brave in your courage."

WILL KEITH KELLOGG (1860–1951)
American Entrepreneur

At the bottom:

1895—Will Kellogg was angry with his older brother, John. For years, Kellogg had worked at the hospital and health spa run by John Harvey Kellogg in Michigan. At the Battle Creek Sanitarium, John Kellogg emphasized the role of nutrition and diet in restoring and preserving good health. He also treated his brother Will like a servant, expecting him to shine his shoes and shave his whiskers. Though John's estate at the time of his death was worth more than $4 million—roughly $100 million in contemporary terms—he paid Will a salary of only eighty-seven dollars a month.

While experimenting with whole grains, the brothers developed a wheat flake that patients enjoyed so much that many asked for boxes of it when they left the sanitarium. Will Kellogg hoped that his brother would agree to produce and market the product on a wider basis, but John insisted that the product only be used for their patients. When C. W. Post, an inventor and farm equipment manufacturer from Texas, came to Battle Creek in the early 1890s after a nervous breakdown, he fell in love with the cereal and became convinced he could duplicate the product. He did, opening his own cereal company almost literally down the street from the Battle Creek Sanitarium.

By the end of the century, C. W. Post had turned Will Kellogg's great idea into a business that sold hundreds of thousands of dollars worth of cereal each year. Even worse for Kellogg, Post's advertisements could be seen in newspapers and magazines everywhere. Post's company, which would eventually be known as General Foods, soon became one of the most recognizable brands of food in the United States. Meanwhile, Will Kellogg continued to work for a brother who'd thwarted his ambition.

At the top:

1946—After building his company into an internationally known producer of grain cereals, Will Kellogg retired as chairman of the board of the W. K. Kellogg Company. Products like Bran Flakes (introduced in 1914) and Rice Krispies (1928) had competed successfully with General

Foods' products and helped transform the way that Americans ate breakfast. Kellogg was best known, however, for his world famous Corn Flakes, a cereal that was imitated by companies all over the world—none of whom could match the Kellogg product. In addition to being a hugely successful businessman, Kellogg was a renowned philanthropist as well, using his foundation to fund projects for children, including hospitals, schools, social services, and recreational opportunities. His philanthropic activities were so successful that the U.S. State Department asked him to develop similar programs for Latin America during World War II.

The comeback:
Although Will Kellogg was disappointed that his discovery had made another man rich and successful, he continued to tinker with the process of making flaked cereals. In 1903, he perfected the recipe for "Toasted Corn Flakes," and in 1906 he finally left his brother behind and founded his own company. At last Kellogg was free to conduct business on his own terms. He advertised more aggressively than any of his competitors—including Post—and within a few years had made his flakes the leading cereal on the market. He gave away free samples and utilized innovative marketing techniques to sell his Toasted Corn Flakes. (One campaign offered housewives a free box of Corn Flakes if they winked at their grocers. Another pleaded with customers *not* to buy Corn Flakes because the demand was so great that the company couldn't keep up with the orders.) By the early 1920s, Will Kellogg was one of the richest men in the United States, and he'd managed to change the eating habits of hundreds of millions of people.

RAY KROC (1902–1984)
American Restaurant Entrepreneur

At the bottom:

1919—Just after World War I, a seventeen-year-old Ray Kroc was work-ing as a salesman for a ribbon company, "peddling rosebuds for farm wives to sew on garters and bed cushions." He enjoyed the work but could not imagine making a career out of it. A self-described bad student, Kroc was an energetic daydreamer who bounced around between several jobs as a young man. In his spare time, Kroc earned extra income as a piano player, performing anywhere he could find a gig, including a briefly playing in a Chicago bordello. Though he eventually landed a job as a paper-cup sales-man—a job he kept for several years—Kroc was not content and hoped that something else might one day come along.

At the top:

1963—Ray Kroc, who now owned a chain of restaurants known as McDonald's, sold his billionth hamburger and celebrated the opening of his five-hundredth franchise. That same year, his company developed a clown character called Ronald to be its mascot; within five years, Ameri-can children would recognize Ronald McDonald in the same way they recognized Santa Claus. Ray Kroc was now the owner of one of the most remarkable success stories in the history of modern American business. His empire was worth hundreds of millions of dollars—a fortune that would only grow in the next twenty years. When he died in 1984, Ray Kroc had seen McDonald's expand overseas, with restaurants opening in Europe, Asia, and elsewhere. His company's business model had been widely imitated by other fast-food chains, but none would be as popular and financially lucrative as McDonald's.

The comeback:

Ray Kroc never stopped looking for opportunity. His job as a paper-cup salesman had led him to a sales position for a milkshake machine manu-facturer, where he worked for almost twenty years before discovering a small but successful hamburger restaurant in Southern California. There, two brothers—Dick and Mac McDonald—had turned a simple idea into a small fortune. Kroc sold milkshake machines to the McDonald brothers and tried to persuade them to open more stores throughout the country. Ray Kroc might have continued to work as a salesman and enjoyed a comfortable retirement, but this plan didn't make his pulse "hammer with excitement," as he recalled in his autobiography.

While the McDonald brothers were satisfied with what they already had, Ray Kroc was always thinking of the next big thing. Convinced he was seeing it right before his eyes, Kroc convinced the two brothers to sell him the rights to build McDonald's franchises wherever he could. For $2.7 million, a fifty-two-year-old milkshake machine salesman had purchased the name and the concept that would soon enough make him rich and famous. He hadn't invented the idea of fast food, but he recognized a brilliant concept when he saw it.

HAROLD KUSHNER (B. 1935)
American Rabbi and Author

At the bottom:

1966—The diagnosis hardly seemed believable. Harold Kushner, a thirty-one-year-old rabbi from Natick, Massachusetts, listened as the doctor explained that his three-year-old son Aaron was suffering from a rare genetic disease called progeria, which causes a child to age so rapidly that they rarely live beyond their teenage years. Kushner was distraught with grief, and he suddenly realized that the usual words of comfort—the advice he gave to members of his congregation during traumatic moments in their lives—were completely useless. He couldn't believe, for example, that God would have any reason to afflict Aaron with such a terrible illness. What had his son ever done to hurt anyone? Aaron was innocent; moreover, he came from a family whose commitment to God was profound. How could this have happened? Kushner had no way to answer the question, and his uncertainty caused him to question whether he could even continue as a rabbi. All he knew anymore was that his precious child was going to die, and that somehow God had allowed this to happen.

At the top:

1984—Harold Kushner never expected to write a best seller, but when Random House published *When Bad Things Happen to Good People* in 1981, he wound up doing exactly that. By 1984, the book had sold more than two million copies, had been translated into eight languages, and had remained on the *New York Times* best-seller list for an entire year. The book featured Kushner's reflections on the meaning of suffering, especially the most common question that people ask during a time of trial: "Why me?" Kushner argued that good people endure terrible events not because God wants them to, but rather because God simply cannot control everything. Rather than ask God why He allowed something terrible to happen, Kushner urged his readers to ask God for guidance on how to use their own suffering as inspiration to bring something good into the world. Following the success of his first book, Kushner has gone on to write eleven more popular titles about religion and the search for meaning. His work has earned him a Lifetime Achievement Award from the

Jewish Book Council, and he remains one of the most popular religious writers of his generation.

The comeback:

When he learned of Aaron's prognosis, Harold Kushner's grief was profound. Rather than walk away from serving his faith, however, Kushner used his son's illness as an opportunity to reflect on his own assumptions about God and the meaning of suffering. By the time Aaron died of a heart attack in 1977, just one day after he turned fourteen, Kushner had come to believe that God was not responsible for his death. Kushner believed that God did not allow bad things to happen—nor could he prevent bad things from happening—but that instead He inspired people to be generous and helpful and brave in the face of challenges.

As Kushner explained in his first book, his son served "by facing up so bravely to his illness and to the problems caused by his appearance. I know that his friends and schoolmates were affected by his courage and by the way he managed to live a full life despite his limitations. And I know that people who knew our family were moved to handle the difficult times of their own lives with more hope and courage when they saw our example. I take these as instances of God moving people here on earth to help other people in need." For his own part, Kushner decided before Aaron's death that he would honor his memory by writing a book that might help others to endure life's most difficult moments.

MARIO LEMIEUX (B. 1965)
American Hockey Player

At the bottom:

1993—In early January of 1993, Mario Lemieux received devastating news from his doctors: he had been diagnosed with Hodgkin's disease. Driving home from Allegheny General Hospital, Lemieux could hardly pay attention to the road. He was scheduled to be married in five months, but now his personal life was in question, his season seemed over, his career threatened, and his life in the balance. He'd lost a cousin to Hodgkin's fifteen years earlier, and he couldn't help but wonder if he'd suffer the same fate.

Lemieux, one of the most gifted scorers ever to play hockey, had noticed a small, rubbery lump in his neck in 1992 but thought nothing of it, even as it grew in size. His team, the Pittsburgh Penguins, was marching toward a second consecutive Stanley Cup, and while Lemieux would spend much of the season dealing with injuries of one kind or another, he would eventually play a key role in bringing the Cup back to the Steel City. When the 1992–93 season began, Lemieux and the Penguins had their sights fixed on a third title, and Lemieux set a pace to break some of the greatest scoring records in the history of the sport.

At the top:

1997—Two days after being inducted into the National Hockey League Hall of Fame, Mario Lemieux bid a tearful farewell to the Penguins and his Pittsburgh fans. Describing his thirteen years with the team as "the best thirteen years of my life," the man known as "Super Mario" watched as his number 66 was retired and hoisted to the rafters of Pittsburgh's Civic Arena. Lemieux had not only defeated cancer—surviving months of brutal radiation treatment—but he'd actually managed to return to the ice before the 1992–93 season was over. Miraculous as his return had been, his level of play never diminished. He was named hockey's most valuable player in 1994–95 and won scoring titles in that season as well as the next—all while suffering from back problems and other injuries that would have kept most players off the ice.. Indeed, Lemieux's drive to succeed was so intense that he came out of retirement in 2000 and played another five seasons before retiring for a second and final time in 2006.

The comeback:

Four days after his diagnosis, Mario Lemieux spoke with reporters and expressed optimism about his chances for survival. "I'm a positive person," he explained. "Sometimes in life, you have to go through tough periods. I haven't been that fortunate. But you climb the mountain. We know this disease is curable." Lemieux's excellent physical conditioning and his boundless optimism helped carry him through his treatments and back to action a mere two months later. He was determined to complete the rest of the season, and to put nothing else on hold while he battled cancer. He even insisted that his wedding (scheduled for June of 1993) not be postponed. Throughout his career, Lemieux struggled back from injuries and illness, and cancer became merely one of the obstacles that he threw aside on his way to one of the most remarkable careers in any sport. Only when he was diagnosed with an irregular heartbeat did Mario Lemieux finally leave the ice for good.

ABRAHAM LINCOLN (1809–1865)

American Politician

At the bottom:

1850—Abraham Lincoln's political career seemed over. After serving as a militia captain in Illinois during the 1832 Black Hawk War, he climbed the ladder of Illinois politics during the 1830s and '40s and eventually served a single term in the US (as opposed to Illinois) House of Representatives from 1847 to 1849. When his term ended, however, Lincoln—a shy but ambitious man—returned to Illinois without much of an idea of what to do other than to return to his legal practice. To make matters worse, Lincoln's marriage was frequently a source of frustration.

In February of 1850, his beloved son Edward died of a respiratory illness at the age of four; and, less than a year later, his father, Thomas Lincoln, passed away. Lincoln's relationship with his father had been strained and distant for many years, and he did not attend the funeral. With Thomas Lincoln's death, Abraham was the only surviving member of his immediate family. His mother had died in 1818 (when Lincoln was nine years old), and his sister had died in childbirth a decade later. With personal tragedy heaped on top of professional frustration, Lincoln sank into one of his occasional bouts of depression.

At the top:

1865—Having won reelection to a second term as President of the United States, Abraham Lincoln now watched as the nation's armed forces struck a final blow against the Confederate states. After four years of unimaginable war and national strife, Lincoln had successfully steered a course to victory while destroying the institution of slavery, which had survived for more than two and a half centuries in North America. In early April of 1865, just days after the Confederate surrender—a few days before his assassination—Abraham Lincoln walked through the streets of Richmond, Virginia, where the Confederacy had set up its government during the war. As cheering crowds of freed slaves greeted him, Lincoln witnessed firsthand the "new birth of freedom" of which he'd spoken in the Gettysburg Address of July 1863.

The comeback:

Lincoln returned to politics during the 1850s as the nation dealt with a series of conflicts over the question of whether slavery should be allowed to expand into new lands. Lincoln argued forcefully—and in the language of common sense—that slavery and freedom were not compatible with each other. Although Lincoln opposed slavery, for political reasons he did not, initially, try to end it entirely. Instead, he wanted to limit its growth and keep new territories in the west free for settlement by farmers working their own land. His eloquent speeches and thought-provoking arguments helped push him into the national spotlight and then the White House. As president, Lincoln presented a vision of national unity that appealed to a broad range of people. His objections to slavery were based on his own moral judgment, but as a leader he always tried to find solutions that brought the greatest benefits to the greatest number of people.

VINCE LOMBARDI (1913–1970)
American Football Coach

At the bottom:

1946—Vince Lombardi, football coach at a small Catholic high school in New Jersey, opened a letter from an old college teammate, hoping for good news. His friend was working as the head coach at a midwestern college, and Lombardi—who'd enjoyed great success at St. Cecilia—was hoping to break into the collegiate ranks as an assistant coach. Though Lombardi projected an image of always being in control, he was in fact constantly doubting his own choices and often changed his mind suddenly.

The previous year, he had nearly left St. Cecilia to take a job at another New Jersey high school before a group of his players pleaded with him to stay through their senior seasons. Lombardi agreed, committing himself to another two years, but he was eager to be more than a high school coach. Unfortunately, the rest of the football world seemed uncooperative. One rejection after another piled onto his desk, until his friend's letter arrived in the mail. It brought another rejection, along with some painful words of advice: "No future in coaching. Try something else."

At the top:

1967—It was New Year's Eve, and the Green Bay Packers were again the champions of the National Football League. In one of the most famous games in the sport's history, Vince Lombardi—who'd led the club for eight winning seasons, including three consecutive league titles—led his team to victory over the Dallas Cowboys in a game played in temperatures as low as –13F. With the Packers behind by a three points, quarterback Bart Starr brought the team to the Dallas goal line. On third down and with a mere sixteen seconds left to play, Lombardi and Starr agreed to run the ball rather than pass it, despite the fact that a failed running play would leave the team unable to stop the clock and attempt a tying field goal. With the Cowboys expecting a pass, Starr kept the ball and lunged across the goal line for the winning score. As Lombardi explained after the game, "We gambled, and we won." Two weeks later, the Packers defeated the Oakland Raiders of the American Football League to win their second consecutive Super Bowl (a game that was less prestigious at the time).

The comeback:

Lombardi's career benefited from his intense work ethic, having high standards for his players, a few helpful pushes from friends old and new, and a commitment to fair (but hard) play on the field. Shortly after his friend turned him down for an assistant coaching job, Lombardi received an offer from his *alma mater*, Fordham University, to serve as an assistant coach for the freshman squad. During his two years at Fordham, Lombardi developed a reputation as a great motivator; he also befriended a New York sportswriter who recognized that the thirty-five-year-old assistant coach possessed talents that were not being utilized to their full potential.

A graduate of West Point, the sportswriter recommended Lombardi for the head coach's job when it became available in 1948. After five seasons with mixed success at West Point, Lombardi migrated to the NFL as an assistant coach for the New York Giants, a team with a losing record and few prospects for success. With Lombardi as offensive coordinator, the team rose to the top of the league three years later; in 1958, Lombardi parlayed his success with the Giants into a head coaching job with the Packers, the worst team in the league.

Lombardi's coaching philosophy and motivation—famously captured in the maxim "winning isn't everything, it's the only thing"—earned him the love and devotion of his players, who knew that if they did everything he asked of them, they'd wind up as winners. At the same time, Lombardi placed great value in sportsmanship and was, in the words of former player Willie Wood, "the fairest person I ever met." Long before such an attitude was fashionable, Lombardi refused to tolerate discrimination of any kind. For example, in a time in which segregated hotels were common, Lombardi refused to allow any players to stay at hotels that did not allow blacks when the team was traveling.

DAVE LONGABERGER (1935–1999)
American Businessman

At the bottom:

1955—At the age of twenty-one, Dave Longaberger held the dubious honor of being the oldest graduating senior in his high school class in Dresden, Ohio. The fifth of twelve children, Longaberger grew up in a family that was happy but nevertheless struggled to get by. His father, who worked at a paper mill, had grown up in a family of German American basket makers, but the family business had closed its doors during the Great Depression. Nevertheless, Longaberger's father continued the craft by making baskets in his spare time, selling them for a few pennies, or (more often) giving them away to friends.

Longaberger himself struggled terribly with school as a young boy. He stuttered and was marked as a slow reader; other kids mocked him openly in class, snickering when he was called on to read out loud. He was held back twice in elementary school, and by the time he finished high school, he was still reading at only a sixth-grade level. He was excited to be finished with school, but he felt "scared" and "inadequate." "What should I do now?" he thought. "Here I am, reading at a sixth-grade level. What could I expect the world to do for me?" It seemed as if he had no good choices.

At the top:

1999—Dave Longaberger probably never expected to be the undisputed king of wooden baskets, but as the twentieth century drew to a close, Longaberger presided over a company that sold millions of high quality, handmade maple baskets each year and whose annual revenue topped $700 million. Though he was struggling with the last stages of kidney cancer, Longaberger remained upbeat and confident. "Big deal," he wrote in a memoir that would be published after his death. "Anyone who lives long enough is bound to have his share [of adversity]." His Newark, Ohio, headquarters—a massive complex that included a two-hundred-fifty-thousand-square-foot plant as well as a thirty-million-dollar, seven-story building built in the shape of a basket—had become a popular tourist destination. The company's signature product had been used many times as gift baskets for the Academy Awards, the Emmy Awards, and the NAACP Image Awards, along with other high-profile events. Collectors of Longaberger baskets had formed a subculture of their own, participating in a vibrant Internet trade with more than a thousand Web sites devoted to Longaberger products. Along with his business success, Longaberger developed a reputation as a great philanthropist and gave millions of dollars over the years to his home community of Dresden, Ohio. The Longaberger Foundation provides grants for educational and health programs for children and families in need. One of Longaberger's daughters ran the foundation while the other one became president of the company.

The comeback:

As Longaberger recounts in his autobiography, his failures at school never convinced him that he would be a failure in life. As a teenager, he took pride in doing a good job shoveling snow for his neighbors or being a valuable stocker at the grocery store where he worked. "I didn't get many strokes in school," he wrote, "so I found ways to get them elsewhere." He was constantly looking for new challenges—whether it was mowing lawns better than any other kid in Dresden, or working the film projector at the movie theater. After finishing high school, Longaberger held a series of jobs that included stints as a Fuller Brush salesman and as a route deliveryman for several bakeries in Dresden. He spent two years in the U.S. Army during the early 1960s and began a career as a small businessman by purchasing a small grocery store and a dairy bar.

In 1973, Longaberger noticed that wooden baskets were selling well at a local shopping mall. Persuading his father to come out of retirement, Longaberger devoted some time over the next few years to selling small batches of baskets that his father and a few others made. In 1978, he developed a new marketing plan that was modeled on the Tupperware company's method of direct marketing. Longaberger hired sales associates who sold the products directly to customers at home basket parties. Using his own family's story as part of the sales pitch, Longaberger quickly saw his sales accelerate.

MUKHTAR MAI (B. 1972)
Pakistani Women's Rights Activist

At the bottom:

2002—"In the name of the Koran, release me!" the woman screamed. Four men stripped the thirty-year-old woman as a group of onlookers danced with joy. All were members of a tribe in the remote Pakistani village of Meerwala, and they had been given permission by the village council to rape the woman as punishment for an affair her brother had been accused of having with a high-status woman. (By custom, family members of someone accused of a crime or social transgression could be punished for those acts.) After her clothes had been torn from her body, Mukhtar Mai was raped by all four men before being forced to walk home naked.

Hundreds of villagers witnessed her humiliation; all of them knew that, by custom, the young woman would soon be obligated to take her own life. In the tribal culture of rural Pakistan, a young woman subjected to such an attack was treated as an outcast. Her stigma would follow her for the rest of her life, and she would never be deemed suitable for marriage. As Mukhtar Mai wrote in her memoir, tribal culture allows men to treat women as objects of "possession, honor, or revenge. They marry or rape them according to their conception of tribal pride." Rape, she explained, "is the ultimate weapon: it shames the other clan forever."

At the top:

2006—Four years after her attack, Mukhtar Mai was welcomed to the United Nations headquarters in New York, where officials had gathered to celebrate her bravery in the face of a terrible ordeal. In the years since her rape, Mukhtar had become a symbol of hope, having become one of the leading advocates for women's education in societies where women were still second-class citizens. "I think it is fair to say that anyone who has the moral courage and internal strength to turn such a brutal attack into a weapon to defend others in a similar position, is a hero indeed, and is worthy of our deepest respect and admiration," said Under-Secretary-General for Communications Shashi Tharoor. Risking her own safety, Mukhtar had remained in the region of her birth and now oversaw a school that taught three hundred girls and two hundred boys. The previous year, the government of Pakistan had honored her with the Fatima Jinnah gold medal for bravery and courage; *Glamour* magazine named her "Woman of the Year" in 2005. Her memoir (originally published in French) had just gone to press and would eventually be translated into numerous languages, allowing millions of readers throughout the world to read her story first-hand.

The comeback:

With the help of her family, Mukhtar Mai ultimately refused to allow an inhumane tribal custom to force her to end her own life. Though she was distraught and humiliated, and she did begin preparations to kill herself immediately after the rape, her parents kept a close eye on her for several days and prevented her from harming herself. When she recovered some of her strength, her attitude shifted from shame to fury. She bravely filed charges against her attackers, surprising the entire nation.

Within a few weeks, the international media—including *Time* magazine in the United States and the British Broadcasting Corporation (BBC)— began covering the story as the case moved toward trial. Human rights groups such as Amnesty International took an interest as well and helped bring the case to the world's attention. In late August of 2002, a Pakistani court convicted six men in the rape of Mukhtar Mai and sentenced them to death. (Three years later, their convictions would be overturned, with the court citing a lack of evidence.) In the meantime, Mukhtar had begun using her case to bring positive changes for young girls in her country.

When a judge awarded the equivalent of eighty-two hundred dollars in compensation for Mukhtar, she put the money toward the creation of a school for girls. "Why should I have spent the money on myself?" she asked a reporter. "This way the money is helping all the girls, all the children." When Nicholas Kristof, a reporter for *The New York Times*, began covering Mukhtar's story, readers contributed more than $430,000 to further her educational work. Through courage and resilience, Mukhtar had survived a brutal attack, defied a terrible custom, and set about on a course that would improve the lives of others like her, enabling them to escape a similar plight.

NELSON MANDELA (B. 1918)
South African Political Activist and Politician

At the bottom:
1964—Nelson Mandela sat in a jail cell on South Africa's infamous Robben Island, a place that had housed lepers, prisoners, quarantined animals, and, most recently, South African political activists. Mandela had just been convicted of plotting and carrying out acts of sabotage against the apartheid government, which denied black South Africans equal rights. A longtime political activist from a distinguished family, Mandela had been the leader of an armed group within the African National Congress, which was campaigning to end racial discrimination and segregation.

When the white-controlled government began to suppress black protests with great violence and went so far as to ban the ANC itself, Mandela believed there were no alternatives left if black South Africans ever were to be free. In 1962, he was arrested and sentenced to five years in prison for leading an illegal workers' strike; two years later, nearly two dozen top ANC leaders were arrested and charged with over two hundred acts of sabotage. In a trial that much of the world condemned, Mandela and twelve other ANC leaders received life sentences.

At the top:
1994—Almost thirty years from the day of his conviction and life sentence, more than sixty thousand people and leaders from 130 nations gathered in Pretoria to watch Nelson Mandela take the oath as South Africa's first black president. "Today," Mandela explained, "all of us . . . confer glory and hope to newborn liberty. Out of the experience of an extraordinary human disaster that lasted too long, must be born a society of which all humanity will be proud." A new national flag was hoisted before the event—the red, white, and blue flag (symbolizing European political control) was replaced with one that included the African colors of green, white, and black. The apartheid system was officially dismantled, as the African National Congress won more than 60 percent of the votes in the country's first multi-racial election. After Mandela had been released from prison in 1990, he remained determined to carry on the struggle against racial injustice. Over the next several years, he and other

ANC leaders negotiated with the government of F. W. de Klerk to bring apartheid to a close and try to build a new, non-racist South Africa. For their efforts, both men received the 1993 Nobel Peace Prize.

The comeback:

In his 1995 autobiography, *Long Walk to Freedom*, Mandela wrote, "I have discovered the secret that after climbing a great hill, one only finds that there are many more hills to climb." Having won his release from prison, Mandela explained, "I can rest only for a moment, for with freedom come responsibilities, and I dare not linger, for my long walk is not yet ended." Mandela led an extraordinary and dangerous campaign against an unjust government, and he was not defeated by his imprisonment. As he explained at the 1964 trial, he was prepared to die for his beliefs.

Throughout his twenty-seven years in prison, he continued to hold onto his conviction that black South Africans must be free. He was offered an early release on at least one occasion during the 1980s, provided that he give up his struggle against the South African government. Mandela refused, explaining that his own personal freedom was not worth surrendering the freedom of others. Mandela and his supporters around the world kept their hopes alive throughout the years he was incarcerated, and their hopes were eventually rewarded—not only with Mandela's release, but also with the emergence of a free South Africa at last.

DIEGO MARADONA (B. 1960)
Argentine Soccer Player

At the bottom:

2005—Anyone catching a glimpse of Diego Maradona would have been stunned to realize they were looking at a man who once had been one of the greatest soccer players in the history of the sport. Born into severe poverty, Maradona had risen from a Buenos Aires shantytown to become an Argentine national hero and international superstar, leading Argentina to a World Cup championship in 1986 and dominating the Italian professional league for much of the 1980s. Along the way, he had dazzled millions of fans with his ball-handling and goal-scoring abilities. The most famous of his goals, scored against Great Britain in the 1986 World Cup quarterfinals, was clearly the result of a handball. When reporters asked about the incident, Maradona described the goal as having been scored "a little with the head of Maradona and a little with the hand of God."

Now, almost two decades since the notorious "hand-of-God" goal, Maradona was grotesquely unhealthy. Measuring a mere 5 feet 6 inches tall, Maradona had ballooned in weight to well over three hundred pounds since his retirement in 1997. When he wasn't eating and drinking enormous quantities of alcohol, Maradona was slowly killing himself with cocaine, a drug he'd begun using during his playing days and which had eventually led to his expulsion from the Italian professional league. (Drugs had also ended his World Cup career in 1994; when routine tests detected ephedrine in his blood, Maradona was sent home, and his team exited the tournament in the second round.) By the age of forty-five, Maradona had endured two heart attacks and kidney disease, and he seemed unlikely to make it to the age of fifty. One of the most remarkable athletes of his era, Maradona had crashed and burned.

At the top:

2009—A triumphant Diego Maradona—now coach of the Argentine national squad—celebrated a thrilling 1–0 victory over Uruguay in a match that guaranteed Argentina a place at the 2010 World Cup finals in South Africa. Before play began in the Uruguayan capital of Montevideo, Argentina was in danger of being eliminated from competition; it would have marked the first time since 1970 that Argentina had failed to reach the World Cup's final round. Had that happened, Maradona's brief career as a coach would certainly have been over. His players, however, managed to score a late goal and pull out the win—the first time in thirty-three years that Argentina had beaten Uruguay in their capital city. "I'd like to thank the players from the bottom of my heart," said a delighted Maradona after the match ended, "because today was the day they made me a coach." He dedicated the win to his family and to all the people of Argentina.

The comeback:

Physical recovery did not come easily for Maradona. He had been treated for cocaine addiction in the early 2000s, but excessive eating and drinking, coupled with severe depression, had jeopardized his health severely. Realizing that he did not want to die, Maradona began his steep climb back to health with a gastric bypass operation in March of 2005. His weight tumbled by more than one hundred pounds by the end of the year, and he commenced a new career as a talk show host. Referring to Maradona's jersey number, the show titled "La Noche de Diez" ("The Night of Ten") became an instant success, dominating the ratings throughout its first and only season.

Maradona experienced several setbacks over the next few years—including two relapses for overeating in 2007 and 2008 that returned him to the hospital—but he has since steered clear of drugs and alcohol and has maintained his weight loss. His return to the Argentinean soccer world seems to have been instrumental in giving Maradona the motivation to stay healthy. For years, Maradona served as a national hero to ordinary Argentineans, a symbol of their own dreams of greatness. Despite his personal problems, he was still adored in his home country and longed to find a way back into the spotlight. In 2005, he served as general manager of the Boca Juniors, a popular pro club from Buenos Aires. When the coach of the national team resigned in 2008, Maradona pushed hard for the job. Despite his thin coaching resumé, he was awarded the position. Maradona and Argentina's national team were at last reunited.

BERNARD MARCUS (B. 1929)
American Entrepreneur

At the bottom:
1978—Bernie Marcus had just been fired by a man whose nickname was "Ming the Merciless." The fifty-year-old son of Russian immigrants, Marcus had scratched his way through school and, after working a few years as a pharmacist, found that he liked the idea of running a store more than he enjoyed working in one. By the late 1970s, he had worked his way to the top of a Los Angeles-based discount hardware chain called Handy Dan, where he served as president and CEO. Handy Dan was doing well and earning excellent profits. Unfortunately for Marcus, Handy Dan was owned by a parent company, Daylin, whose top executive was rumored to be worried that Bernard Marcus might one day succeed him. So while Handy Dan was the only division of Daylin that was turning out impressive profits, "Ming the Merciless" reminded everyone of why he had earned his nickname. On a Friday afternoon, he fired the top three executives at Handy Dan. For good measure, he told the press that Marcus and the others had been guilty of labor law violations—allegations that turned out to be without merit. Now at the age of fifty, Bernie Marcus was unemployed and nearly broke.

At the top:
2002—On the day of his retirement as Chairman of Home Depot, Bernie Marcus presided over one of the top twenty public companies based in the United States. With outlets in the United States, Canada, Mexico, and China, Home Depot's sales reached $58 billion in 2001. More than 160,000 men and women were employed in more than two thousand "superstores"—massive warehouse facilities that averaged 105,000 square feet each. In addition to founding and leading a successful home improvement retailer for over twenty years, Marcus and his business partners also changed the way that Americans approached home improvement projects. By offering an extremely wide selection of supplies and tools, as well as short, simple workshops in basic home improvement tasks, Home Depot made it possible for almost everyone to "do it yourself." Beyond his astounding business success, Bernie Marcus had also become one of

the nation's top charitable donors. Among other causes, Marcus established an institute that provides services to children with developmental disabilities; established a think tank that focuses on issues of democracy in Israel; and provided almost all the funding for the Georgia Aquarium, which opened in 2005.

The comeback:

Shortly after his dismissal from Handy Dan, Bernard Marcus spoke with a friend and investment banker, Ken Langone, who reminded him of an idea that Marcus had shared with him a few years earlier, when Marcus had thought that a national chain of warehouse-sized home improvement centers would be a good idea. But Marcus was content at the time and had no reason to explore his idea, at least not until he later lost his job. Though Marcus was humiliated by the firing, Langone was optimistic. "This is the greatest news I have heard," he told this friend. "You have just been kicked in the ass with a golden horseshoe." After Langone helped Marcus find a group of enthusiastic investors who liked his business plan, Marcus and his business partner Arthur Blank opened a handful of stores in Atlanta in 1979.

The first few warehouses did not immediately make an impact, but within two years business began to tick upward. Within a decade, the company had almost $3 billion a year in sales and employed about twenty thousand people. Known for its outstanding customer service, Home Depot also established itself as a company that treated its employees well. Marcus encouraged his managers and employees to think creatively and bring new ideas into the company. Home Depot's unique employee training programs give everyone in the company the background to understand and sell the products they carry. He also compensates his employees well, offering wages that exceed industry averages by 20–25 percent; generous health and dental benefits; and options to purchase discounted Home Depot stock. As Marcus explains, he and his partners were in "the right place at the right time with the right philosophy . . . . We surrounded ourselves with good people and we believed in them."

JOHN McCAIN (B. 1936)
American Naval Officer and Politician

At the bottom:

1968—At the age of thirty-one, John McCain found himself a prisoner of war in North Vietnam. A naval aviator, McCain had been shot down over the North Vietnamese capital of Hanoi in October of 1967. He managed to eject himself from the plane before it crashed, but he was badly injured and nearly drowned when he came down in Truch Bach Lake. After being beaten by civilians who dragged him from the lake, McCain was transported to Hoa Lo Prison, where North Vietnamese doctors told him that it was "too late" to save him. He remained in horrific physical condition for weeks, with unattended broken limbs and a case of dysentery that nearly killed him. (He eventually received medical treatment when his captors learned that McCain's father was a very high-ranking officer in the United States Navy.)

McCain, like other American prisoners, was kept in solitary confinement at the prison. The food was nearly inedible, and McCain lost fifty pounds within a few months. By August of 1968, North Vietnamese interrogators began torturing him on a daily basis, demanding that he confess his "crimes" against the Vietnamese people. Eventually, at what he later described as the lowest point of his life, McCain reached his breaking point and signed a "confession," excerpts of which were later read on Radio Hanoi.

At the top:

2008—John McCain stood at the podium at the Xcel Center in St. Paul, Minnesota, where he had just accepted the nomination as the Republican Party's candidate for President of the United States. "I don't mind a good fight," he told the crowd. "For reasons known only to God, I've had quite a few tough ones in my life." Since 1983, McCain had served in the U.S. Congress—first as a representative from Arizona's First Congressional District, and then as one of the state's two senators. During his years in Congress, he had worked on issues such as campaign finance reform and had earned a great deal of visibility as an opponent of "pork barrel spending." Having served in Vietnam, he had taken the lead on numerous issues related to veterans' affairs; he recounted his experiences as a prisoner of war in a 1999 memoir titled *Faith of My Fathers*. He had run for the GOP nomination in 2000 but finished second to George W. Bush; a second run in the 2008 campaign had initially seemed like a failure. In mid-2007, his campaign had nearly run out of money and he was far behind in the polls. But a year later, after the dust settled, McCain had dominated the primary process, winning a vast majority of his party's delegates and sewing up the nomination by early March 2008. Although he would eventually lose the general election to Barack Obama, McCain had secured a place in history as one of the most important political figures of his era.

The comeback:

John McCain always regretted signing a coerced "confession," but he was not alone among his fellow POWs in succumbing to torture. In his memoir, McCain admitted that in his shame, he contemplated suicide; instead of taking his own life, however, McCain actively resisted his captors. He refused to sign a follow-up "confession" and was subjected to months of additional physical abuse as a result. McCain spent two years in solitary confinement, yet he and his fellow prisoners managed to communicate by tapping on the bars of their cells. During the five years he remained at the "Hanoi Hilton," McCain gained a reputation as a leader among the other prisoners. Though he had numerous opportunities to secure an early release, he refused to leave before all those men who ranked beneath him had been let go.

When the war ended and he returned to the United States, McCain received an array of honors, including the Silver Star, the Legion of Merit, several Bronze Stars, a Navy Commendation Medal, and the Purple Heart. Motivated to understand his experiences as well as the wider circumstances of the Vietnam War, McCain pursued graduate studies at the Naval War College before serving as a congressional liaison for the navy during the late 1970s.

Though he had been profoundly shaped by the five and a half years he spent in captivity, McCain was determined to move beyond that experience and not allow his life to be defined by it. During his service as a congressional liaison, McCain realized that he had an interest in public service and began pondering a career in politics. Aided by the financial assets of his second wife, Cindy—the heiress to the Hensley and Company beer fortune—McCain ran for a seat in the U.S. House in 1982 and won, setting in motion the next major phase of his life.

ARTHUR MILLER (1915–2005)
American Playwright

At the bottom:

1944—As his first play flopped after less than a full week of performances, Arthur Miller must have wondered why he titled it *The Man Who Had All the Luck*. Only six years earlier, Miller had graduated from the University of Michigan with high hopes for his future as a novelist and playwright. While at Michigan, he had won two Hopwood Awards—a prestigious prize awarded to the best aspiring writer at the university—and had been a runner-up for the award once as well. After graduation, he moved to New York City and took a job with the Federal Theater Project, where he expected to make a quick mark on American drama. Unfortunately, the Federal Theater Project closed shop a year after Miller arrived, and he found himself having a difficult time getting his work published or staged.

He managed to find work writing for radio dramas and was hired to work on a screenplay about the war journalist Ernie Pyle, but Miller was not at all satisfied. He seemed to have gotten his big break, however, when *The Man Who Had All the Luck* was accepted as a Broadway production—something that was unheard of for a first play by such a young talent. Miller's triumph, however, turned to bitter disappointment when the play opened in November of 1944. Critics scorned it. Five of the seven daily newspapers in New York trashed the play, with one describing it as "incredibly turgid in its writing and stuttering in its execution." With poor attendance and a cold critical reception, the producers had little choice but to shut Miller's play down after four performances.

At the top:

1949—It was opening night for Arthur Miller's new play, *Death of a Salesman*, and as the final curtain dropped, Alan Hewitt—one of the cast members—wondered how the audience would respond. "There was a long, deathly silence," he remembered. "I held my breath for what seemed like an eternity and then the whole audience exploded. They cheered, hollered, clapped, hooted and screamed and would not stop. Even after the actors stopped taking curtain calls, they milled around and wouldn't leave." The audience that night had witnessed the opening of one of the greatest plays in the history of American drama. In 1949 alone, Miller's play would go on to earn the Pulitzer Prize for Drama, a Tony Award for Best Author, and the New York Drama Circle Critics' Award. Whereas his first play had folded after a handful of performances, *Death of a Salesman* would run for several years, with 742 performances in all before the run concluded. It has since been performed hundreds of thousands of times in theaters across the world, including in China, where Miller took the play in 1983.

Miller would go on to write several dozen celebrated works of drama, the best known of these being *The Crucible* and *The Price*. (He would also spend five years in a different sort of drama, as the husband of Marilyn Monroe.) In an interesting twist of fortune, Miller's first play—the one that flopped so badly—would later receive greater critical appreciation and would be staged successfully in London as well as on Broadway. After his death in 2005, Miller was hailed as one of the century's great playwrights, a man whose works, as one critic observed, "will always stand with the masterpieces of Ibsen, Shakespeare and Sophocles."

The comeback:

Miller's first play was a terrible disappointment, and Miller himself was never completely happy with the project, even as it was being readied for its debut on Broadway. But as he was writing it, he stumbled upon a theme—the relationship between fathers, sons, and brothers—that would be central to his work for the rest of his career. "*The Man Who Had All the Luck,*" he explained years later, "through its endless versions, was to move me inch by inch toward my first open awareness of father-son and brother-brother conflict." Once he realized that he was interested in these family tensions, he felt "an indescribable new certainty that I could speak from deep within myself, had seen something that no one else had seen." While the failure of the play was a great disappointment, Miller was able to look beyond the immediate moment and see that he had happened upon an important source of inspiration that would serve him well in the coming years.

GRANDMA MOSES (1860–1961)
American Artist

At the bottom:

1927—Anna Moses, a sixty-seven-year-old farm wife from upstate New York, had just buried her husband, Thomas, a former farm worker to whom she'd been married for forty years. Coming from a poor family, Moses had worked hard all her life, first as a farmhand and then as a tenant farmer with Thomas in Virginia, where they lived for about sixteen years during the late nineteenth century. The Moses family was no stranger to heartbreak, as Anna and Thomas suffered through the deaths of five of their ten children. After their farmhouse burned down in 1905, they returned to New York and established a small dairy farm, which brought them a modest income but took a physical toll on Anna and Thomas.

Thomas Moses worked until the day he died of a heart attack, while Anna Moses continued to labor each day even as her hands began to feel the symptoms of arthritis. Several of her children remained on the farm to help with the daily routine, but at her age—and at a time when American farmers were experiencing a long period of hard times preceding the Great Depression—Anna Moses faced an uncertain future.

At the top:

1960—On Anna Moses's one-hundredth birthday, New York Governor Nelson Rockefeller proclaimed September 7 to be "Grandma Moses Day," in honor of the woman who had become the most popular female artist in American history. By that point, Anna Moses had over thirty-six hundred paintings to her credit, almost all of them featuring scenes of rural farm life—the only life she had ever really known. A self-taught artist, Moses nevertheless captivated critics, collectors, and the general public, who found her simple, pleasant visions appealing at a time of tremendous historical change and amid the deepening tensions of the Cold War.

Moses's work brought her viewers back to a time that seemed more innocent and less complicated, a world defined by small town virtues and a lifestyle untouched by commercialism. (Ironically, Moses's work was used by the Hallmark company—no stranger to commerce—on numerous greeting cards over the years.) In the two decades since her art became known to the world outside her family and hometown, Moses had become an international sensation.

The comeback:

Anna Moses's husband and several of her children had always admired her skill with a sewing needle, and they knew that she had an interest in painting as well, that she had been unable to pursue as much more than an occasional hobby. In the first few years after her husband's death, Moses spent some time doing some embroidered pictures, but she eventually had to abandon the craft as her arthritis worsened. She could still hold a paintbrush, however, and in 1935—at the tender age of seventy-five—she began to paint more frequently, even exhibiting some of her pictures at local events including fairs and charity sales. She gave away much of this early work, having no intention of making money from it; indeed, at the county fair one year, she earned a prize for her preserves but nothing for her paintings.

In 1938, an amateur art collector named Louis Caldor happened to see some of Moses's work displayed in a drugstore. He tracked down Anna Moses and urged her to submit some of her work for a show at the New York Museum of Modern Art. Moses and her family laughed when Caldor promised that he could help her achieve fame in the art world.

Though initially many of New York's art critics and collectors were not enthusiastic about investing in the work of an elderly amateur, within two years her work had begun to make a mark. Thomas Watson, IBM's founder, purchased one of her pieces, as did singer Cole Porter. Before World War II was over, "Grandma" Moses's work was being exhibited throughout the United States, with a traveling show that would circulate throughout the country until 1963, two years after the artist's death. For millions of elderly Americans, Moses's life has offered proof that "second acts" are possible and that it's never too late in life to start a new career.

LIZ MURRAY (B. 1980)

American Author and Motivational Speaker

At the bottom:

1996—By the age of fifteen, the Bronx-born Elizabeth Murray had watched her mother die of AIDS. Both Murray's parents were cocaine addicts who neglected her and her sister, and squandered what little money they had on their shared drug of choice. As a child, "Liz" frequently watched them shooting up in the kitchen; the walls were spattered with drops of blood from their clumsy efforts to find usable veins. At the age of eight, she earned much of the family's income by working off the books at a grocery store and pumping gas for tips.

When her mother died in 1996, Liz and her sister had nowhere to turn. Their father had been living on the streets for some time and was incapable of providing for them. Liz Murray soon joined the ranks of New York's homeless population. She had rarely attended school—she was too embarrassed by her personal appearance and her poverty—and seemed to be heading toward a life of struggle and desperation.

At the top:

2008—A little over a decade after living on the streets of New York, Liz Murray received her bachelor's degree in psychology from Harvard University. Her remarkable life had been the subject of a 2003 television movie, "Homeless to Harvard: The Liz Murray Story," and Murray's memoir of her youth, *Breaking Night,* had been published in 2005. She was a widely sought motivational speaker and appeared frequently at schools, where she recounted her story and encouraged her audiences to spend time every day trying to improve their own lives. "The reason I'm standing here in front of you today is because I chose the higher road," she told a college audience in early 2009. "I chose the higher road which is available to each of us."

The comeback:

The death of her mother proved to be a turning point in Liz Murray's life. Although she quickly found herself without a place to live, she refused to give up hope that a better life existed somewhere. Although her parents had been hopelessly addicted to drugs, Murray knew that they loved her; instead of being bitter toward them, she drew on their few positive influences. The most important of these was perhaps her father's love of reading. Even when she was not attending school, Liz read encyclopedia volumes that had been discarded from a local library. She decided to return to school and plunged herself into her studies, encouraged by a few influential teachers who believed in her. She slept on friends' couches and sometimes on the subways; she took a double load of courses and managed to finish high school in two years.

During her senior year, she won a *New York Times* scholarship awarded to students who had overcome daunting obstacles to finish school and received twelve thousand dollars per year for college. When her class visited Harvard in 1999, she was enthralled and decided to apply. "Why can't this be mine if I really want it?" she asked. "What makes everyone else in this place different?" Her academic achievements and her compelling personal story impressed Harvard's admissions board. When she received her acceptance letter in early 2000, she screamed with delight. "I felt like I had wings," she explained. "I felt like I could do anything," The road to a Harvard degree was not without its detours. She took several years off to care for her dying father, but she returned to Harvard in 2007 and completed her degree.

BARACK OBAMA (B. 1961)
American Politician

At the bottom:

2000—Barack Obama was not doing well. "I knew in my bones that I was going to lose," he wrote in his second book, *The Audacity of Hope*. "Each morning from that point forward I awoke with a vague sense of dread, realizing that I would have to spend the day smiling and shaking hands and pretending that everything was going according to plan." After serving three years in the Illinois State Senate as a representative of the thirteenth district in Chicago, thirty-nine-year-old Barack Obama was running for U.S. Congress, challenging the Democratic incumbent, Bobby Rush, in the party's March primary.

Though he'd lived in the city for less than a decade, Obama sought to move onto the national stage by replacing Rush, a longtime Chicago political activist who had served three terms in the House of Representatives and was an overwhelming favorite to keep his seat. Obama was eager and ambitious but was unknown to many voters, and the fifty-three-year-old Rush was able to portray him as a young, inexperienced outsider. "Barack Obama went to Harvard and became an educated fool," Rush commented during the race. He argued that Obama had neither the experience nor the community roots necessary to serve in Congress. Rush handily defeated Obama, who received a mere 30 percent of the vote. "He spanked me," Obama recalled several years later.

At the top:

2009—At noon on a sunny Tuesday, Barack Obama looked out into a massive crowd, including many of the most powerful and famous Americans and an ocean of other well-wishers, who chanted his name as they prepared to watch him take the oath as the forty-fourth president of the United States. After winning the Democratic Party's nomination following a difficult and bitter campaign against Hillary Clinton, Obama defeated Arizona Senator John McCain, winning 53 percent of the popular vote and almost 70 percent of the electoral tally. In the midst of a terrible economic crisis, the nation's voters had elected an inexperienced

African American—a "skinny kid with a funny name," as Obama had described himself—to lead them.

The comeback:

Obama's crushing loss to Bobby Rush turned out to have many silver linings. He introduced himself to a wider political audience and developed friendships and political alliances that would serve him well over the next decade. Obama possessed great political skill and an ability to connect with ordinary people, so it was only a matter of time before the right opportunity emerged. In 2003, Obama announced that he would run for the U.S. Senate against Republican Peter Fitzgerald; when Fitzgerald decided not to run and the Republican front-runner dropped out following the release of embarrassing details about his divorce, Obama cruised to an easy victory. Meanwhile, his national stature had increased when he delivered a widely praised keynote address at the Democratic National Convention in 2004, where he expressed his belief in the "audacity of hope" that Americans could face uncertainty and difficulty together. It was a theme he returned to many times over the next few years, and it helped carry him to an unlikely presidential victory in 2008.

GEORGIA O'KEEFFE (1887–1986)
American Artist

At the bottom:

1909—Georgia O'Keeffe hadn't attended art school in New York and Chicago so that she could spend her days drawing lace embroidery for magazine advertisements and being paid by the piece. Ever since the age of twelve she had dreamed of being an important artist, and her talent was visible to her teachers, who recognized her with several small awards and scholarships during her art school years. But by 1908 her family's increasingly difficult financial situation spurred O'Keeffe to find work—any kind of work—that would allow her to make a living on her own. As a freelance illustrator, O'Keeffe fulfilled that minimal goal. The work was dull, though, and she hated every minute of it.

By the end of each day, she was too exhausted to work on her own art—the smell of paint and turpentine only frustrated her further, a reminder of the artistic drive that she'd once possessed but had somehow lost by her early twenties. She continued as a freelancer for a year before contracting a severe case of measles that harmed her eyesight badly enough that she could no longer continue. She moved back to her family's home in Virginia, where her father struggled to keep his farm and small business alive and her mother endured the early stages of tuberculosis. Before long she wrote a letter to a friend, telling him that she was giving up painting for good.

At the top:

1928—Georgia O'Keeffe's annual show at the Room—a New York gallery founded by the photographer Alfred Stieglitz—was a stunning and historic success. In the midst of a general decline in the art market that year, O'Keeffe sold six small paintings of calla lilies for the price of twenty-five thousand dollars, an amount that represented the largest amount ever paid for a group of paintings by a living American artist. Her work was not simply financially rewarding, however. The famous art critic Henry McBride heaped praise on O'Keeffe's work in the pages of *The New York Sun*, describing the "simple, smooth surfaces" in her work that "change so slowly in tone that it sometimes appears as though a whole earth would be required to make them go all the way around." O'Keeffe would enjoy the same combination of critical and financial success for the next six decades, as she evolved into one of the most important American painters of the twentieth century.

The comeback:

Georgia O'Keeffe didn't touch a paintbrush for two years, but in early 1911 a family friend—an art teacher at a private high school—asked her to teach some art classes there. She agreed and quickly discovered that she was a talented teacher. Moreover, the process of teaching others to paint reminded her of her own youthful enthusiasm for art, and she began to consider the possibility that she might be able to make a career out of it after all. She imagined herself living in the Virginia countryside, teaching and painting and enjoying a quiet life, but when she took a summer class at the University of Virginia in 1912, she so impressed her professor that he insisted she continue taking his courses.

Within a few years, she had been hired as his teaching assistant, a job that soon led to her appointment as an instructor at West Texas A&M. Her professor at Virginia also passed along some of her work to Alfred Stieglitz, a renowned photographer and one of New York's most important art promoters during the early twentieth century. In 1916, Stieglitz exhibited some of O'Keeffe's work at his gallery; the next year, he offered O'Keeffe a solo show. Following these initial successes, O'Keeffe moved to New York and began her rise within the American art world. As an added bonus, she and Stieglitz fell in love and were married in 1924.

SUZE ORMAN (B. 1951)
American Investment Advisor

At the bottom:

1981—Suze Orman tried to wrap her mind around the fact that she had just lost fifty thousand dollars of someone else's money. The child of Russian-Jewish immigrants, Orman had grown up in a working-class Chicago neighborhood without much exposure to real wealth and where many people—her parents included—had constant financial troubles. Making matters worse, as a child Orman had a speech impediment that diminished her confidence and convinced many of her teachers that she was not a bright student. As she remembered years later, she always "secretly felt dumb" and was surprised when the University of Illinois admitted her as an undergraduate.

With only a few credits to go before completing her social work degree, Orman left Illinois and moved to California with some of her friends in 1973. A few years later, as she approached her thirtieth birthday, Suze Orman was making four hundred dollars a month as a waitress at the Buttercup Bakery in Berkeley, California. She hoped to follow in her parents' footsteps and own her own small restaurant, but though she had plenty of ideas, she had no savings and no investors. That's when a long-time customer heard of Orman's dreams and offered her fifty thousand dollars to get started. Orman knew almost nothing about investing and turned the entire sum over to a broker who managed to squander it all within four months. "I didn't know what to do," she wrote years later. "I knew I owed a lot of money, and I knew I had no way to pay it back.

At the top:

2009—Ranked at number 18 on Forbes' list of "Most Influential Women in Media," Suze Orman has become one of the most popular financial experts in the United States. Her mini-empire of television shows, books, and DVD and CD-ROM packages have turned a four-hundred-dollar-a-month waitress into a popular financial guru with a net worth of about $25 million. In addition to her television show on CNBC (*The Suze Orman Show*) and her numerous specials produced for public television, Orman is the author of six books on personal finance, including *The Road to Wealth* and *Women and Money*, all of which have been best-sellers. Orman is especially popular with women between the ages of eighteen and forty-nine, who come from modest economic backgrounds and might be struggling to manage debt of one kind or another. Orman's fans credit her with being able to put the complexities of personal finance into plain language that provides clear direction and encouragement.

The comeback:

Orman's dream of owning a bakery may have been shattered, but she was determined to pay her investor back. Moreover, she wanted to learn how to avoid a similar catastrophe in the future. Returning to the Merrill Lynch office where her broker worked, Orman applied for a job. Before she knew it, she was on her way toward being a broker herself. As a broker, Orman built a strong reputation quickly. "My clients made out like bandits," Orman explained once, "and I was propelled pretty quickly to become one of the top brokers." Having learned a painful lesson from experience, she paid attention to her clients' needs and vowed never to deceive them.

From Merrill Lynch, she moved to Prudential Bache before founding her own firm in 1987. Orman paid special attention to the problem of investing for retirement, and the seminars she led on the topic became quite popular in Northern California. Before long, a mid-sized publisher, Newmarket Press, caught wind of her success and asked her to publish a book based on her retirement planning seminars. The book, *You Earned It, Don't Lose It*, came out in 1995 and has sold nearly three million copies. The book introduced Orman to a national audience that has continued to grow.

THOMAS PAINE (1737–1809)
English Political Essayist

At the bottom:

1774—Thomas Paine had pursued a variety of occupations as a young man. He had worked as a corset maker, an excise officer, a schoolteacher, and a tobacco shopkeeper. By the age of thirty-seven, Paine had failed to find success at anything. His first wife and child had died in childbirth, and his second marriage brought him little happiness. In 1774, he lost his job as an excise inspector and saw his tobacco business collapse. To evade a sentence to debtors' prison, Paine sold all his possessions and left for the American colonies. While in transit, he contracted typhoid fever and arrived in North America too weak to leave the ship under his own power.

At the top:

1776—Paine arrived in America in the early stages of the revolution. His most important contact in the colonies happened to be Benjamin Franklin, who helped him get a job as an editor of the *Pennsylvania Magazine*. As an editor, Paine flourished and committed himself fully to the cause of independence. In early January of 1776, he published an anonymous, revolutionary tract by the title of *Common Sense*. The pamphlet urged colonists to declare their independence from Great Britain, the "mother country" he claimed was no longer looking out for the best interests of its North American "children." The tract was immensely popular and sold more than half a million copies throughout the year—an astonishing number given that the population of the American colonies was roughly 2.5 million. Written in clear and persuasive language, *Common Sense* helped rally public opinion and made Paine one of the most important voices for liberty during his time.

The comeback:

Thomas Paine took the opportunity to make a fresh start in the American colonies, and he was willing to give up everything to do it. He used the only resource at his disposal—his acquaintance with Benjamin Franklin—to make a new career for himself, and he recognized that the colonists in North America were looking for new opportunities of their own. Paine had a very keen sense of injustice, perhaps as a result of his many past failures, and wrote passionately. Because he had been such a failure, he had much less to lose than others in speaking up about his beliefs, and his outspoken passion about the rights of the colonists brought him the success that he had not found in any other endeavor.

JAMES PENNEBAKER (B. 1950)
American Psychologist

At the bottom:

1983—James Pennebaker was a thirty-three-year-old assistant professor of psychology when he received the worst possible news for a young professor: he was being denied tenure and would no longer have a place at the University of Virginia, where he had been employed since finishing graduate school six years earlier. One of the complaints made by the university—one of the reasons for his failure to earn tenure—was that he lacked a clear research program and that his work was not likely to make a mark on the field of psychology. He was devastated, feeling crushed by a school he cared about and where he had expected to spend the rest of his career. Years of hard work had seemingly just gone up in smoke.

For a professor, the denial of tenure not only represents the loss of a job, but it also provokes a deep, emotional sense of rejection. Because the tenure decision rests on the evaluation of a faculty member's research, teaching, and university/community service, a negative outcome is almost always interpreted as a judgment on one's suitability for the profession. Pennebaker was humiliated and angry. He wondered if Virginia's decision would affect his future employment prospects, since a failure to earn tenure can become a black mark beside an academic's name. Maybe he'd find another job, maybe not. If he hadn't been so stunned and depressed by the news, he might have been overwhelmed with fear.

At the top:

2010—The author of eight books and sole or coauthor of more than two hundred articles, James Pennebaker—now a full professor at the University of Texas—has become one of the most recognizable psychologists in the United States. His research (incorporated in books like *Writing to Heal* and *Opening Up*) has explored the use of expressive writing as a tool for physical and mental health and as a means of confronting traumatic experiences. His studies have noted that physical health and work performance can be aided by simple writing or talking exercises. As he explained in *Opening Up*, "holding back our thoughts and feelings can be hard work," producing stressors that can affect the workings of the immune system, the heart, and the brain. More recent research has made Pennebaker an unlikely contributor to the war on terror; at the request of the Federal Bureau of Investigation, he has used his research on language to examine the speeches, letters, and videotapes sent or delivered by Al Qaeda, with the goal being to learn something about the psychology and mindset of the organization's top figures, including Osama bin Laden himself.

The comeback:

Pennebaker still gets upset by memories of his tenure denial. "This is a major blow to one's self-esteem, let me tell you," he explained in *Psychology Today* in 1993. However, he found writing about the ordeal to be therapeutic. "Seriously," he explained, "I wrote to help get an understanding of what had happened." In the course of writing about the experience, however, Pennebaker discovered an intriguing set of ideas for future research. His private writings—journal entries and letters—inspired him to think in a broader way about how people actually deal with difficult situations, including job loss, the death of loved ones, or any other event that disrupts a person's life or traumatizes them.

Though he was initially focused on his own travails, he broadened his focus and embarked on a research project that not only earned him jobs at Southern Methodist and the University of Texas, but also gave him the focus his early career had seemed to lack. Like so many of the others we profile in this book, his attempt to understand his own problems led to solutions that helped many other people.

ROSS PEROT (B. 1930)
American Businessman and Politician

At the bottom:

1962—Ross Perot stared at the telephone, wondering when he'd catch the break he needed. After four months of being in business for himself, he'd failed to land a single contract. More than seventy times, he'd heard, "No, thanks," from potential clients. The son of a Texas cotton farmer, Perot had served in the United States Navy as a young man before joining the sales force at IBM in 1957. Gainfully employed yet frustrated with the prospect of scaling IBM's corporate ladder, Perot left the company after five years and—on the day he turned thirty-two—founded Electronic Data Systems with one thousand dollars he had borrowed from his wife. EDS was created to serve companies that were beginning to use computers in their offices, but Perot was curiously unable to land any clients. To pay the bills, he offered consulting services to Blue Cross. At some point, Perot must have wondered if he'd made the right decision in leaving IBM.

At the top:

1992—After his initial difficulties with EDS, Perot began to land contracts, and before long his company skyrocketed to the top, making him one of the wealthiest men in the nation. By the late 1980s, Perot had sold EDS to General Motors for nearly $1 billion, after which he went on to found Perot Systems, which became a major success in its own right. Already one of the most successful businessmen in the United States, Perot made a spirited run for the presidency in 1992. His infomercial-style campaign spots turned him into a household name and drew millions of enthusiastic followers to his economic ideas (especially his concern over the deficit and job losses) as well as his critiques of Washington "gridlock." After leading in many polls during the summer of 1992, he eventually wound up receiving nearly 20 percent of the popular vote—the strongest showing for a third-party candidate in eighty years.

The comeback:

A journalist once described Perot as someone driven by a ferocious sense of certainty. "Once he is convinced that he is right," Peter Elkind explained, "he will never give in." It was this spirit that gave Perot the confidence to leave a comfortable job with IBM and start his own company. He'd tried to persuade his bosses to listen to his ideas about providing customized computer information services to business clients; when his bosses ignored his ideas, Perot founded EDS to bring his vision into reality, and he made a fortune.

Perot's success was due in no small part to his boundless energy and attention to detail, as well as his ability to stay grounded in the family and business values he grew up with. As an executive, Perot created a "straight-arrow" culture within EDS, and he maintained high expectations of his employees. He also took a personal interest in the people he employed, and former EDS employees often recall the ways he was able to stay connected to ordinary working people.

Though Perot experienced setbacks along the way—losing half a billion dollars in a stock market downturn, losing $60 million in a failed venture with DuPont—he learned from his mistakes but never swayed from his approach to doing business. Indeed, when he was running for president in 1992, much of his success was based on the sense many voters had that Perot—one of the hundred richest people in the United States—understood the concerns of regular folks.

AZIM PREMJI (B. 1945)
Indian Entrepreneur

At the bottom:

1966—Azim Premji was studying for summer school finals when he received a call from his mother, who delivered devastating news. His father, she told the stunned young man, had just dropped dead, the victim of a massive heart attack at the age of fifty-one. Premji, who was set to begin his senior year as an electrical engineering major at Stanford University, immediately booked a flight back to Mumbai, India, where he had grown up as the son of a vegetable oil manufacturer. Premji's father had founded Western India Vegetable Products ("Wipro") in 1947, and he had done well enough to provide a decent standard of living for his family. He had, after all, been able to send Azim to an expensive and prestigious American university. By the mid-1960s, however, his company was struggling to survive.

When Azim Premji returned for his father's funeral, he learned—much to his distress—that his father had selected him as his successor. Though he had expected to return to Palo Alto to complete his studies, Premji knew that he could not refuse his late father's wishes. He had no choice but to stay in Mumbai for a while to see if anything might be done to save a dying business.

At the top:

2004—By the turn of the century, Wipro had not only survived as a manufacturer of vegetable oils and laundry soap, but it had diversified into numerous other areas of production and customer service. Its most notable area of growth was in information technology. In 1979, Wipro had begun producing computers and software, and by 2002 Wipro was ranked seventh in the world on the Infotech 100 list. Its clients included Hewlett-Packard, Lehman Brothers, Boeing, Toshiba, Cisco, IBM, Best Buy, Microsoft, Sony, and nearly five hundred other major corporations from every corner of the world. With thirty offices and more than twenty-one thousand employees, Wipro was generating well over $3 billion worth of annual sales. Premji himself had become one of the wealthiest people in the world, with a net worth of more than $14 billion. With his business success, Premji was able to establish a foundation dedicated to expanding school facilities and improving educational opportunities for India's least affluent children.

The comeback:

At twenty-one years old, there were many other things that Azim Premji wanted to do with his life, but he also wanted to carry on his father's work and did not wish to see the family business collapse. He was not well prepared to be a businessman, and at such a young age was an unlikely candidate to lead a wilting company back from the brink. One of Wipro's investors demanded that he sell the company, since there was no way a "twit" could run it. The doubters only made him more determined to succeed. As he explained years later, "It's like being thrown into a swimming pool. To avoid drowning, you learn to swim quickly."

Though he wasn't a trained business leader, Azim Premji was ambitious and immediately set out to expand the company's range of products. He bought a stack of business management textbooks and spent the next year reading them. (He also grew a mustache to give himself a more mature appearance.) Within a decade, the company had begun manufacturing soaps, toiletries, and baby care products, and its profits grew rapidly. Over the next few decades, Premji's uncompromising stand on corporate ethics, combined with his insistence on the highest standards of customer service, gave Wipro a valuable edge over its competitors.

AYN RAND (1905–1982)
American Author and Philosopher

At the bottom:

1923—Alissa Rosenbaum, an eighteen-year-old senior at the University of Petrograd, watched in horror as the world around her disintegrated. In the aftermath of the Russian Revolution, Rosenbaum's country descended into a brutal civil war that would last five years. As someone who did not come from the proletariat—her father had been a successful pharmacist and business owner—Rosenbaum was among those groups of students whom the Bolshevik party viewed with suspicion: Her middle class background had perhaps infected her with intolerable "bourgeois" ideas.

As the Bolsheviks tightened their grip on power, academic freedom was destroyed in the name of safeguarding the revolution. Professors and students who did not fit the party's ideological criteria were purged from the universities and sent into exile, while others were shipped to work camps in Siberia. Rather than focus on their studies, students whispered nervously about arrests and executions carried out by the Soviet secret police. Meanwhile, disease flourished throughout the land, with epidemics of typhus, cholera, influenza, and pneumonia thinning the population and adding another layer of instability to an already fragile society. Rosenbaum wondered if she would make it through the year alive, much less finish her degree.

At the top:

1957—On October 13, 1957, Ayn Rand, the former Alissa Rosenbaum, received the news that her fourth novel, *Atlas Shrugged*, had reached position number 4 on the *New York Times* best-seller list. The book had been released only three days earlier, and despite mostly negative reviews from literary critics, *Atlas Shrugged* proved to be enormously popular among readers who were drawn to Rand's philosophy of "Objectivism." In her novels, Rand highlighted her belief that reason, individual creativity, and rational long-term self-interest were the best means of achieving individual happiness and thwarting the rise of a totalitarian society. *Atlas Shrugged*, which offered the clearest expression of Rand's philosophy, would continue to sell well throughout the rest of the twentieth century.

Moreover, Rand's philosophical notions inspired the emergence of "Objectivist" societies that devoted themselves to exploring her ideas and applying them to contemporary social, economic, and moral problems. Her work has never been out of print, and by 2008, more than twenty-five million copies of her books had been sold. One of the few fiction writers to effectively convey complex philosophical ideas, Rand remained one of the most influential and popular writers of her time. Her books had a strong influence on libertarian political and economic ideas, and enjoyed a recent resurgence among those opposed to the economic policies of the Obama administration.

The comeback:

Rosenbaum managed to dodge the university purges and graduated with a degree in history in 1924. After studying film for a year, she decided to leave the Soviet Union forever. She secured a visa to the United States, where she told authorities she would be visiting her relatives in Chicago; she had no intention, however, of ever returning to a society she believed could no longer support meaningful existence. In the United States, she moved to Hollywood, chose a new name—Ayn Rand—and struggled to make ends meet for several years before at last finding somewhat regular work as a screenwriter.

Her 1929 marriage to actor Frank O'Connor allowed her to remain in the States as a permanent resident, and she became a citizen two years later. Throughout the 1930s and '40s, Rand was vocally critical of the Soviet Union at a time when such views were not popular among intellectuals in the United States. Knowing what life was like on the inside of a totalitarian state, however, she stuck to her point of view, producing screenplays and other works of fiction (including We the Living and Anthem) that railed against "collectivism" as an assault on individual freedom.

Her first major novel, The Fountainhead, was rejected by twelve publishers, and it might never have been published except that an editor, Archibald Ogden, threatened to quit if his company did not buy the manuscript, for which Rand was given a thousand-dollar advance. The success of The Fountainhead assured Rand of an audience for her magnum opus, Atlas Shrugged, as well as the nonfiction work which further articulated her philosophy.

RACHAEL RAY (B. 1968)

American Cook and Entertainer

At the bottom:

1995—Rachael Ray had grown up in upstate New York and believed, like so many other young people, that she could make it in the Big Apple. The daughter of successful restaurant owners, Ray entertained vague dreams of becoming a hit in her own right in the competitive atmosphere of New York City. She was able to find work—first at the candy counter at Macy's Marketplace, then as a manager at an upscale grocery store—but she was young and didn't have a clearly defined career plan. Then the twenty-seven-year-old Ray was mugged outside her apartment in Queens.

As she explained to a journalist years later, "This kid comes in behind me—next thing I know he shoves my face up against the door, jams a gun into my back and says, 'Give me your bag.'" Ray managed to escape after spraying him with mace, but the mugger returned the following weekend, dragged her down an alley, and struck her numerous times with the handle of his gun. Ray was terrified, but her attacker fled when a dog began barking in a nearby apartment. Spooked by the experience, Rachael Ray left New York City for good a week later and returned to her mother's house in Lake George, the tiny upstate community where she'd grown up. Lacking a college degree and without much experience outside of working in grocery stores, Ray was now just another young woman living back home.

At the top:

2009—Though she had never received any training as a chef, by 2009 Rachael Ray was perhaps the most popular cook in the United States. With more than fifteen best-selling cookbooks to her credit—including *30-Minute Meals* and *Yum-O! The Family Cookbook*—Ray had become a franchise, with three shows on the Food Network, a magazine (*Every Day with Rachael Ray*), and numerous product endorsements. In 2008, she even introduced a line of pet foods. Her earnings by the end of the decade had reached between $15-20 million a year, with *Forbes* magazine naming her as one of the one hundred most powerful celebrities in the world. In 2008 and 2009, Ray earned back-to-back Daytime Emmy Awards for Outstanding Talk Show/Entertainment.

The comeback:

While living with her mother, Ray once again bounced around from one job to another before winding up as a food buyer for a gourmet store in Albany. After a while, Ray noticed that grocery sales were going down, even though she was stocking what she believed to be some of the best food in the world. "I started asking my customers why they didn't buy the great stuff I was bringing in," she recalled. "Their universal response was, 'We don't cook, we don't know how to cook, and we don't have time to cook.'"

To help address her customers' needs, she began to offer short cooking classes at the store, and she quickly gained a following. Even though she had no training as a chef, a fact that bothered her a little at first, she was energetic and understood that her students wanted to know how to prepare quick, nutritious, and tasty meals. Her "hook" was to teach people how to make dinner in less than thirty minutes, and it was a hit locally.

Before long, a local television station in Albany signed her on to do a weekly evening segment. She won two local Emmy awards over the next few years and sold more than ten thousand copies of a self-published cookbook before the producers of NBC's *Today* show got wind of her story and asked her to appear on the show in 2001. When the president of the Food Network saw her performance, he saw her potential and signed her to a $360,000 contract for her first show.

JUDY RESNICK (B. 1942)
American Investment Advisor

At the bottom:

1983—Judy Resnick had always enjoyed the easy life. Born into a wealthy Los Angeles family, Resnick had always counted on her father to take care of her financially. She married (and divorced) at an early age, but she never needed to work and never wondered how she might pay the bills so long as daddy was around. When he died suddenly of a heart attack, however, Resnick lost her major source of income. Though he left her with 5 percent of one of his businesses, the income she received was minimal, and after a few years her father's old partners simply stopped paying her. Meantime, her investment broker had managed her small inheritance poorly, trading mostly in options, and he lost a good portion of it by the early 1980s. With two teenage daughters to support and no meaningful work experience, Resnick found herself broke at the age of forty-one, with no prospects for a sustainable career, and without even the most basic office skills.

At the top:

1994—Judy Resnick, owner of her own investment firm in Beverly Hills, was honored with an Entrepreneur of the Year award, sponsored by some of the largest companies in the United States. Founded in 1989, Resnick-Dabney consisted of six employees when it opened for business and within a mere four months of opening it had paid off all its debts. By 1992, her firm was making extremely good returns on its high-yield bond portfolios and had expanded to eighty employees. In 1994 the firm did more than $1 billion in business, focusing on leveraged buyouts and corporate restructurings. Lacking formal training in business, Resnick liked to joke that parenthood had taught her everything she needed to know about running a successful company. "If you can get your employees to play well with others, share their toys and remember the golden rule, you'll do OK." A regular columnist for *Forbes* magazine, Resnick later authored a successful book on investing and money management, titled *I've Been Rich, I've Been Poor—Rich is Better.*

The comeback:

Much like Suze Orman, Resnick's interest in financial markets was in part a result of the poor investment decisions her own broker had made. She couldn't help but notice that he continued to make money in commissions even as he squandered what she'd entrusted to him. "Even I could do that," she told herself. After being turned down for entry-level positions with Merrill Lynch and Shearson Lehman, she met a woman who worked as a broker with Drexel Burnham Lambert. Introduced to the broker's manager, Resnick impressed him with her enthusiasm and received a job offer as a broker trainee. "I don't know what it is," the manager explained, "but you've got something. And I'm going to give you a chance."

She quickly made a list of everyone she knew and began calling them. Within her first year, she sold enough Treasury bills and municipal bonds to bring in over one hundred thousand dollars in commissions. By year three, she had been transferred to Beverly Hills and had proven herself to be one of the top female brokers in the business. In 1988, she sold $200 million worth of bonds.

As her business partner Neil Dabney explained, Resnick simply lacked the fear of failure or rejection that grips most people, not even allowing it to "enter her mind." Resnick "believes in herself and those around her and that we will succeed even if it looks overwhelming on the surface." Resnick also had a scrupulous sense of honesty. When Drexel Burnham Lambert began pushing dubious bonds on their customers, Resnick refused to play along and decided (with Dabney) to strike out on her own.

JUAN "CHI CHI" RODRIGUEZ (B. 1935)
Puerto Rican Golfer

At the bottom:

1942—One of six children living in horrific poverty in Rio Pierdras, Puerto Rico, Juan Rodriguez had gone without food more times than he could have counted. "Chi Chi," as the young Juan was called, suffered from rickets and tropical sprue, brought on by vitamin deficiencies that would leave several of his fingers permanently crooked. By the time he was seven years old, he had joined his father working in the sugarcane fields, where he carried water to other workers for a dollar a day. At a time when the Puerto Rican economy had not yet emerged from the global depression of the 1930s, there was no reason for Rodriguez to imagine that his future would be much different from the sort of life his father had.

At the top:

1992—Chi Chi Rodriguez could hardly believe how far his life had taken him. He had just become the first Puerto Rican elected to the World Golf Hall of Fame, capping a career in which he had won eight PGA Tour events, and another twenty-two championships after joining the seniors' tour in 1986. His combined lifetime earnings totaled more than $7 million—placing him in elite company with superstars like Jack Nicklaus and Arnold Palmer—though his winnings told only part of the story. In a sport usually known for its stodgy characters, Rodriguez was a charismatic performer who wore colorful outfits and was known for his endless stream of jokes and (most famously) the "sword dance" he would do with his putter after finishing a hole. He was also extremely generous, giving away huge portions of his winnings to charity and raising millions more for his foundation, which aids at-risk youth through educational and athletic programs.

The comeback:

For Chi Chi Rodriguez, success could be attributed to the lessons he learned from his father, his own inventiveness and drive for success, and the support of those who invested in his talents. Chi Chi learned a great deal about life from his father, Juan, who taught him the value of hard work and the virtues of generosity. While the elder Juan never earned more than eighteen dollars a month in the Puerto Rican sugarcane fields, he never missed a day of work and never complained. He always made time for his family and would spend a half hour with each of his children every night before he went to bed. Though Juan knew nothing about the sport of golf, he did not discourage his young son when he began fashioning crude golf clubs from guava tree branches, which Chi Chi would use to swat tin cans like the golfers he saw at the course near the cane fields where he worked.

Juan allowed Chi Chi to earn extra money as a caddie and smiled as his son dreamed about earning enough money as a golfer to purchase a bicycle. By the time Rodriguez was twelve years old, he had begun playing the game—using actual golf clubs and balls—and was shooting well enough to attract notice from the professionals who worked at the resort where he caddied. At the age of seventeen, he finished second in the Puerto Rican Open. Trained by longtime PGA pro Pete Cooper—and assisted financially by one of the owners of the resort—Chi Chi Rodriguez became a professional golfer in 1960.

THEODORE ROOSEVELT (1858–1919)
American Politician

At the bottom:

1884—On Valentine's Day in 1884, two days after the birth of his first child, Theodore Roosevelt experienced an unthinkable loss when both his wife and his mother died on the same day. Stricken with grief, Roosevelt wrote in his diary that "the light has gone out of my life." He tried to resume his work as a New York state assemblyman—an office to which he'd been elected three years before at the age of twenty-three—but Roosevelt had lost his zest for the political life he'd chosen. At the 1884 Republican National Convention, Roosevelt and his like-minded party members watched as his party nominated a candidate who was not interested in reforming political corruption. Disappointed and still aching from the loss of his wife and mother, Roosevelt left office and retired to a ranch he'd purchased in the Dakota Territory.

At the top:

1904—Twenty years later, Theodore Roosevelt had returned to public life in a big way. After several years on the frontier, he moved back to New York and returned to politics. He served as president of the board of the New York City Police Commissioners, Assistant Secretary of the Navy, and Governor of New York before receiving the vice-presidential nomination in 1900. Along the way, he had fought in the Spanish-American War and had become a national hero for leading his men to victory at the famous Battles of San Juan and Kettle Hills.

When President William McKinley was struck down by an assassin's bullet in 1901, Roosevelt became the youngest president in U.S. history at the age of forty-two. He was an energetic and reform-oriented leader, and he was tremendously popular with the general public. In 1904, Theodore Roosevelt was elected president in his own right, and over the next four years he solidified his record as one of America's greatest presidents, with a particular emphasis on conservation and creating vast new public parks.

The comeback:

Though Roosevelt had been a sickly child, he compensated with a feisty personality and he never retreated from difficulty. After several years in the Dakotas, Roosevelt was determined to overcome his grief and to make a difference in politics. He dealt with his personal losses by working hard not to think about them and by not dwelling on circumstances he could not change. When he returned to politics, he pushed for changes that were not always popular with those in power, but which he believed were in the best interests of ordinary people.

J. K. ROWLING (B. 1965)
English Author

At the bottom:

1993—Penniless and wracked by depression, a young, aspiring English writer and single mother named Joanne Rowling considered taking her own life. Although doing so would deprive her infant daughter of the only parent she'd truly known, Rowling wondered if her baby wouldn't have a better chance in life with someone else—someone who could pay the rent, someone who could keep a marriage together, someone who could offer the emotional and financial stability that Rowling believed herself incapable of providing on her own. Having recently separated from her husband, Rowling had left Portugal (where she and her husband had met and married) and returned to Britain in December of 1993, taking up residence in a flat near her sister in Edinburgh, Scotland. The change of scenery did her little good. Even writing failed to provide relief, as she found herself unable to work on the novel—a fantasy tale about a boy wizard named Harry Potter—that she'd begun writing three years earlier.

At the top:

2007—At the stroke of midnight on July 21, 2007, J. K. Rowling's seventh and final book in the *Harry Potter* series went on sale and promptly sold eleven million copies before the day ended. Rowling's novels had become an empire unto themselves, worth more than $15 billion in revenue from films and merchandising, and Harry Potter himself became one of the most successful characters in children's literary history, with an astonishing one hundred twenty million copies from the seven-book series having been sold worldwide. Translated into more than five dozen languages, Rowling's books took her from Great Britain's welfare rolls to the *Sunday Times Rich List* as one of the wealthiest women in the nation. With her fortune estimated at nearly $800 million, Rowling also established herself as a notable philanthropist, donating millions to charities for single mothers as well as to research on multiple sclerosis, the disease that took her own mother's life a year before Rowling considered ending her own.

The comeback:

With her marriage falling apart and no viable source of income, Rowling saw little reason for hope during the difficult months following her return to Great Britain. Her family, however, helped save her from the bottom. As Rowling explained in 2008, "[My] mid-twenties life circumstances were poor and I really plummeted. The thing that made me go for help . . . was probably my daughter. She was something that earthed me, grounded me, and I thought, this isn't right, this can't be right, she cannot grow up with me in this state."

Although she remained "on the dole" for much of the next year, Rowling found the energy to return to her novel, spurred on as well by her sister's encouragement. In time, she began receiving small grants to support her writing, and she pulled through the darkest period of her life. A dozen publishing houses rejected the novel, but *Harry Potter and the Philosopher's Stone* was eventually picked up by a small press, Bloomsbury, whose publisher warned Rowling that children's books never made their authors any money. After an initial press run of five hundred copies, the book received numerous favorable reviews as well as a National Book Award and a Nestlé Smarties Prize, both of which helped propel the book and its author toward wider recognition.

WILMA RUDOLPH (1940–1994)
American Sprinter

At the bottom:

1945—It was a miracle she ever made it to her first birthday. Born two months premature in June of 1940, Wilma Rudolph was the twentieth of twenty-two children in her family (her parents each had children from previous marriages as well as from their own). At the time, preterm babies like Wilma (who weighed less than five pounds) frequently died within their first year. As an African American living in a small, segregated Tennessee town, Rudolph faced additional risk factors in her early life, including deep poverty and substandard medical care.

By the age of four, she had survived viral pneumonia, mumps, measles, whooping cough, and scarlet fever. A bout of polio, however, had lasting effects, twisting her left leg, turning her foot inward and leaving her partially paralyzed. Coincidentally, the U.S. president at the time, Franklin Roosevelt, had survived polio as a young man, but afterward he had never again been able to walk under his own power—and he had come from a very wealthy family, which afforded him the best medical care. At best, doctors said, Wilma might learn how to walk with the aid of a leg brace.

At the top:

1960—Eight years after shedding her leg brace, crutches, and corrective shoes, Wilma Rudolph stood on an Olympic medal podium, where an official draped a gold medal—her third of the Rome games—around her neck. Earlier that afternoon, more than one hundred million television viewers around the world had joined eighty thousand fans at Stadio Olympico as Rudolph and three other American women took first place in the 4 x 100-meter relay. The teams from the Soviet Union, Great Britain, and West Germany had been favored in the competition, but all eyes were on the Americans. If Rudolph—who had already won gold in the 100-meter and 200-meter events—could bring her team across the finish line first, she would become the first American woman to win three gold medals during a single Olympic Games. As a black woman, Rudolph was inspired by the mark set by black American Jesse Owens in 1936, when he shocked the Nazi hosts of the Berlin Games by winning four gold medals. With the civil rights movement stirring in the United States, she hoped to provide a similar model of achievement to young black women. Running on a sprained ankle, Rudolph nearly dropped the baton at the start of the race's final leg. Although the Americans were in third place at the time, the young woman from Tennessee soon managed to sprint past the other racers, bringing the United States the gold medal.

The comeback:
As Wilma Rudolph acknowledged many times in her life, she was depressed and broken by her physical handicap. She felt isolated from other children, many of whom teased her, and her feelings of loneliness were awful. But her family gave her the strength and determination she needed to overcome the brutal effects of the polio virus. "The doctors told me I would never walk," Rudolph explained years later, "but my mother told me I would, so I believed my mother."

During the most difficult years of Rudolph's young life, there were plenty of helping hands around the home, and her siblings took turns carrying her from room to room. Beginning in 1946, Rudolph's parents would take her on a Greyhound bus twice a week to receive treatment fifty miles away in Nashville, where the doctors believed heat and water therapy might enable her to walk someday. Eventually, her family's encouragement wore off on young, shy Wilma. By the age of eight, she was secretly taking off her braces when her parents weren't around; she practiced walking on her own, hoping that she might one day be able to run and jump with the other kids.

At last, not long after her twelfth birthday, she was able to remove the braces for good. As if making up for lost time, Rudolph began playing basketball every waking moment that wasn't spent in school. Though she was an excellent all-around player, her unbelievable speed distinguished her from her peers. Before long, Rudolph came to the attention of Ed Temple, the legendary track coach at Tennessee State University who produced forty Olympic athletes and twenty-three Olympic medalists in his career. He recognized her unique abilities and took her under his wing, setting her on a road that ultimately would lead to Olympic glory.

CHARLES M. SCHULTZ (1922–2000)
American Cartoonist

At the bottom:

1950—Charles Schultz was fed up. The young artist from St. Paul, Minnesota was unhappy with the treatment his work was receiving from the *Pioneer Press*, his hometown newspaper. For the past three years, the paper had been running a weekly series of his called "Li'l Folks," a single-panel cartoon featuring a collection of small, clever children and a beagle. He had sold a few cartoons on the side to *The Saturday Evening Post*, but his efforts to place "Li'l Folks" in syndication had come to nothing. Meantime, Schultz was unhappy with the ten dollars he received each week from the *Pioneer Press*, and he had recently asked the editors to move his work from the "women's page" to the comics section. Without much of an explanation, his requests were turned down. So Schultz decided to quit the only newspaper that seemed willing to publish his work.

At the top:

2000—When Charles Schultz announced his retirement a half century after leaving the Pioneer Press, "Peanuts"—the daily strip that had made him the world's most famous comic artist—ran in more than twenty-six hundred newspapers in seventy-five countries, with a daily readership of 150 million. The strip's central figures, including Charlie Brown and Snoopy, had evolved from their "Li'l Folks" days into some of the most recognizable characters in popular culture, joining the likes of Mickey Mouse and Ronald McDonald as emblems of twentieth-century American life.

The gang from "Peanuts" starred in several animated holiday specials as well as a Broadway production (*You're a Good Man, Charlie Brown*) that became a staple of youth theater in the United States. Thanks to Charlie Brown, Lucy, Linus, Sally, Snoopy, and the rest of his creations, Schultz earned more than $1 billion during his lifetime. In 2005—five years after his passing—Schultz's work was still earning $35 million a year. A lifelong hockey fan and tireless promoter of ice sports in general, Schultz was also inducted into the U.S. Hockey Hall of Fame as well as the U.S. Figure Skating Hall of Fame. A few months after his death on February 13,

2000—the night before his last strip appeared in print—Schultz received the Congressional Gold Medal, the highest civilian honor bestowed by the United States Congress.

The comeback:

Schultz didn't have to wait long for his big break. A few months after leaving the *Pioneer Press*, his work was picked up by United Feature Syndicate, which had rejected him several times before. But Schultz was persistent, and UFS eventually agreed to place his new four-panel daily strip—which they named "Peanuts"—in seven newspapers across the country. For his first month's worth of strips, Schultz earned ninety dollars. Within eight years, the strip's popularity had grown, appearing in more than 350 papers in forty countries. By then, Schultz and his family had relocated to Sebastopol, California, where he lived for the rest of his life.

For Schultz, the key to his success rested in having a routine that he followed every day for decades. Every day after he woke, he had breakfast at the ice rink he and his wife had built. There, he watched the skaters before returning to his studio for a long morning session of drawing. After breaking for lunch, he returned to his studio and worked until dinner. Schultz loved his work and never wavered from his routine, even as his strip grew in popularity and branched out to include television specials, greeting cards, toys, and merchandise. Though "Peanuts" made him a very wealthy man, Charles Schultz never wanted anything more than the chance to introduce his characters to an everyday readership.

CHARLES R. SCHWAB (B. 1937)
American Stockbroker

At the bottom:

1971—Charles R. Schwab stared at his desk, wondering how everything could have gone so wrong with his life. The young stockbroker watched helplessly as his first company—a partnership formed with two other men—collapsed, brought down when the partners neglected to register some of their securities with Texas financial regulators. The state insisted that Schwab and his partners provide refunds (with interest) to everyone in Texas who had purchased their unregistered financial products. When the company, at Schwab's insistence, decided to fight the case, the Securities and Exchange Commission stepped in and blocked the brokerage from selling anything to anyone, anywhere in the United States. The partnership soon disintegrated, leaving Schwab more than one hundred thousand dollars in debt. His reputation was destroyed, and his marriage soon followed. At thirty-four, Schwab was a bust.

At the top:

2008—When Charles Schwab, an avid golfer, stepped up to the tee on a late July morning, only fifty-four individuals in the United States could claim to be wealthier than him. Schwab had just stepped down as the CEO of his own company, taking with him a trusted reputation and assets valued at more than $6.2 billion. It was the second time that Schwab had given up the title of CEO, having initially stepped down in 2003; when his successor veered away from what Schwab called the company's "heritage" of attention to individual investors, Schwab returned to set the company back on course. He did just that, helping raise the value of Schwab stock by more than 150 percent as its client assets rose to nearly $1.5 trillion. In addition to being one of the wealthiest and most successful figures in the financial world, Charles Schwab had also become an important philanthropist, creating a foundation to help children struggling with learning difficulties, including dyslexia, with which Schwab himself struggles.

The comeback:

Bailed out by an uncle who agreed to pay his nephew's debts, Schwab started a new brokerage partnership soon after the debacle that nearly ruined him. Schwab's uncle wondered if he'd ever get his money back and grew irritated by what he perceived as an unclear business plan. After some fits and starts, Schwab eventually assumed control of the entire operation and focused his energy on filling an emerging need in the financial services industry: the discount brokerage, which appealed to small investors who were not welcomed by investing giants like Merrill Lynch.

It was a bad time for the stock market in the mid-1970s, and the economy was treading water, but Schwab liked the idea of reaching out to the "little guy." By offering lower commissions than their competition and pioneering the no-load mutual fund, Schwab soon owned the largest discount brokerage in the country, with branches all over the United States and half a million accounts under its management. By refusing to follow the conventional path to success in the financial world, Schwab saw an emerging opportunity and blazed his own path to the top.

MARSHA SERLIN (B. 1949)
American Entrepreneur

At the bottom:
1978—Marsha Serlin was a twenty-nine-year-old mother of two from Northbrook, Illinois. She had recently divorced, and her family faced a mountain of unpaid bills and credit card debt. She fell behind on her car payments and discovered one day that her car had been repossessed; even worse, she was unable to keep up mortgage payments on her house, and the bank began the foreclosure process. Her only source of independent income was a part-time job taking care of houseplants for businesses and a handful of wealthy clients. While she enjoyed the work, it provided nothing close to a sufficient income to support her and her children. Her forays into the job market were fruitless. She tried selling insurance, but still the income was insufficient to keep her family afloat. When it seemed her situation couldn't get any worse, it did—the IRS got in touch with her and informed her that she and her ex-husband owed $250,000 in back taxes.

At the top:
1996—"I'm not a quitter," Marsha Serlin told her audience in Washington, D.C. "I don't like to fail, and I see this as a tribute to the American dream, to the fact that if you work hard enough, long enough and are focused enough, you can do just about anything." Serlin had just received her award as National Small Business Subcontractor of the Year (awarded by the U.S. Small Business Administration). A few months later, United Scrap Metals—the metal recycling firm she'd founded in 1978—was judged by the accounting and consulting firm Arthur Andersen to be one of the top companies in the United States for customer service.

As president and founder of USM, Marsha Serlin sat atop a highly successful company that employed 120 people and had more than $40 million in annual revenue, figures that would continue to rise throughout the rest of the decade. In 2008, USM brought in an astonishing $215 million, a five-fold increase from just a decade before. As Serlin explained recently, "I never looked at where I started, because it's always where you're going to end up that's important. I hope I can inspire someone else, a young woman who decides she can do whatever she wants without barriers."

The comeback:

While Marsha Serlin was trying to figure out how to keep her utilities from being shut off, she remembered one of her former clients, a man named Ray Ebbinger who lived in an expensive luxury apartment but seemed to have a schedule that allowed him to be home during regular business hours. She called him up and found out that he made a good living in scrap metal but was taking a break from the business. "Teach me everything you know in twenty-four hours," she asked him. Ebbinger obliged, and with two hundred dollars and a rental truck, Serlin began driving all over the Chicago area, scouring the landscape for scraps.

She got her first big break when she learned that a Del Monte canning factory had accumulated so much scrap metal that they might need to shut down for a few days to clean it up. She called the company and asked if she could have the job. She and her brother cleaned up the plant and were immediately rewarded with a long-term contract. The work was hard and dirty, and in a business dominated by men, Marsha Serlin was an unusual newcomer. But she stuck with it and by 1981 had purchased a small building in Cicero (just west of Chicago) and set up new headquarters there.

For the next ten years, she slowly added more buildings and hired more employees. Indeed, one of the keys to Serlin's success has been her ability to create a family atmosphere that forges a close-knit feeling among her employees. In an industry that typically sees annual turnover rates of 30 percent, USM loses less than 8 percent of its employees a year. As recently as 2006, 90 percent of Serlin's employees had been with the company for more than five years, and half had been with Serlin for a decade or longer. USM offers its employees annual bonuses, a retirement plan, health insurance, flextime, university tuition reimbursement, and onsite English classes for its employees, about two-thirds of whom speak Spanish as their first language.

FRANK SINATRA (1915–1998)

American Singer and Actor

At the bottom:

1952—The career of Francis Albert Sinatra was marked by numerous ups and downs. He was expelled from high school in Hoboken, New Jersey for rowdy behavior and arrested for having an affair with a married woman, a criminal offense at the time. But Sinatra emerged during World War II as one of the biggest musical stars in the United States. After a three-year stint with Tommy Dorsey—who led one of the most important bands of the swing jazz era—Sinatra moved on to a solo career that delivered one hit after another. A box office success as well, Sinatra costarred in several films with the great Gene Kelly.

By the early 1950s, however, Sinatra's promising career had begun to slide. He gave in to the crass commercialism of the music industry by joining the radio series *Your Hit Parade*, in which he sang the top hits of the week, which were often vapid, forgettable tunes. Now in his late thirties, his appeal to younger audiences faded somewhat, and in January of 1950 he suffered vocal strain and hemorrhaging at a concert in Hartford, Connecticut. A stormy and ultimately unsuccessful marriage to Ava Gardner followed in 1951, and in 1952 the Columbia record label canceled his contract. Frank Sinatra was on his way to becoming a B-level performer.

At the top:

1994—A seventy-eight-year-old Frank Sinatra choked back tears as he accepted a Legend Award at the 1994 Grammy Awards ceremony, offered in recognition of his lifetime of achievements in music and film. After a thunderous and lasting ovation from the audience, Sinatra thanked everyone and joked that he hoped they might get together again from time to time and do it all over again. His career was winding down, but over the past four decades Sinatra had released more than fifty Top 20 albums, a streak that had continued with his two *Duets* albums, released in 1993 and 1994 to great popular and critical acclaim. *Duets II*—which featured Sinatra performing with Stevie Wonder, Willie Nelson, Jimmy Buffett, and many others—reached position number nine on the Billboard chart and won a 1995 Grammy for Best Traditional Pop Vocal Performance. In the past several years, he had celebrated his seventy-fifth birthday with an elaborate and sold-out national tour, and he had received one honor after another—and continued to prove himself to be one of the top concert draws in American music. By the time of his death in 1998, Sinatra had been honored with three Academy Awards and four Golden Globes; thirteen Grammy Awards; a Lifetime Achievement Award from the NAACP; a Congressional Gold Medal; and a Presidential Medal of Freedom.

The comeback:

Though many performers from the 1930s and '40s saw their careers decline as rock and roll grew to dominate the airwaves and draw young audiences, Frank Sinatra made his comeback by returning to the musical style that brought him success in the first place. He'd seen what crass commercialism could do to someone's career. Rather than surrender to new cultural shifts, Sinatra scornfully dismissed rock as a "rancid-smelling aphrodisiac" and continued to make music his own way.

With the help of friends who refused to believe his career was over, Sinatra got a new record contract with Capitol Records in 1953. He weathered a brief career slide during the 1950s and emerged more popular than ever. Sinatra was known as a tireless performer who used his vast array of talents to reach audiences through his music and film performances. "You have to scrape bottom," he told a friend, "to appreciate life and start living again."

O. BRUTON SMITH (B. 1927)

American Racetrack Developer

At the bottom:

1961—Working as a car dealer, Ollen Bruton Smith had grown accustomed to the ups and downs of a life in business, but nothing could have prepared him for the disappointment of watching his first racetrack fail within two years. There had been problems with the project from the very beginning, when Smith teamed up with a lumber baron and stock car driver named Curtis Turner to build a facility in Charlotte, North Carolina, to host contests sponsored by the National Association for Stock Car Racing (NASCAR). As a child, Smith had dreamed of racing cars for a living and was racing and promoting stock car events by the age of eighteen. He quit the sport at his mother's request: "She started praying I would stop. You can't fight your mom and God, so I stopped driving." Still, Smith loved the sport and continued to work as a regional promoter.

When the chance came to build a new "superspeedway" in Charlotte, Smith jumped in with both feet. Financed by Smith's wealthy brother-in-law, the project broke ground in 1959. Within a few weeks, excavation workers had struck a massive slab of solid granite—a half million square yards of it—that increased the cost of the speedway by hundreds of thousands of dollars. When the track opened the following year, the surface crumbled after a few races. Combined with poor turnout, the costly repairs sent the shareholders into a mad frenzy, leading to Smith being ousted from the company. Broke and discouraged, Smith declared bankruptcy and left North Carolina altogether in 1962. The Speedway was turned over to a wealthy furniture dealer, and Smith headed off to Illinois.

At the top:

2007—One of the wealthiest people in the United States, O. Bruton Smith couldn't help but marvel at the road he'd traveled since his bankruptcy almost a half century before. His induction into the International Motorsports Hall of Fame was simply the latest honor in a career filled with great risks and even greater rewards. The chairman and CEO of Speedway Motorsports, Inc., Smith oversaw six major NASCAR tracks, including his first very first track, the former Charlotte Motor Speedway, now

Lowe's Motor Speedway. He also owned tracks in Atlanta, Tennessee, New Hampshire, Las Vegas, Kentucky, California, and Texas, where in 1996 Smith opened the second largest track in the nation, the $250 million, 150,000 seat Texas Motor Speedway. With a net worth of $1.5 billion, Smith owned some of the most important racing venues in the United States, as well as nearly two hundred car dealerships.

The comeback:

After the failure in Charlotte, Smith went back to selling cars for a living, eventually building up a chain of ten dealerships in Illinois. He set aside a large amount of his income, however, and within a few years began purchasing stock in his old racetrack. By 1975, he'd regained control over Charlotte Motor Speedway and returned to the sport at the right moment, when tobacco giant R. J. Reynolds launched an unprecedented sponsorship deal with NASCAR and helped turn a regional sport into one with a wider, national fan base. Though he had failed the first time around, Smith couldn't leave behind the abiding passion of his life. As he joked to a reporter in the late 1990s, "All of us who were in the business [had] tried to kill it, but it would not die. So I figured it must be a hell of a sport."

Throughout his career, Smith devoted a huge amount of energy to promoting the sport he loved, trying to convince others that it was in fact a "hell of a sport." He spent millions on improvements at his racetrack, adding luxury suites and upscale restaurants while improving the landscaping and adding lights for night racing. Smith staged lively pre-race events, featuring Elvis impersonators and a car-crushing mechanical giant called "Robosaurus." In short, Smith dedicated himself to something he loved and tried to figure out how to bring others to the show. His dedication had much to do with making NASCAR one of the most popular spectator sports in America today.

EARL STAFFORD (B. 1948)

American Entrepreneur

At the bottom:

1990—For the family of Earl Stafford, the holiday that December was almost completely lacking in good cheer. Stafford, who had founded an information technology company just two years before, had just lost the only two contracts he'd been able to secure. He had been forced to lay off his entire staff, and his income had fallen to zero, almost literally overnight. His electric and phone bills were unpaid, and he was trying to figure out a way to explain to his children that he would be unable to buy them any Christmas presents. Two years before, everything had been going well for the twenty-year U.S. Air Force veteran. After retiring from the service in 1988, he'd taken a good job with a company that provided personnel and aviation services to the Federal Aviation Administration.

But Earl Stafford was restless and decided after only a few months that he would launch his own company At the age of forty, he was moving into a comfortable second career as the founder of Universal Systems & Technology (UNITECH). His first two years brought a three-hundred-thousand-dollar subcontracting job to work on NASA's Hubble Space Telescope. Things were looking up for Stafford and UNITECH until problems with Hubble were discovered shortly after its launch in the spring of 1990. Though UNITECH had nothing to do with Hubble's flaws, Stafford—along with scores of other contractors and subcontractors—lost their contracts. By fall of that year, Stafford's only other contract was gone as well. Two years into his new career, Earl Stafford was broke.

At the top:

2006—A little more than sixteen years after he'd fallen on his face as an entrepreneur, Earl Stafford had turned UNITECH into an eighty-million-dollar company that employed more than three hundred people who provided telecommunications and computer services to military agencies as well as private companies. By 2006, UNITECH had become a leader in the development of simulation and training software; its projects included developing an M-16 simulator for the United States Navy and a Light Armored Vehicle simulator for the U.S. Marines. Recognized as one of the top African American executives in the United States, Earl Stafford also used his wealth and power within the black community to fund anti-drug efforts in Maryland, Virginia, the District of Columbia, and elsewhere. In 2008, shortly after the election of Barack Obama, Stafford purchased a one-million-dollar hotel package through Marriott and used it to bring wounded, disabled, and terminally ill veterans to the 2009 Presidential Inauguration.

The comeback:
Even after losing all his contracts and shedding his entire staff, Earl Stafford refused to give up his entrepreneurial dream. He stubbornly and patiently sought new contracts and proved himself willing to do almost any kind of work in order to get his foot back in the door. After losing his first two contracts, his next contract required UNITECH to provide janitorial services in addition to consulting services. Now, however, Stafford was the only employee of UNITECH. And so he wore a suit during the day, attending meetings and working with a variety of other professionals. At the end of the day, he waited until everyone had left, then changed into work clothes and spent the rest of the evening straightening offices, emptying the trash, and making sure that copies of sensitive documents were disposed of. Stafford never told anyone that he was working on every part of the contract by himself; when the company that hired his services found out, they were impressed and soon afterward awarded him a contract for $2.5 million, which helped get UNITECH permanently back on its feet. Stafford's determination and flexibility had saved his company and allowed him to take a huge step toward fulfilling his dream.

JOHN STEINBECK (1902–1968)
American Author

At the bottom:

1925—Struggling and shouting furiously, a twenty-three-year-old aspiring writer named John Steinbeck was dragged out from the Robert McBride and Company building and shoved back onto the street by security guards. A trail of typed pages fluttered behind him, littering the hallway and lobby of the publishing firm that had just rejected Steinbeck's collection of short stories. A native of Salinas, California, Steinbeck had ventured to New York City the previous year, hoping to make his way as a writer. While sending his stories around town and waiting for his break, Steinbeck took a series of ill-fated jobs. For a while, he worked at the construction site where Madison Square Garden was being erected, but he quit after a coworker fell from a high scaffold and died. Steinbeck also tried his hand as a reporter, but he regularly got lost while trying to cover the news. Before long, he was fired.

At last, he received word that an editor at McBride was interested in his work. Overjoyed by the prospect of publishing a book, he immediately threw himself into his stories, writing at a mad pace to complete a collection of short fiction. When he brought his completed manuscript to the office, however, the editor who liked them was no longer employed there—and no one else at the company was interested in publishing the stories. Enraged, Steinbeck began screaming and cursing. After being evicted from the building, Steinbeck shut himself off from the world. "My friend loaned me a dollar," he explained later, "and I bought two loaves of bread and a bag of dried herrings . . . . I was afraid to go out on the street—actually afraid of traffic—the noise." He soon returned to California.

At the top:

1962—Four decades after his unpleasant eviction from the McBride offices, John Steinbeck addressed the Swedish Academy and thanked them for their decision to grant him the Nobel Prize for Literature. A humble man, Steinbeck believed there were other literary voices more worthy of the recognition, but he accepted the honor graciously and urged his fellow writers to work for the betterment of a dark and dangerous world. As he explained, "I hold that a writer who does not passionately believe in the perfectibility of man has no dedication nor any membership in literature." The prize he received that day was a tribute to his major works, including *East of Eden*, *Of Mice and Men*, and *The Grapes of Wrath*, the latter of which received the Pulitzer in 1939 and would earn a place as one of the greatest American novels. His depictions of life among ordinary workers helped to define the cultural tone of the Great Depression, and his work as a war correspondent during World War II inspired him to write numerous screenplays and novels about confrontations between regular people and the forces of evil unleashed by the war. By the time of his death in 1968, Steinbeck had written twenty-seven books, most of which were translated into dozens of languages and reprinted throughout the world.

The comeback:

Recognizing that he had come to New York in pursuit of a dream that was heading toward a dead end, Steinbeck changed course and returned home, where he was more comfortable as a writer and as a person. New York was of course a fabled destination for American writers, but Steinbeck never felt comfortable there. He later described his brief time in the city as a "thin, lonely, hungry time" in which he was "scared thoroughly." Taking the first opportunity to leave—he accepted a job on an ocean freighter—Steinbeck returned to California.

Though his father tried to convince him that no one could earn a decent living as a writer, Steinbeck refused to listen. Someone had thought his work was worth publication, and it was only a matter of time before someone else agreed. Taking a job as a caretaker for an estate in Lake Tahoe, Steinbeck enjoyed his newfound solitude and returned to the typewriter. When the Depression struck a few years later, Steinbeck—who'd always been interested in and attuned to the lives of ordinary people—saw others who were underfed, lonely, and scared for the future. Had he remained in New York, he never would have witnessed the struggles of farm workers in California, whose struggles became the focus of The *Grapes of Wrath* and *Of Mice and Men*.

JAMES STOCKDALE (1923–2005)
American Military Officer

At the bottom:

1966—It was New Year's Day, and Navy Squadron Commander James Bond Stockdale lay in a North Vietnamese prison in Hoa Lo, where he'd been held since being shot down in September of 1965. "I was shivering," Stockdale recalled years later, "legs in stocks, hands in cuffs, lying in three days of my own excrement." Conditions only grew worse from there. Stockdale, like most Americans captured during the war, was tortured on a regular basis. To emphasize their inferior position, captives like Stockdale were prohibited from looking anywhere but toward the ground, and they were even forced to bow at the waist when greeting the guards and officers who brutalized them. Stockdale lived under these unimaginable conditions for the next eight years, during which time his North Vietnamese captors shattered his legs, broke his back, and yanked his shoulders from their sockets.

At the top:

1987—On March 16, 1987, forty-five million Americans tuned in to watch "In Love and War," a television movie based on the letters Jim Stockdale wrote to his wife Sibyl during his years of captivity. The film, and the book on which it was based, chronicle the story of a husband and wife struggling to maintain hope in the face of tremendous adversity. By the late 1980s, Stockdale had become a well-known and respected figure in academia, having served a brief and rocky tenure as president of The Citadel military college in South Carolina before moving on to Stanford's Hoover Institution, where he had studied foreign relations in the early 1960s before his service in the Vietnam War.

Although he was not an especially gifted public speaker, he was an elegant and thoughtful writer whose views on leadership—forged out of his compelling personal story—made him a sought-after figure at university graduations and business conferences. He would eventually achieve even more recognition as Ross Perot's vice presidential candidate in 1992, though his confused debate performance left many viewers with an inaccurate perception of his intellect. After his death in 2005, Stockdale was honored by the United States Navy, which named a missile destroyer in his honor and erected a statue of him at the Naval Academy in Annapolis, Maryland.

The comeback:
In the years after his 1973 release from North Vietnam, Stockdale credited the Stoic philosophers, particularly a first-century Greek named Epictetus, with giving him the perspective he needed to endure his captivity. Stockdale learned from the Stoics that individual misfortune could be overcome by trying to adhere to timeless, universal virtues. As Stockdale explained in a 1993 speech, Epictetus taught him that people cannot be truly victimized by anyone but themselves. "To the Stoic," he wrote, "the greatest injury that can be inflicted on a person is administered by himself when he destroys the good man within him." As a prisoner, Stockdale realized that while his captors might attack his body, they could not destroy his moral integrity; therefore, even as a prisoner, Stockdale recognized that he could control his own destiny, that he was not defeated. After his ordeal was over, Stockdale built a career of writing and teaching that showed people how to prevail over misfortune and how to lead others along a path of personal development.

JIM STOVALL (B. 1959)
American Entrepreneur

At the bottom:

1988—Jim Stovall had withdrawn completely from the rest of the world. Day after day, he sat in the smallest room in his house, ignoring his wife and refusing to speak with anyone. A former national champion and Olympic-caliber weightlifter, Stovall had married and settled into a comfortable life as an investment broker in Tulsa, Oklahoma. But he was slowly losing his eyesight. Diagnosed with macular degeneration as a teenager, Stovall chose to ignore the progress of the disease as best he could, even when he could no longer read for himself. In fact, he met his future wife, Crystal, when they were both in college at Oral Roberts University; Crystal volunteered as a reader for the visually impaired, and she was assigned to Stovall one day.

As his career got underway, Crystal continued to help her husband with his work, going so far as to join him in the office each day as his assistant. But when the darkness came at last, Jim was twenty-nine and unable to cope. "I remember waking up one morning," Stovall explains, "and I stepped into the bathroom and turned on the bright light and looked in the mirror, and I couldn't see anything . . . the bright light, the mirror, nothing. And I realized, that's it, I have now reached the bottom of this. And I actually went into this little room at the back of my house. And I really fully intended never to walk out of that little room again."

At the top:

2007—Nearly two decades after losing his sight forever, Jim Stovall had become a popular motivational speaker, newspaper columnist, and author as well as the founder of the Narrative Television Network (NTN), a service for blind people that adds plot narration to films and television programs. NTN reaches millions of blind and visually impaired people throughout the United States and eleven foreign countries. An Emmy-Award-winning service, NTN is carried by more than twelve hundred broadcast and cable affiliates and brings in revenues of more than $6 million a year. For Stovall, though, NTN was just one part of his success story. By 2007, Stovall was reaching more than 500,000 people annually as a motivational speaker at business meetings, conventions, and sporting events; he'd shared the stage with people like Colin Powell, Barbara Bush, Paul Harvey, and Christopher Reeve. Along the way, he'd been named an International Humanitarian of the Year and one of the Ten Outstanding Young Americans by the Jaycees, had received a National Entrepreneur of the Year award from Ernst and Young, and had been the winner of the U.S. Chamber of Commerce National Blue Chip Enterprise Award. To top it all off, one of his novels, *The Ultimate Gift*, had just been turned into a motion picture starring James Garner and Abigail Breslin.

The comeback:

For Jim Stovall, the comeback began when he decided to walk to the mailbox. One morning, he told a reporter in 2007, "I just woke up and realized whatever it is out there that I'm afraid of, can't be a lot worse than spending the rest of your life in this little 9 x 12 foot room. And as soon as the fear of not trying gets to be bigger than the fear of failing, we move. And the first day I walked out of that room, I didn't get a Gold medal or an Emmy award, I walked 52 feet to the mailbox. And that was the day that changed my life."

Before long, he joined a support group for visually impaired people. There, he met a woman named Kathy Harper who—like Jim—had recently lost her vision. Both Stovall and Harper shared their frustration with not being able to enjoy movies and television programs, even ones they had seen before. Neither knew the first thing about television or film production, but they soon realized that millions of other people could benefit from a service that provided narrative descriptions of what was going on between character dialogue. Although supposed experts told him his idea would never work, Stovall ignored their doubts and had launched NTN by 1989; the next year, he received an Emmy for NTN's technological contributions to television.

The key for Stovall was to recognize that while his blindness had cut him off from the world that was familiar to him, it had opened up connections to other people who were facing the same challenges. By thinking beyond his own struggles and despair, and by overcoming his fear of the unknown, he was able to make a huge difference in the lives of millions of people.

JONI EARECKSON TADA (B. 1949)
American Author

At the bottom:

1967—On a hot July afternoon, seventeen-year-old Joni Eareckson dove into the Chesapeake Bay near Baltimore, not realizing how shallow it was. Her head struck the bottom, and the impact crushed her fourth cervical vertebra, leaving her paralyzed from the neck down. Her arms and legs were completely lifeless, and the doctors told her there would be almost no chance of recovery. Eareckson was angry and filled with despair. She begged numerous friends to help her commit suicide. As she recalled years later, she begged them "to slit my wrists, dump pills down my throat, anything to end my misery." She had a lifetime yet to live, and she wanted none of it. She couldn't imagine a life in which she couldn't swim or ride horses—two of the things she loved most. Instead, she was trapped in a body she couldn't control. Friends and family tried to reassure her that her accident had happened for a reason and that she would someday be able to make sense of it all. Joni didn't believe them. "I was numb," she remembers, "desperately alone, and so very, very frightened."

At the top:

2004—Nearly four decades after being confined for life to a wheelchair (and twenty-two years after marrying her husband, Ken Tada), Joni Eareckson Tada had become one of the most popular Christian authors in the United States. With more than thirty books to her credit—books that had been translated into dozens of languages and distributed in more than fifty countries—she had also become a familiar radio voice, having produced twenty-two years of daily radio programming that reached a million listeners each week throughout the world. Joni Eareckson Tada's charity, "Wheels for the World," distributed thousands of wheelchairs each year through Christian ministries in more than a dozen countries. For her writing, broadcasting, and charity work, Tada had received numerous awards, including the Courage Award from the Courage Rehabilitation Center; the Award of Excellence from the Patricia Neal Rehabilitation Center; and the Victory Award from the National Rehabilitation Hospital.

The comeback:

Religious faith had nearly everything to do with the rebirth of Joni Eareckson's passion for life, and it encouraged her to share her story with others. After her accident, she spent a lot of time questioning the reasons for her predicament; by her own admission, she lost the faith she had before breaking her neck. During her recovery, several friends came to visit her and began leading her through passages in the Bible that might help her understand why all this had happened to her. With their help, she came to believe that God had allowed this horrible thing to happen for a reason—she just needed to figure out what that reason was.

Before long, her occupational therapist encouraged her to take up painting, showing her how she could use her mouth to hold a brush. This creative outlet gave Joni a sense of purpose and accomplishment, and it opened up a realm of creative ability she didn't know she possessed. She also began to work with other disabled young people, using her newly found religious faith as a means of reaching people experiencing the same kind of despair she'd overcome in her own life. She spoke in churches, met with youth groups, and visited the sick and disabled at hospitals. As she told her story, she attracted interest from evangelical Christian publishers like Zondervan, which published her best-selling autobiography in 1976. In 1979, she founded "Joni and Friends," an outreach ministry that has served as the basis for her work ever since.

HARRY TRUMAN (1884–1972)
American Politician

At the bottom:

1922—After only three years in business, Harry Truman's Kansas City clothing store was in deep trouble. Truman and his friend Eddie Jacobson had returned from their service in World War I and opened the store in a prime downtown location, where they planned to sell a full line of "gents furnishings," including shirts, socks, ties, belts, and hats. Truman had grown up as the son of a farmer and livestock dealer in the nearby town of Independence, but he had no taste for the farming life. During the war, he and Jacobson had run the canteen at Ft. Sill during their training, and they did such steady business that they decided to try their hand at running their own store.

At first, the operation was a roaring success; the partners doubled their investment, selling seventy thousand dollars worth of goods their first year (roughly $760,000 in today's dollars). By 1922, however, the nation's economy was suffering from the effects of a deep post-war recession. Farmers experienced the worst of it, as wheat prices dropped by nearly half; because the economy of Kansas City was so closely linked to the agricultural market, businesses like Truman's and Jacobson's suffered as well. Their earlier, flourishing success had disappeared. They were now tens of thousands of dollars in debt. With their business on the verge of ruin, Harry and Eddie closed up their shop for good. At the age of thirty-eight, Harry Truman seemed pretty well washed up.

At the top:

1948—When the final election returns came in, Independence burst into spontaneous celebration. Bells and whistles, sirens and car horns sounded throughout the November night as the small Missouri town cheered the victory of its native son, Harry Truman, who had just been elected president of the United States. Truman, who had been vice president for only ten weeks, had assumed the presidency in April of 1945 after president Franklin Roosevelt died of a brain hemorrhage. Though he lacked foreign policy experience, Truman successfully managed the nation through the final months of World War II and stood firm against the Soviet Union over the next three years as the Cold War evolved. Even so, after sixteen years of Democratic control of the White House, political experts widely expected Truman to lose the 1948 election to Republican candidate Thomas Dewey. After a fierce campaign, during which Truman toured the country by train and rallied his supporters with one speech after another, President Truman defeated his challenger by two million votes.

The comeback:

The closing of Truman & Jacobson wounded Harry deeply, and he never forgot the sting of failure. Remarkably, however, he chose not to erase his debts through bankruptcy; instead, he was determined to pay back his creditors. It took him fifteen years to do it, and it meant that he was constantly strapped for cash, but Truman eventually cleared all his debts. In the meantime, his friendship with the nephew of Tom Pendergast—the boss of Kansas City's Democratic political machine—led Harry Truman into his first political job as a county commissioner. Elected to the office a few months after the clothing store shut its doors, Truman quickly gained a reputation as a loyal member of the party and (more importantly) as a scrupulously honest public official.

Though Pendergast dismissed Truman's ambitions for higher office, Harry was patient and spent the better part of the next decade trying to persuade his doubters that he could handle higher responsibilities. During the early 1930s, Truman oversaw the redevelopment of Kansas City through public works programs that brought a series of roads, public monuments, and a new courthouse to the county. By 1934, Pendergast finally agreed to promote Harry Truman as a candidate for the U.S. Senate. His huge victory that year—defeating the incumbent by twenty points—vaulted him into national politics.

In the Senate, Truman overcame the doubters once again. He held investigations of government fraud and mismanagement of defense contracts, and he once again built a reputation as an honest, hard-working public servant. When Roosevelt was seeking a new running mate in 1944, the party turned to Harry Truman. Though he had been underestimated at every turn—by Tom Pendergast, by his own colleagues in the Senate, and even by President Roosevelt (who more or less ignored him even after he became vice president)—Truman never doubted his own abilities and stubbornly refused to allow the doubts of others to become his own.

HARRIET TUBMAN (1822–1913)
American Abolitionist

At the bottom:

1849—Born in Eastern Maryland sometime between 1820 and 1825, Harriet Tubman was to grow up facing a life that was gravely limited by virtue of her status as a slave. During her younger years, she suffered a terrible head injury when her master, Edward Brodess, clubbed her for refusing to help arrest a fellow slave who had left his plantation without permission. For the rest of her life, she suffered headaches, nausea, and seizures as a result of the trauma from that assault. Her illness eventually reduced her value as a slave, and in 1849 Brodess attempted to sell her; when he died later that year, his widow resumed the search for a buyer. Fearful that she would be sold and shipped far away from her family, Harriet Tubman reached a state of near despair.

At the top:

1865—By the end of the Civil War, the institution of slavery was no more, and Tubman herself had played no small role in bringing about its destruction. Shortly after Edward Brodess died in the spring of 1849, Tubman and her brother fled to Pennsylvania, where slavery had been abolished since the 1820s. Not satisfied with obtaining only her own freedom, Tubman returned to Maryland numerous times over the next eleven years and led dozens of enslaved people through the "Underground Railroad" to freedom. Tubman placed herself at great risk throughout these years, and slaveholders in the region tried desperately—though without success—to capture her.

When the Civil War broke out, Tubman worked as a nurse and a scout for the Union army in South Carolina. In June of 1863, Tubman even served as an adviser to Colonel James Montgomery during an armed attack on a plantation along the Combahee River. More than seven hundred slaves were liberated in the raid. Tubman never received a regular salary for her work and did not receive a military pension until 1899. Nevertheless, her bravery was recognized throughout the country, and Harriet Tubman became one of the great heroes of her era.

The comeback:

Harriet Tubman became legendary due to her selflessness and her insatiable belief in the right of all people to be free. Rather than take comfort in the success of her own escape, Tubman put herself in harm's way again and again as she helped rescue family members and other enslaved people. Tough anti-fugitive laws during the 1850s made her work especially dangerous. She might have remained in Ontario, Canada, where she'd settled with other escaped slaves (including her parents, whom she'd brought northward in 1857) had she not felt a higher calling. She believed, in fact, that she was on a mission from God, and other opponents of slavery soon began referring to her as the "Moses of her people." Though she was nearly captured many times during her years of work on the Underground Railroad, Tubman valued the freedom of others over her own personal safety. She understood that she was essential to the cause, and she trusted in her own ability to prevail.

TINA TURNER (B. 1939)
American Singer

At the bottom:

1976—Ike and Tina Turner were among the most important rhythm and blues performers during the 1960s and '70s, but their success (and marriage) had always been hindered by Ike Turner's violent temper, drug use, and refusal to allow anyone to help manage or guide their careers. Ike's erratic and domineering temper drove away one musician after another. After producing a long list of hits—including a famous cover of "Proud Mary" by Credence Clearwater Revival—the couple faded from view after 1973. Ike's abusive behavior toward his wife grew worse, and Tina finally left him in July of 1976. She had less than a dollar in her pocket; to make matters worse, she owed hundreds of thousands of dollars to tour promoters as well as to the IRS.

At the top:

1991—Fifteen years after leaving her husband (and quite possibly her career) in the rearview mirror, Tina Turner was inducted into the Rock & Roll Hall of Fame. After her breakup with Ike, Turner released several solo albums that sold poorly. She remained popular in Europe, however, and continued performing to large audiences there while trying to reconnect with the American market. At last, in 1984, Tina Turner released *Private Dancer*, an album that sold well over ten million copies worldwide while spawning several Top 10 hits. Her success grew even further in the coming years, as her music earned one award after another while her live performances broke attendance and sales records across the globe. As a solo artist, Tina Turner has sold more than 200 million records worldwide and is listed in the *Guinness Book of World Records* for selling more concert tickets than any other individual performer.

The comeback:

Tina Turner lived in fear of her husband, yet she also believed—mistakenly, it turns out—that she could not survive as a performer without him. After she returned to the top, Turner frequently credited her religious faith with giving her the strength to start a new life. In the two years before her marriage ended, Turner had become a Buddhist; when she left Ike, her religion was "the only tool I had." Though she didn't have a place to live and spent her time hopping between friends' houses, she felt liberated by her decision to leave her marriage. She was determined, moreover, to make a career for herself and to stand on her own two feet. Just before her career took off again in 1984, Turner cleared off a wall in her home where her old gold and silver records and other awards had been displayed. Turner looked at the empty wall and thought, "Alright, I am going to see what I am going to do." Within two years, the wall was filled again.

ARMANDO VALLADARES (B . 1937)
Cuban Political Dissident

At the bottom:

1960—It was the simplest of acts that landed Armando Valladares in the hands of the authorities: As an employee of the Ministry of Communications, he had discussed his opposition to Communism with his friends. Citizens in a free society would have nothing to worry about due to such statements, but Valladares happened to be living in Cuba during the aftermath of Fidel Castro's revolution. A two-hour trial—which featured no actual witnesses or evidence against him—resulted in a swift conviction and thirty-year sentence for "counter-revolutionary activities."

A few days after his conviction, the young prisoner was transferred to the Isla de Pinos, which the revolutionaries had turned into "the Siberia of the Americas," where conditions resembled those of Stalinist-era Soviet facilities. There, Valladares witnessed fellow prisoners being tortured; he listened to the defiant cries of condemned men moments before volleys of rifle fire tore through their bodies. His companions were mutilated and/or murdered. In time, he would be tortured repeatedly as well. Prison officials placed tons of dynamite around each building—an insurance plan of sorts that guaranteed that an attack on Cuba would, in the very least, fail to liberate its most "dangerous" political dissidents.

At the top:

1987—A few months after becoming a naturalized citizen of the United States, Armando Valladares was appointed by President Ronald Reagan to serve as the U.S. representative to the United Nations Human Rights Commission, giving him the rank of ambassador. It was a tremendous honor, one that acknowledged the importance of his voice in the global human rights community. Having been freed in 1982, Valladares wrote an acclaimed memoir of his imprisonment. Published in 1985, *Against All Hope* provided a searing indictment of Castro's regime and an important touchstone for human rights and democracy activists across the globe. Ronald Reagan's daughter Maureen read the book and urged her father to take notice of Valladares's story. Other officials in Reagan's administration were equally impressed, and he became one of numerous exiled Cuban dissidents who helped the United States turn greater attention toward the denial of basic human freedoms under Castro's government.

The comeback:

Valladares survived twenty-two years in prison thanks to the power of his own faith, the endurance of his creative spirit, and the aid he received from loved ones and strangers alike. "I felt myself neither alone nor abandoned because God was with me inside that jail," Valladares wrote three years after his release. "The greater the hatred my jailers directed at me, the more my heart brimmed over with Christian love and faith." Valladares refused to allow himself the luxury of hating his captors. Though his body was confined, beaten, and deprived of nutrition, he did not allow Castro's prisons to destroy his soul.

He refused to be politically "rehabilitated" and refused to recant his beliefs, which he knew were crimes only in the eyes of a dictator. He wrote poetry on small scraps of paper; he used his own hair to paint tiny images, some no larger than stamps or cigarette wrappers; and he somehow managed to smuggle his work outside the prison, hiding it in toothpaste tubes and anything else that might be useful to the task. His wife, Martha, waited for his release the entire time he was in prison. While refusing to abandon him, she published his work throughout the world and ensured that Valladares would remain one of the most celebrated victims of Castro's regime. Her work on her husband's behalf also led directly to his release in 1982, after the French government, to whom Martha had appealed vigorously for help, urged Castro to relent.

KURT WARNER (B. 1971)
American Football Player

At the bottom:

1995—It was a terrible day to move into a new apartment, and an even worse day for Kurt Warner's worthless car to die. It was the coldest day of the year, and snow had been falling since the previous day in Cedar Falls, Iowa. Drifts piled up around the wheels as Warner tried to figure out how he was going to move all his stuff without a car. He wondered how on earth he'd wound up in this position. Just a few months earlier, he was throwing passes at the Green Bay Packers training camp, working his way toward a spot as an NFL quarterback. The former University of Northern Iowa star was sure that he'd be a standout in the pros, so he was stunned when the team cut him. The quarterbacks' coach told him he had talent but wasn't ready for the big time.

Disappointed, Warner returned to Cedar Falls to live with his girlfriend, Brenda, and her children. He waited for another shot at an NFL roster spot, but no one called. He waited by the phone on draft day for the World Football League, but no one wanted him. Desperate for a job—any job—Warner found work at a Hy-Vee grocery store, where he stocked shelves for minimum wage and bought his groceries with food stamps. When officials from the Arena Football League called to see if he would join an expansion team in Iowa, Warner ignored the offers, believing arena football was a last resort. Now, as he stood in the middle of a blizzard with a useless car and no direction in his life, Warner wondered if things could get any worse.

At the top:

2000—Warner stood at midfield at the Georgia Dome and raised the silver Lombardi Trophy into the air, celebrating as the St. Louis Rams became world champions for the first time. Warner, who had already received the league's Most Valuable Player award, had just been named MVP of the Super Bowl, having passed for more than 400 yards and 2 touchdowns. He had begun the season as a backup quarterback, but when the starter fell to injury, Warner stepped in and became one of the more unlikely heroes in the history of professional sports. He led his team to a surprising 13–3 record, throwing 41 touchdowns and accumulating more than 4300 passing yards—a remarkable feat for any quarterback, much less one who had only played in one NFL game before the 1999–2000 campaign. Warner followed up the regular season by marching the Rams through the playoffs and leading them to a close win over the Tennessee Titans in one of the most exciting Super Bowls ever. Warner would bring the Rams back to the playoffs (and to another Super Bowl) over the next two years before moving on to play with the New York Giants and the Arizona Cardinals, where he served mainly in backup roles while his teams groomed younger quarterbacks for the starting job.

In 2009, Warner put together another remarkable season when he brought the Arizona Cardinals—a team that had not won a playoff game since 1947—to their first Super Bowl, where the underdogs lost on a last-second touchdown to the Pittsburgh Steelers. With stellar play during 2009 and previous playoffs, Kurt Warner had secured himself a place as one of the great quarterbacks in NFL history.

The comeback:
Warner had turned down offers from the Arena League because he believed he was capable of doing better. He soon realized, however, that the last resort is sometimes the only resort, and after six months of stocking groceries, he took a job as quarterback of the Iowa Barnstormers, a new team that he took to the league championship game each of the next two seasons. During the 1996 season his girlfriend, who became his wife the next year, helped guide him toward a religious awakening. He became a born-again Christian, an experience he believes helped strengthen his character as well as his personal life. During his years in the Arena Football League, Warner continued to believe he still had a shot at the NFL. He inched closer in 1998 when the Rams signed him and sent him to play for a season with the Amsterdam Admirals in the NFL's European league. There, he led the league in passing yards and touchdowns—which was enough to earn him a backup job in St. Louis the next year. Many football observers were stunned by what happened in 1999, but not Warner, who had been steadily working toward his chance for stardom for years.

ERIK WEIHENMAYER (B. 1968)
American Mountain Climber

At the bottom:

1981—Erik Weihenmayer would not be able to look forward to the same sorts of teenage experiences his friends would enjoy. Having been diagnosed with a rare eye disease called retinoschisis ten years earlier, the thirteen-year-old Weihenmayer was losing his last remaining bit of sight as his retinas slowly split. Doctors were powerless to stop the slow progress of the disease. "Each morning," he wrote in his memoir," I woke up to a new level of diminished vision and the lessened expectations that went with it." His world was shrinking each day, but he had no idea when his retinas would finally give way to the pressure building up behind them. The world he saw was filled with "dim, dark shapes" that hovered on the periphery of his vision. "Nothing I saw was real and, as my vision flickered, I imagined monsters with scaly bodies and bulging eyes waiting just out of view." By the time he turned fourteen, his vision was completely gone.

At the top:

2001—Erik Weihenmayer slowly ascended the dreaded Hillary Step, the narrow forty-foot rock face that separated climbers from access to the true summit of Mt. Everest. Tibet lay ten thousand feet below him on one side; Nepal was a slightly closer seven thousand feet below on the other side. The slightest misstep would send him tumbling into one country or another, but Weihenmayer made it to the top along with eighteen other climbers in May of 2001. It was not the first major summit of his life. He had already scaled Mt. McKinley in 1995, El Capitan (in Yosemite National Park) in 1996, Mt. Kilimanjaro in 1997, Argentina's Aconcagua in 1999, and Polar Circus—a three-thousand-foot-tall ice waterfall in Canada's Banff National Park—in 2000. At the age of thirty-four, Weihenmayer became one of the small number of individuals—less than one hundred total—who have climbed the "Seven Summits," the tallest peaks on all seven continents. Widely sought as a motivational speaker, Weihenmayer also authored *Touch the Top of the World*, a popular memoir and account of his Everest climb.

The comeback:

When Weihenmayer was in the last stages of losing his vision, he learned about the Canadian runner Terry Fox, who had lost his right leg to cancer and yet had embarked on a mission to run across the continent. A national hero in Canada, Fox's story served as inspiration to Weihenmayer, who decided to take up the sport of wrestling not long after total blindness set in. He continued to wrestle while attending Boston College, but he soon wandered toward a new interest in climbing. As he told an interviewer in 2004, his blindness actually challenged him to do more with his life than he otherwise might have. "One thing that blindness enables you to do in the modern world is to be more of a pioneer," he explained. "I don't want to sound nostalgic, but it's exciting to be the first to see if it can be done. That's 50 percent of the reason why I find things exciting." Blindness, he added, "isn't a death sentence. Everything you need is inside you."

SIDNEY WEINBERG (1891–1969)
American Investment Banker

At the bottom:

1907—Sidney Weinberg was a sixteen-year-old boy from Brooklyn who never finished high school, dropping out after the eighth grade at the age of thirteen. One of eleven children born into the family of a struggling bootlegger, Weinberg was scarred by his upbringing in the most literal of ways—his back was marked by the evidence of several knife fights he'd gotten into before he was even a teenager. After leaving school, he worked at a variety of odd jobs, including shucking oysters and selling newspapers to ferry-goers arriving from Manhattan. By 1907, he was working as a porter's assistant in Lower Manhattan, where he drew a paycheck of three dollars per week from the investment firm Goldman Sachs & Company.

At the top:

1956—There were almost too many milestones to count in Sidney Weinberg's career at Goldman Sachs. After being handed the reins of the firm in 1930, as the nation tumbled into the Great Depression, Weinberg provided leadership that helped to restore confidence in the stock market while steering the company into the top tier of the nation's investment banking hierarchy. Throughout the Depression and into World War II, Weinberg played an important advisory role to the administration of Franklin Roosevelt, offering insights into securities reform policies as well as helping to review defense contracts with industries vital to the war effort.

Over these years, Weinberg served as a director of literally dozens of companies—he sometimes lost track of how many—while establishing a reputation as one of the most honest and ethical men in American business. Nicknamed "Mr. Wall Street," Weinberg was perhaps best known as the man who orchestrated the Ford Motor Company's first public stock offering in 1956. Involving more than $650 million worth of stock, the Ford deal was, at the time, the largest initial stock offering (IPO) in American history. For his efforts, Weinberg earned a fee of one million dollars (A substantial fee at the time, but far less than the 6% that modern investment banking firms charge for the same service.) Though he was certainly a very wealthy man—one of the great rags-to-riches stories of the century—Weinberg nevertheless lived relatively modestly. Indeed, until his death in 1969, he and his wife still lived in the home they had purchased in 1923.

The comeback:

Though Stanley Weinberg lacked much formal education, he always seemed drawn to the world of business. (He was also fortunate to live in an era before graduate degrees were a prerequisite for a career in finance.) Before starting out as a janitor at Goldman Sachs & Company, he had worked as a messenger for a few smaller brokerage houses in New York City—before being fired when his employers learned he was also working for their competitors. Using his own meager income, he had also taken a few night courses at Browne's Business College, and he showed evidence of higher career aspirations.

He landed the job at Goldman Sachs after seeking out the tallest building in the financial district. Starting at the top floor and working his way down, he asked for jobs on every floor until he reached the second floor, where he finally found one of the lowest-paying jobs in the building. Weinberg slowly worked his way into a job as an office boy, but his coworkers knew him as a youthful prankster, and it took more than a decade before he truly became serious about his career.

He took a leave from the firm to serve as a cook in World War I, but he returned in 1919 and took a job as a commercial paper trader, where he proved himself to be one of the most skilled men in the company. Within a few years he had earned greater responsibilities and was placing bonds for Sears, Roebuck and Company, Proctor & Gamble, and other top Goldman clients. By 1925, he was able to buy a seat on the New York Stock Exchange—at a price of $140,000—and two years later was promoted to partner in the firm.

MICHAEL KENNETH WILLIAMS (B. 1966)
American Actor

At the bottom:

1991—As he bled from two long gashes in his face and neck, Michael Kenneth Williams was unsure if he would live to see the next day. It was Williams' twenty-fifth birthday, and his friends had just rushed him to a Brooklyn hospital after he'd been attacked outside a bar where they were celebrating the occasion. Outside the bar entrance, one of Williams' friends had been surrounded by a group of men who were attempting to rob him. As Williams told an interviewer years later, "I stuck my nose in . . . [and] the gentlemen didn't take too kindly to me sticking my nose in their business." They attacked Williams, slashing him with razor blades and putting his budding career, if not his life, in danger.

Williams—who had grown up in a rough Brooklyn housing project— had been pursuing a career as a dancer and model and had recently begun getting small jobs dancing in music videos and modeling hip-hop fashion. "I was going happily in the direction the universe was taking me," Williams remembers, when the bar attack changed everything. Even with plastic surgery, he would likely have permanent scarring.

At the top:

2008—Michael K. Williams held a shotgun, demanding that the young man at the poker table surrender the ring on his finger. The man looked up at him without moving. "Boy," said Williams, "you must have me confused with a man who repeats himself." As the HBO crime drama *The Wire* completed its fourth season, Omar Little—played to perfection by Michael K. Williams—was one of the show's most popular characters, and Williams's portrayal of the character had received almost universal acclaim from critics. As Little, Williams played a stick-up artist with a peculiar moral code: He only robbed drug dealers like Marlo Stanfield, the ruthless kingpin whose ring Little took midway through the fourth season. "If you'd have told me seven years ago that this character was going to warrant this type of attention," Williams told National Public Radio's Terry Gross in 2008, "I'd have said get the hell out of here. But the fact that this character has been so well received has been humbling. It's an honor to be a part of something so beautiful and so revered within the industry." For his work in the fourth season, Williams would receive an NAACP Image Awards nomination for Best Actor in a Drama Series. *The Wire* itself received consistently high reviews; numerous critics regarded it as the best show on television. During his presidential run in 2008, Barack Obama told a newspaper reporter that *The Wire* was his favorite show and that Omar Little was his favorite character.

The comeback:
Michael Williams's comeback came in fits and starts. He survived the birthday attack and he was surprised to discover after his wounds healed that some photographers and music video directors were still interested in him, though for different reasons. Strangely enough, his new scars were intriguing from a certain vantage point. Though Williams would not recommend that people disfigure themselves to get acting work, the scars "definitely got the ball rolling." He no longer received offers to appear as a dancer, but he earned a few small roles—usually playing thuggish characters—in music videos. Eventually, he made appearances in episodes of *Law and Order* and *The Sopranos*, but he was still waiting for his break.

In 2001, he returned to Brooklyn and was working in a daycare facility his mother managed when he received a call to audition for the character of Omar in a new series being produced for HBO. Initially, Williams assumed his character would survive for only a few episodes, but he eventually realized that Omar was being written in as a major character. Though his role had stabilized, Williams himself was still adjusting to the new career turn. He didn't manage his money well at first, and in 2002 he fell behind on his rent and was evicted from his apartment. He moved to Los Angeles and slept on friends' couches while awaiting the next season of *The Wire*. He received several other roles in the meantime, including one in a series of rap videos by the artist R. Kelly that earned him a sizable income and got him back on his feet.

OPRAH WINFREY (B. 1954)
American Talk Show Host and Entrepreneur

At the bottom:

1968—Oprah Winfrey's young life had completely unraveled by the age of fourteen, when she discovered that she was pregnant. Having been born out of wedlock herself to a young woman in Kosciusco, Mississippi, Winfrey grew up in one of the bleakest parts of the poorest state in the nation. "I was raised with an outhouse, no plumbing," she explained once. "Nobody had a clue that my life could be anything but working in some factory or a cotton field in Mississippi." Her mother and father were not an intimate part of her early childhood; her father left Mississippi and moved to Nashville around the time of Oprah's birth, and her mother soon after headed north to Milwaukee.

Raised until the age of six by her maternal grandmother, Hattie Mae Lee, Winfrey was a bright child who nevertheless grew up lonely, without any friends to speak of and surrounded by severe adults who expected children to be quiet and well behaved. Craving some form of companionship, she read stories and talked to the pigs in the barn.

When she was six, Oprah moved to Milwaukee to join her mother, a poor woman who was putting in long hours as a domestic worker. Oprah felt unwanted, resented her lighter-skinned half sister, and grew to hate her mother, whom she blamed for the sexual abuse she suffered from one of her mother's male friends as well as from one of her uncles. Increasingly hard for her mother to control, Oprah was at last sent away once more, this time to Nashville to live with her father. By this time she was already pregnant; the result, not of abuse, but of her own adolescent promiscuity. She gave birth to a premature baby who died after only two weeks of life.

At the top:

2008—Oprah Winfrey would not have been surprised to learn that she'd made *Forbes* magazine's list of the four hundred wealthiest Americans. After all, she'd made the Forbes 400 every year since 1995, and there was no reason to assume she'd fall off the list anytime soon. Her afternoon television talk show, which had turned her into a household name more than two decades earlier, had served as the foundation for a media empire that included a film production company, two magazines, a Web site that draws six million users per month, a satellite radio channel, and a cable television channel. With a net worth of more than $2 billion and an annual income of nearly $300 million, Winfrey had become without question the wealthiest African American in U.S. history. With an enormous, loyal, and dedicated fan base, Winfrey's cultural influence is extraordinary, as she's helped shape her audience's views on social issues, religion, literature, film, and music. As a philanthropist, Winfrey has given more than $300 million to a variety of causes and in 2005 was ranked by *Business Week* as one of the fifty most generous philanthropists in the United States.

The comeback:

Winfrey credits her father, Vernon, as the primary positive influence that kept her young life from ruin. "When my father took me," she explained later, "it changed the course of my life. He saved me . . . I was definitely headed for a career as a juvenile delinquent." Though her father was as poor as anyone else in Winfrey's family, he provided an example of someone whose hard work and dedication had eventually paid off. With the money he'd earned scrubbing dishes at a restaurant and working as a custodian, Vernon had saved enough to buy a small barbershop in Nashville. As a deacon at his church, Vernon would also instill in Oprah the religious faith and personal discipline that would serve her throughout her adult life.

She had always been a smart child who did well in school and, living in Nashville under her father's care, Winfrey became one of the first black students to enroll at the formerly all-white East High School. Vernon urged his daughter to always remember that she was a trailblazer who had a great responsibility to do her best and make the most of the opportunity she'd been given. An honor student, she soon became active in drama and student government, and by graduation had won numerous debate tournaments. She had also begun working in radio, reading the news several times a week for a local radio station. By the time she entered college at Tennessee State, Oprah Winfrey had already begun making a mark in the world while leaving her troubled youth behind.

CONCLUSION

Reality Check: What Do You Really Have to Do to Make a Comeback?

How did they do it? What can we learn from these profiles, and perhaps apply to our own lives? Are there any common themes among the approaches that those we profiled used to bounce back? It goes without saying that those who staged these amazing comebacks were very persistent and determined. But there is so much more we have discovered.

Physical Location Matters

In the age of the Internet, digitized information, and the "Global Village," there is a temptation to think that physical location no longer matters, or at least not as much as it once did. The idea that we can use e-mail or cheap phone conversations to work with others anywhere in the world may be something of an illusion: Many of the individuals we profiled made some significant, physical move as part of their comeback. Einstein graduated from college in Switzerland but returned to Italy to take a job at a patent office; Barack Obama grew up mostly in sunny Hawaii, but attended schools in Jakarta, went to college in California and New York, and completed his education at Harvard Law School in dreary Boston; John Steinbeck had to leave New York and return to California to find his roots; many other Americans left their homes in other parts of the country to try to make it in New York.

Charles Darwin found much of his inspiration far from home in the Galapagos Islands. The Dalai Lama had to flee Tibet into India to avoid bloodshed. While movement is most often seen as the solution, it can also be a problem; for example, a young James Earl Jones was traumatized when his family moved from Mississippi to Michigan. But overall, location still matters, and ambitious people move when they think it will advance their aims. The Internet is an amazing and useful tool, but if you want a career in contemporary art or high finance, your odds of very high level success are still much better if you work in London or New York.

America Matters

Despite all its manifold problems and injustices, America is still the place for the ambitious and the oppressed. Thomas Paine was a complete failure in England before emigrating to America and changing history. Ayn Rand left Russia to become an important American writer. Andy Grove fled Hungary as Soviet tanks roared in, and he was always amazed that Americans did not resent, but rather celebrated, his great success as an immigrant in the United States. People from countries all over the world who have faced terrible political oppression; Armando Valladares in Cuba, Nien Cheng in China, Joseph Brodsky in Russia—all sought refuge in the United States after being released from prison in their native countries. Even when there has been oppression in the United States, as in the case of former slave Harriet Tubman, the solution has most often been to move from one part of the country to another, rather than emigrate. Corazon Aquino and her family had fled from the Philippines to Boston to escape the Marcos regime. When her husband was assassinated she returned, reluctantly, to the Philippines and was elected president. Guy Gabaldon became a very unlikely American hero on the Japanese island of Saipan; years later he returned to Saipan to open a successful seafood business.

America has had a historically variable but generally open immigration policy, and far more of the world's best and the brightest choose to move to the United States than to leave it. America is a relatively open society politically, economically, and culturally. For many of those we profile, that freedom has been critical to their success. There has been much talk about the economic vitality of developing nations like China, India, Russia, and Brazil, and some of those whom we profile have been very successful in those countries. But, at this time, none of the emerging countries have nearly the level of political freedom or economic opportunity that is available in the United States, and the emerging countries of the world are not nearly as open to foreigners. It's far more likely that a woman born in India will become successful in New York than it is that a woman born in New York will become successful in India.

School, Not So Much

There are countless surveys you can read that posit a correlation between educational attainment and higher incomes, and no doubt they are correct, on average. But truly exceptional achievement seems to have very little to do with academic success. Albert Einstein and Charles Darwin are universally acknowledged as two of history's most profound and influential thinkers, thanks, respectively, to their theories of relativity and evolution. Einstein was a bright student who did not care for rote learning; he failed an entrance examination for a science school in Zurich and, even after eventually obtaining a degree, he was unable to secure a faculty position at a university. Darwin was a curious child, but he was not interested in formal education; he was a poor student who disappointed his parents and teachers. Real profound change is made by those who, like Einstein and Darwin, challenge fundamental assumptions in creative ways, and formal educational institutions are not really designed for such people. Truly creative people are often bored by formal education or may simply not fit within its parameters.

Winston Churchill was a lousy student and failed his officer's test—twice. Buckminster Fuller was expelled from Harvard—twice. Sidney Weinberg dropped out of school at thirteen before going on to become the most important investment banker of his time. Jim Clark dropped out of high school before eventually founding the company that started the Internet stock boom. While he eventually earned a PhD in computer science and spent years as a teacher, he actually discovered his thirst to understand the world while serving in the United States Navy. Dave Longaberger graduated from high school at age twenty-one, reading at a sixth-grade level. Susan Boyle was nicknamed "Susie Simple." Joe Dudley was labeled a "slow learner." Richard Branson, a poor student, is now the most interesting entrepreneur in the world, with more than three hundred ventures to his name.

While it's true that Michael Bloomberg has a MBA from Harvard, that didn't stop him from being fired from Salomon Brothers. Although Barack Obama did very well at Harvard Law School, he was called an "educated fool" by his opponent in a congressional primary, which Obama lost by a wide margin. Azim Premji was forced to drop out of Stanford when his father died, which is when his real education began. Ruth Fertel was a brilliant woman who had graduated from Louisiana State University at the age of nineteen with a dual major in physics and chemistry, but formal, scientific education seems completely irrelevant to her eventual decision to buy a steakhouse.

One can find many examples of very successful people who hold advanced degrees from leading universities, but it's important not to confuse correlation with causation: Just because two things occur together does not mean that one caused the other. Bright, ambitious people tend to seek out well-known educational institutions because that often seems like the most obvious route to success, but such people tend to do well even if they drop out of school or end up following some other path. Each of the one hundred people we profile achieved amazing success in some endeavor, but only a few were really top-notch students at leading schools.

Religion

Like America, religion certainly seems to have its critics, but it is nonetheless a force that gives enduring strength to many who find themselves in deep distress. Armando Valladares and Nien Cheng both relied on their Christian faith to help them through almost unimaginable hardships as political prisoners. Tenzin Gyatso's belief in Buddhism, and the power of nonviolent action to achieve change, sustained his resistance to the Chinese takeover of Tibet. Harriet Tubman risked her life to save other slaves because she thought she was on a mission from God. Bethany Hamilton, having suffered the loss of her arm, learned to surf again with the help of her devout Christian faith. Joni Eareckson Tada, paralyzed from the neck down, at one point was begging her friends to help her commit suicide. But she ultimately triumphed after that dark period due to her religious convictions.

Some survived incredible brutality in other ways. James Stockdale had the most tangible and immediate suffering possible; he spent eight years as a prisoner of war in Vietnam, where he was tortured many times. Yet his consolation was the ancient Greek philosophy of the Stoics, and in particular a first-century Greek named Epictetus, whom he credited with giving him the perspective he needed to endure his captivity. For John McCain, it was his desire to adhere to a military code of honor that enabled him to refuse offers of early release that had been presented due to his father's rank. Religion is the most common form of philosophy, but there are non-religious philosophies that also enable people to adhere to their own beliefs and codes, even under the most brutal circumstances.

Family

One's family can be salvation, the root of the problem, or both. Both of Liz Murray's parents were drug addicts, and she was left to fend almost completely for herself from the age of eight, but she learned a love of reading from her father. In some cases, the death of a parent gives a child or young adult a new lease on life; Winston Churchill decided that his destiny was in his own control when his father died. Twenty-one-year-old Azim Premji, who was forced to take over the family business when his father died, did so reluctantly, but with extraordinary success. Abraham Lincoln was surrounded by death: his mother died when Lincoln was nine; his first love, Ann Rutledge, died of typhoid fever while they were engaged; his son Edward died of a respiratory illness at the age of four; his father died a year later; his sister died in childbirth; and his son Willie died at age eleven during Lincoln's first term in the White House. For Lincoln, it would seem that family was much more of a source of tragedy and sadness than comfort, but he was a man who had to learn to deal with death, as he was Commander In Chief of the Union armies during one of the bloodiest wars in American history.

Wilma Rudolf had twenty-one siblings, but far from being neglected as one of many, she received great strength from her family, with her brothers and sisters taking turns carrying the disabled Rudolf from room to room. She would later win three gold medals as a sprinter in the 1960 Olympic Games.

Generally, it might seem that having a family member manage an entertainer's career would be a recipe for disaster, but not in our research; rapper Mary K. Blige was helped in her recovery from drug abuse by having her sister become her manager. At the opposite end of the musical spectrum, Tony Bennett also staged a comeback from substance abuse, in large part thanks to having his son take over management of his career.

Will Keith Kellogg developed the idea of a wheat-flake cereal with his brother, but he had to part ways with him to develop that product. On the other hand, Walt Disney's brother, Roy, was cofounder of the Walt Disney Company and responsible for much of the business success of the company, leaving Walt free to focus on the creative side. Charles Schwab was bailed out of debt by his uncle; Richard Branson was bailed out of trouble, and a potential jail term, by his parents.

Families can be an encouraging or discouraging force. J. K. Rowling's sister encouraged her to keep writing when J.K was depressed, unknown, and poor. Headed for nothing but trouble living with her mother, Oprah Winfrey moved in with her father, and that made all the difference: "When my father took me," she explained later, "it changed the course of my life. He saved me . . . I was definitely headed for a career as a juvenile delinquent." On the other hand, Winston Churchill's father was pretty sure he would amount to nothing, and he told him so.

Modern American parents are encouraged to provide a protective, supportive atmosphere for their children, but we wonder if that really helps build the sort of resilience found in our profiles. One thing the individuals we profile all lack is a sense of entitlement, so common among modern American kids and children from affluent households around the world. Almost universally, the one hundred people presented here realized that if they wanted something, they had to go to great lengths to earn it. When Richard Branson was a small child his mother left him alone in a forest to try to develop his independence; how many parents would do that today? It's not an easy, cosseted life, but a hard one, that leads to the ferocious kind of hunger that fuels very high-level achievement. On the other hand, it seems that there is a great deal of evidence that having at least one parent who provides encouragement for the ambitions of a child can help sustain that child, and later the adult, through many trials. A child must believe that dreams really can come true, but they must also realize that ambition requires tremendous work, resilience, and sacrifice.

A Moment of Truth

How does a comeback begin? For Mary K. Blige, seeing a none-too-flattering picture of herself served as a wake-up call. For Andre Agassi, it was a failed drug test. For Diego Maradona and Tony Bennett their experiences with substance abuse would climax in near death experiences before they faced the need for dramatic change in their lives. For some, a release from prison is a new beginning. For others, like Paula Deen, just getting very tired of their self-imposed prisons led them to make a change.

A Fighting Spirit

Ulysses Grant was a drunkard who had failed as both a farmer and a bill collector, but he ultimately helped save the Union, and became Lincoln's favorite general, by being willing to take the fight to the enemy, unlike the Union's more timid generals. Theodore Roosevelt was devastated when his wife and mother died on the same day, but a spirit of feisty determination and a sort of muscular resilience led him back to an active life and, eventually, the U.S. presidency. When Mukhtar Mai was ritually gang-raped, she was expected to commit suicide, but her shame was transformed into a life-giving rage. "I've always been a fighter," Nien Cheng recalled. "When I'm confronted with a difficult situation, my first reaction is not to get frightened, it's Oh, wonderful, here's a situation that really calls on me to do something." While gentleness works for some, the will to live is often the will to fight.

Accidents

Terrible accidents played a role in many of those we profile. Douglas Bader lost both his legs in a flying accident, yet he went on to become one of the greatest pilots of World War II. Larry Ellison was so hardheaded, literally and figuratively, that it took not one but two life-threatening accidents, plus a major business implosion, for him to make some changes in his life and business. Jami Goldman was trapped in a car for eleven days and lost both legs due to frostbite. Trying out one of Buckminster Fuller's early inventions, the driver died and two investors were seriously injured. Glassblower Dale Chihuly lost one eye, and with it his depth perception, in a car accident. He responded by creating a whole new kind of glassblowing that made him one of the most famous artists of our times. In each case, an incredible amount of pain and suffering resulted from the accidents, but so too did significant life change and remarkable achievement.

Disease

Much like the case of horrific accidents, for some of these achievers disease has led, in very different ways, to unexpected accomplishment. Physicist Stephen Hawking was diagnosed with Lou Gehrig's disease, and while in the hospital he watched a young boy die of leukemia; his realization as to how sudden death could be led him to make the most of his remaining life. Laura Hillenbrand had a mysterious, debilitating disease, but by throwing herself into writing about a comeback horse, Seabiscuit, she was able to forget some of her own problems and create a story that captivated millions. Though Erik Weihenmayer gradually went blind, he was able to see his blindness as a chance to become a pioneer—which he certainly was, becoming the first blind person to scale Mount Everest. Jean-Dominique Bauby suffered a sudden massive stroke, but his imagination led him to create one of the most remarkable accomplishments in the history of literature, when he dictated a best-selling book using only the movement of one eyelid.

Fixing a Problem

Einstein and Darwin focused on very abstract universal and fundamental issues in science. But far more people have become successful focusing on issues of immediate personal concern, which later led to wider applications. Both Suze Orman and Judy Reznick were broke after their investment advisers lost all their money, and both ended up becoming very successful as a result of trying to figure out what happened. Amilya Antonetti spent two years trying to figure out why her baby would not stop screaming, and, when she discovered the answer, she built a company around that solution. When James Pennebaker was denied tenure, he was devastated, but in examining his own feelings he came up with a new area of research that saved his career. As a rabbi, Harold Kushner was used to dispensing advice and consolation, but when his own child died he realized that he had to find a new approach to dealing with grief. Victor Frankl was a trained psychiatrist, but his seven months as an inmate at Auschwitz, and the loss of his entire family, forced him to analyze human suffering in a new way. Jim Stovall didn't know the first thing about television or film production, but, because of his blindness, he soon realized that millions of other blind people could benefit from a service that provided narrative descriptions of television shows and movies.

Refuge

In some cases, having a quiet place and the time to think and develop ideas served as a catalyst for success. For Einstein, this refuge was a boring job in a patent office. Chester Carlton also took a routine job in a patent office, but it gave him an income and time to develop the process of document copying, later known as Xerox. For Buckminster Fuller, a teaching job at a small college served as an intellectual safe haven. For some, a steady source of income can allow them to perform their required duties but still have the time and mental energy left to develop more demanding ideas in their off hours.

Physical Appearance

In only a very few cases was physical beauty a great aid to those we studied. While it's generally believed that physical attractiveness is very helpful to both men and women, especially in the entertainment professions, our selection of subjects included only a few really physically beautiful people. Michael Kenneth Williams was an aspiring model and actor when he got stabbed in the face, leaving a large permanent scar. To his surprise, the scar actually increased his bookings and led, in part, to his standout role as a moralistic drug dealer and thief in the television show *The Wire*. Agents didn't take the rather ungainly looking Carol Burnett seriously when she auditioned for leading lady roles, so she created her own ensemble and became a famous comedian. Whoopi Goldberg is another actress who is far from being a classic beauty, but that didn't stop her from winning an Academy Award.

Tina Turner is certainly an attractive woman, but her outward appearance doesn't seem to be the key ingredient in her singing success, which only grew as she aged. Richard Branson is a very handsome man, but it is his sense of fun and adventure which is his real charm. Rachel Ray has certainly been aided in her television career by her looks, but looking at Susan Boyle on stage might have led many in the audience to have expected her appearance to be a bad joke—until she began to sing. Tyra Banks is a former supermodel, a true beauty with a stunning figure, but her talk show is not nearly as successful as that of Oprah Winfrey, who constantly battles weight problems.

Given a choice, we would all probably choose to be physically beautiful, but beauty doesn't seem to be a key ingredient in staging a great comeback. In fact, because everything in life comes easier to those who are really good-looking, it may be that such people are less equipped to stage comebacks if something goes terribly wrong. The less attractive among us are forced to develop other skills, like a sense of humor, perspective, and persistence, that may make it more likely for them to rebound from failure.

Money

At least half of those we profile had pressing financial problems at some point in their lives. Diego Maradona, the great soccer player, rose from severe poverty in Argentina. Albert Camus was born into a peasant family in Algeria; his father died fighting in World War I when Albert was a baby and his mother was an illiterate domestic worker. Michael Kenneth Williams and Whoopi Goldberg grew up in New York City housing projects. Liz Murray, also from New York, pumped gas and worked in a grocery store trying to make some money when she was just eight years old and living with her drug-addicted parents. Chester Carlson grew up sleeping outside a chicken coop.

Many others were broke as adults and had families to support. As a single father with a young son, Chris Gardner spent a number of nights sleeping in the men's room of a transit station in San Francisco. Francis Ford Coppola was a failure whose screenplays had flopped. By 1966, Coppola was badly in debt and, on top of that, had blown all his savings—twenty-thousand dollars—on a stock market gamble gone awry. "I was broke," Coppola remembered. "I'd lost all my money. I owed the bank $10,000. And I had two kids and a wife to support. . . . I was very depressed." Ruth Fertel was a brilliant, well-educated woman who was divorced and needed to figure out how to pay for her kids' college education. J. K. Rowling was broke, depressed, and on the dole, with a young daughter to support. She is now one of the richest women in England. As a young man, Buckminster Fuller was a "throwaway," a man who had become "discredited and penniless."

We also include some who were rich, even before their real ascent began. Mike Bloomberg was fired, but was paid $10 million for his partnership interest in Salomon Brothers. But that was a tiny amount compared to the billions he would later make as a media kingpin. Larry Ellison was a very rich man even when he was poorly managing Oracle; but he became one of the world's richest when he made some changes. Winston Churchill was born to great wealth; his father was Lord Randolph Churchill, the

7th Duke of Marlborough, but that didn't stop him from running out of money later in his life.

Age

Helen Keller was only nineteen months old when she contracted a disease that took her sight and hearing; she was eighty-four when she received the Presidential Medal of Honor for a lifetime of accomplishment. Anna Moses did not even start to be taken seriously as an artist, or take her own art seriously, until she was seventy-eight. Bernard Marcus was a successful business executive who was fired at fifty due to corporate infighting, yet he went on to cofound Home Depot. At thirty-eight, Harry Truman was just another failed small businessman. In this book we try to pick a low point and a high point for each individual, but these are somewhat arbitrary. For most, both success and failure came in incremental doses.

Others had a series of high points and low points: When Winston Churchill was twenty his father told him he was a washout, yet at age twenty-five he had become a national hero, having escaped from prison during the Boer war; in his late fifties he was isolated and abandoned within his own party, but by his late sixties he was leading England to victory against great odds; and in 1945 he was defeated for reelection, but in 1951, at age seventy-seven, Churchill again became the British prime minister. Great comebacks can occur at any age, young or old; if they occur more often in younger people, it is only because older people give up the fight due to self-imposed, and culturally reinforced, ideas about aging. As life spans around the world increase, hopefully more people will realize that a great comeback is, to paraphrase Dylan Thomas, about raging into the night, not going gentle into the dying light.

Incarceration

Although at least twelve of those we profile saw the wrong side of a jail cell, in most cases they were innocent of any wrongdoing. Nien Cheng, Armando Valladares, Rebiya Kadeer, Joseph Brodsky, and Nelson Mandela all spent years as political prisoners under brutal conditions. James Stockdale and John McCain were both prisoners of war during the Vietnam War and tortured repeatedly by their captors. Douglas Bader was held as a POW after being shot down in World War II, but continued trying to escape, undeterred by the loss of his legs. Victor Frankl spent seven months as a prisoner at Auschwitz. Chris Gardner was incarcerated for ten days in San Francisco for multiple outstanding parking violations; while the reason behind his imprisonment, and its duration, seems laughable compared to the others, it was no laughing matter to him. Richard Branson was arrested for tax evasion and went to jail. He was spared a prison sentence by accepting a large fine, which his parents paid by taking out a second mortgage on their home. Several others whom we profile could easily have ended up in jail, or seemed headed that way, before their lives took a different direction.

Rejection and Failure

For those in creative fields, rejection is part of the process. Walt Disney's first animation studio failed; the failure toughened him up. Ayn Rand's first major novel, *The Fountainhead*, was rejected by fourteen publishers before finally being published; it went on to become a best seller, and, in the opinion of some, The Great American Novel. Charles Schultz got fed up with his ten-dollar–a-week deal and was rejected by syndicators several times before his eventual success with "Peanuts," Charlie Brown, Snoopy, and the rest of the crew. Francis Ford Coppola's early screenplays were flops. Arthur Miller was excited about his first major play entitled *The Man Who Had All the Luck*, but it closed after lousy reviews and four performances. A dozen publishing houses rejected a children's book called *Harry Potter and the Philosopher's Stone*, and when it was finally accepted, it had a first printing of only five hundred copies; the Harry Potter series has since gone on to sell more than 400 million copies. Grandma Moses entered both her preserves and paintings in a county fair one year; the preserves won a prize; the paintings, nothing.

Vince Lombardi was told there was no future in coaching, he should try something else. Kurt Warner was cut by the Green Bay Packers, and even the World Football League would not draft him. At 5 feet, 9 inches tall and 210 pounds, Rocky Bleier was viewed by many pro scouts as being too small and too slow to play in the NFL. Despite his size and despite being ripped apart by a grenade in Vietnam, he ended up as a key player on four Super Bowl winning teams.

The idea that failure is not defeat as long as you don't give up is a concept that Americans embraced long ago. Abraham Lincoln was defeated for the state legislature in 1832 and failed in business in 1833. He had a nervous breakdown in 1836 and was defeated trying to become Illinois's house speaker in 1838. In 1843 he was defeated in his bid for Congress. In 1849 he was rejected in his application to become a land officer and in 1854 he was defeated in his bid for the United States Senate. In 1856 he was defeated in his attempt to get the nomination for vice president and in 1858 he was again defeated in a Senate bid. In 1860 he was elected president of the United States and proceeded to save the Union. Ulysses Grant failed as a farmer and a bill collector before begging his father for a job in a leather shop in 1860. Shortly thereafter, he joined the Union Army, rose to become its commanding general, and proceeded to help Lincoln change the course of American history.

But the roots of American resilience go much further back than the Civil War. Thomas Paine's pamphlet *Common Sense* was instrumental in building support for the Revolutionary War. In England, Paine had worked, and failed, as a corset maker, an excise officer, a schoolteacher, and a tobacco shopkeeper. In 1774, he lost his job as an excise inspector and saw his tobacco business collapse. To evade a sentence to debtors' prison, Paine sold all his possessions and left for the American colonies, and that is how the great Thomas Paine became a famous American patriot. In more recent times, Earl Stafford, Bruton Smith, Charles Schwab, and Ross Perot were all failed entrepreneurs who eventually became very successful entrepreneurs.

Marriage, Divorce, and Single Parents
Lincoln's marriage provided more frustration than consolation—his wife eventually went mad. Frank Sinatra was married to glamour queen Ava Gardner; but not for long—they divorced in 1951. J. K Rowling's young marriage ended early—leaving her a single mother. In fact, single-parenting is a pretty common theme throughout our profiles, because the persons profiled were either single parents themselves or they were raised by a single parent, or both. While living with her mother, Oprah Winfrey became pregnant at fourteen, but her child died only two weeks after birth. Whoopi Goldberg was raised by a single parent and then became one herself at nineteen when her marriage collapsed a few months after

her baby was born. James Earl Jones was raised by his grandparents while his mother searched for work during the Great Depression. Chester Carlson's mother died from tuberculosis when he was in high school, leaving him to care for his father, who also had tuberculosis. James Clark's father abandoned the family at a young age, paving the way for Clark's troubled school years. Chris Gardner, having been abandoned by his father and abused by his stepfather, was determined to give his own son a better life. But when he returned from a short jail term he found his girlfriend had taken their son and left. She then returned him when she couldn't handle being a single mother, leaving Gardner as a single father. Mary Kay Ash was left with three young children to raise after her husband left her. In many cases it appears that children were both a burden and an inspiration for single parents who were forced to find a way to support not only themselves, but their children as well.

Starting a Business

The most common way that the people whom we profile overcame their obstacles was by starting a business. So, how did they get started? Michael Bloomberg started with the most—$10 million that he received for his partnership interest when he was fired from Salomon Brothers. Mary Kay Ash had saved five thousand dollars over the years as a successful cosmetics salesperson; not much, but enough to plant the seed for Mary Kay Cosmetics, which by 2008 had sales of $2.8 billion. Ross Perot founded EDS with one thousand dollars he borrowed from his wife.

Rachel Ray got her start by giving cooking classes in the food store where she worked, showing people how to cook tasty meals in less than thirty minutes, and she eventually self-published her first cook book, which sold ten thousand copies. James Clark established his credentials by getting a PhD, and spending years teaching computer science, before founding Silicon Graphics; funding for tech ventures is generally available for those with a good idea and the right background. Sidney Weinberg started at Goldman Sachs as a janitor in 1907 when he was sixteen years old. Through hard work, intelligence, and a reputation for honesty, he was able to work his way up in the firm to become a partner. That type of ascent would not be possible today, as the leading investment banks have become caste-driven institutions open to men and women from all over the world, but only those who have done well in a top tier MBA program. Ruth Fertel had no experience running a business and had shown no passion for entrepreneurship, but she was able to get a loan for eighteen thousand dollars to buy the first and, at the time, the only, Chris's Steak House in 1945. In many cases, a would-be entrepreneur started out as an employee, and then continued in the same line of work on their own; this was the case with Joe Dudley, who got his start selling Fuller Hair Care Products. Bernard Marcus had a successful career in retail management, despite being fired, before he cofounded Home Depot. Ross Perot had a comfortable management job and tried to persuade his bosses at IBM to listen to his ideas about providing customized computer information services to business clients; when his suggestions were ignored, Perot founded EDS to turn his vision into reality.

Amilya Antonetti could not convince grocery stores to carry her nontoxic soaps so she took out small newspaper ads and sold directly to other mothers; eventually she was offered a guest spot on a weekly talk show that provided a much wider audience for her products. Marsha Serlin might have had the smallest capital base among our group: she began her scrap metal business with two hundred dollars and a rental truck. She got her first big break when she learned that a Del Monte canning factory had accumulated so much scrap metal that they might need to shut down for a few days to clean it up. She called the company and asked if she could have the job. She and her brother cleaned up the plant and were immediately rewarded with a long-term contract. After Chris Gardner finally got a job as a stockbroker, he built his business the old-fashioned way— making hundreds of cold calls each day.

Paula Deen began making and selling boxed lunches to downtown office workers in Savannah, Georgia. After building up a base of customers, she decided to open a small restaurant and watched it grow into a local attraction, which led to other opportunities. Suze Orman was also going to open a restaurant, until her stockbroker lost the fifty thousand dollars that an investor had given her, which prompted Orman to focus on the financial world rather than restaurants. Azim Premji inherited the family business when his father suddenly died, but he was completely unqualified to oversee it, so much so that one of Wipro's investors demanded that he sell the company, since there was no way a "twit" could run it. Bruton

Smith built his first racetrack with financing from his wealthy brother-in-law. But when the track ran into cost overruns he was forced out, then declared bankruptcy, only to buy the track back years later. Using nearly all of his modest savings and eventually quitting his day job as an advertising artist, Walt Disney purchased a Universal camera for three hundred dollars and began hiring young animators for his new studio. Debbi Fields convinced her husband, Randy, to help her get a small business loan, but even he wondered if she'd last more than a month or two. He even bet her that she'd fail to sell fifty dollars worth of cookies the first day; she won the bet, but not by much.

Timing

According to popular lore, success is all about being in the right place at the right time. That was certainly true in the case of the most powerful person in our group, Barack Obama. In his 2003 senate race, the Republican front-runner opposing him dropped out when embarrassing details about his divorce were released, and Obama cruised to an easy victory. Despite having not even served one full senate term, he was able to handily win the presidential election in 2008, largely as a result of the financial crisis that was unfolding that year, severely damaging the incumbent Republican Party and John McCain's candidacy. Having been badly beaten in his 2000 congressional campaign, Obama has won only two national elections in his political career, and in both cases circumstances outside his control were major contributing factors. But it's never quite as simple as that. Obama is a very effective orator, and he ran a strategically brilliant campaign against Hillary Clinton, the clear favorite, to win the Democratic nomination for president in 2008.

It is in the political arena where timing seems to have the most impact. Most types of success happen in small bits and pieces over time, but elections happen on a single day, so the circumstances of the time immediately preceding election days tend to have a huge impact on a politician's career. Max Cleland won his race for the senate by only thirty thousand votes in 1996; he lost a similarly close vote six years later. A small change in the political environment in the days leading up to the election could have reversed the results in either one of those elections.

But overall, timing seems to have been less critical in these comebacks than one might suppose. Generally, there was no single leap to success that had to happen at a certain time. Laura Hillenbrand, fighting a debilitating illness, could do more some days, less other days, as she worked on the story that would eventually become *Seabiscuit*. Dave Longaberger spent several years making baskets in small quantities before really launching his company. The amazing comebacks of Temple Grandin and Helen Keller from childhood disabilities were long, slow, painful processes. Jim Stovall was severely depressed and wouldn't leave the house when creeping blindness finally took the last of his eyesight. His comeback began the day he decided to try to walk to the mailbox, the first step on a long road back.

After thinking he was too good for the Arena Football League, Kurt Warner realized that sometimes the last resort is the best resort, and his success in the Arena league led to NFL's European League, which finally led to Warner's NFL success in America. It's true that Chris Gardner was inspired to become an investment adviser by a chance encounter with a successful stockbroker, but his actual road to success was about diligence, not timing. Susan Boyle's appearance on *Britain's Got Talent* was a real and immediate springboard to success, but was more about opportunity than timing, as well as the nature of her profession. It only takes a minute to tell if a singer is really good or not; this is not true of other professions, business for instance, where talent is much less transparent. While timing plays some role in everyone's life, the ability to stage a great comeback seems to be more dependent on taking a large number of small incremental steps over a period of years.

A Specific Activity

In a number of cases, there was a passion for a specific activity that drove success. Both J. K. Rowling and Ayn Rand were determined to be writers from an early age and stayed on that path despite many obstacles. Former athletes Diego Maradona and Billy Beane both staged comebacks when they returned to the sport they loved as coaches. Running changed Jami Goldman's life. Painting helped Joni Eareckson Tada overcome her paralysis. For Tony Bennett and Frank Sinatra it was about returning to the music they loved, and finding a way to appeal to younger audiences while still staying true to their musical roots. Feeling like a failure, Debbi

Fields made a business of the one thing she really enjoyed; baking cookies. Most people don't have a ruling passion, but if you do, you should do your best to build your life around it.

Help from Others

What role does the help of others play? Michael Bloomberg was already a very rich and successful man, but his candidacy for mayor of New York City had little chance of success until he was endorsed by the very popular incumbent mayor, Rudy Giuliani. Helen Keller's comeback was absolutely dependent on support from her parents and an extraordinary teacher, Anne Sullivan. "The most important day I remember in all my life," Helen Keller wrote in 1902, "is the one on which my teacher, Anne Mansfield Sullivan, came to me." Yet it still took an almost mind-boggling effort for Helen Keller to learn to communicate. Teachers inspired Georgia O'Keeffe to return to painting after having given it up. It was also a teacher who got a young James Earl Jones to start talking again.

For political prisoners like Nelson Mandela and Armando Valladares, organized political pressure from groups like Amnesty International were very important in securing their eventual release; yet they both still spent decades in prison. J. K. Rowling received a number of small grants and positive reviews that helped her early writing career along, as well as encouragement from her sister. The friendship of Democratic Party boss Tom Pendergast helped start, and kept, Harry Truman on the road to political success. Ayn Rand glamorized the idea of standing alone against the world, and to a large extent she did. Nonetheless, she was aided by her marriage to Frank O'Connor, enabling her to stay in the United States, and by the tenaciousness of Archibald Ogden, an editor who threatened to quit if his firm rejected *The Fountainhead*.

Conclusion

If there is a single common denominator among these profiles, it is no surprise: resilience and a sense of optimism, although this can take many different forms. Ross Perot was guided by a "ferocious sense of certainty." John Bogle had a stubborn unwillingness to accept defeat. Walt Disney stayed consistently upbeat in the face of failure. Ruth Fertel said "I've always had a lot of confidence in my ability to do anything that I set my mind to." Mary Kay Ash made a list of all the good things that had taken place over the twenty-five years she'd been working in business. As she wrote in one of her numerous books, "Forcing myself to think positively did wonders for my spirit." Albert Camus had "a flair for being happy." Four days after his diagnosis with Hodgkin's disease, Mario Lemieux spoke with reporters and expressed optimism about his chances for survival. "I'm a positive person," he explained. "Sometimes in life, you have to go through tough periods. I haven't been that fortunate. But you climb the mountain. We know this disease is curable." Judy Reznick simply lacked the fear of rejection that grips many people.

There are also some less obvious commonalities. Everyone in this book has successfully combined reason and irrationality. In every single case, it would have been very unrealistic to expect the level of success that was, in fact, eventually obtained. Rocky Bleier said he had "an ability to persuade myself that reality is not what it seems." If he had been "realistic" he would have given up football after his injuries. It was unrealistic for Einstein, who couldn't even find a university faculty job, to think of having a broad impact on science with his theories. It was unrealistic for Douglas Bader to think he could have a normal life after losing his legs, much less become a superstar flying ace. It was unrealistic for Barack Obama to think he could be become president, or for Oprah Winfrey to think she could become much of anything.

But these people did more than dream; they had crazy ideas, but very sane ways of achieving them. The dreams were wild, but the steps that got them to the dreams were carefully calculated and eminently practical. No one is a greater dreamer than Richard Branson, with his head in the skies—he has flown balloons around the world and one of his companies is now offering space flights. But in his early days his feet were firmly on the ground and he was focused on how to get out of debt. Oprah Winfrey now has her own television network; when she was in high school she was focused on winning debate tournaments, getting good grades, and her role in student government. In 1968 Francis Ford Coppola invested his own money in *The Rain People*, which he wrote and directed. While not a big success, it allowed him to develop and showcase his talents. Ayn Rand was intent on changing the world, and her magnum opus, *Atlas Shrugged*, is twelve hundred pages long. But her much earlier novel, *Anthem*, is less than one hundred pages. Obama spent years as a state senator before running for national office. It takes lots of little realistic steps to make big unrealistic dreams come true.

It's important to note that there is no relationship at all between the level of eventual success these people achieved and the degree to which their comeback should be admired. In fact, the wealthiest and most powerful people in this book, still living, are Barack Obama, Larry Ellison, and Michael Bloomberg. They each faced great obstacles, but, relatively speaking, their paths were easy compared to some of the others we profile. Our greatest respect is not for those who have achieved great wealth or power, but for those who were able to survive with honor as political prisoners or prisoners of war, and for those who overcame seemingly insurmountable physical disabilities. Most of these people aren't very famous, but they should be.

The things most commonly cited for success—good health, education, appearance, and timing—don't seem to be of overwhelming importance in making a great comeback, although they tend to be very important in achieving a high degree of conventional success. What matters is that someone believes, for whatever reason, that change is possible. A belief in change requires, perhaps more than anything else, a sense of imagination; you have to believe that life can be something other than what it appears at the moment. Ayn Rand, John Steinbeck, and J.K. Rowling are storytellers by profession; Joseph Brodsky was a poet. Walt Disney used animated characters to create stories; Charles Schultz, cartoon characters. Jean-Dominique Bauby, a magazine editor, was completely paralyzed, but instead of wallowing in self-pity, he focused on all the places he could go in his imagination.

You would expect writers and artists to have a well-developed sense of imagination. But where did their sense of imagination come from, and is it present in the others? We don't have the data to prove it, but we suspect that reading some sort of fiction, or being told stories, or having to create your own entertainment as a young person has much to do with developing the sense of imagination required to overcome great odds. Oprah Winfrey read stories and talked to the pigs in the barn. Laura Hillenbrand had read about Seabiscuit as a child. Liz Murray, living on the streets, read books that had been discarded by the local library. Almost none of the people profiled in this book had the constant sort of stimulation from TV, the Internet, cell phones, video games and so on that is prevalent among children the world over today. It may well be that imagination develops as an escape, or a tool for those that have to create their own entertainment. Children who are ill, or in a rural environment, or living in poverty, may be forced to develop their imaginations in ways that are far less common in the modern, affluent, stimulation rich environment.

Generally speaking, those who have been able to come back from failure have been bright and creative, but not brilliant students. They might be attractive or moderately attractive, but rarely beautiful. Some have received critical help from others or their family, others have not. Many have started businesses, usually with modest capital. Most have had to move at some point in their lives in pursuit of their objectives, either across the world or across the country. Timing appears to be overrated; if they were in the right place at the right time, it was because they traveled to the right place and waited for the right time. Many either had unhappy marriages or were the children of unhappy marriages. Many, perhaps most, were on the brink of insolvency at some point in their lives. They have an amazing, and increasingly uncommon, ability not to be defined by trauma in their lives, but to move on.

They almost universally share a long-term point of view, the ability, and willingness, to ignore present pain while working towards a better future. They often went through periods of depression, but generally they did not spend much time wallowing in self-pity or bitterness. If anyone knows life is unfair, it is these one hundred individuals, but they don't focus on that unfairness or let it define them. They rarely saw themselves as victims. Instead, they focused on one of two great skills; creativity or the ability to connect to others. The writers, artists, and other creative thinkers used their abilities to create new worlds, fired by imagination. The scientists used imagination to think of theories that could encompass the earth, or even entire galaxies.

The other skill that deserves attention is the ability to connect to others; to get people to share your dream, or your plight, or to persuade others to join your battle. The entrepreneurs and the politicians we cover have to convince large groups of people to join their quest, whether as voters, customers, campaign workers, investors, or employees. Because they have faced adversity, and because they are often not the most gifted in terms of inherited wealth, physical beauty, or academic credentials, they have been forced to develop the ability to persuade. If you can combine imagination with persuasiveness, you can change the world.

Ultimately, it is the ability to imagine and persuade, combined with optimism and endless determination, more than beauty, education, wealth, health, or timing, that makes for the great comeback.

We'll leave you with some words from Vince Lombardi:

> The real glory is being knocked to your knees and then coming back. That's real glory. That's the essence of it.

SOURCES

Agassi, Andre

"Agassi Says He Used Crystal Meth in '97." ESPN.com (October 28, 2009) <http://sports.espn.go.com/sports/tennis/news/story?id=4600027>

"Agassi Fights Back to Capture First Title at Roland Garros." Sportsillustrated.cnn. com (June 9, 1999) <http://sportsillustrated.cnn.com/tennis/1999/french_open/ news/1999/06/06/french_final/index.html>

Andre Agassi. *Open: An Autobiography.* New York: Alfred A. Knopf, 2009.

Andrews, Julie

Richard Stirling. *Julie Andrews: An Intimate Biography.* New York: Macmillan, 2008.

Antonetti, Amilya

Amilya Antonetti. *Why David Hated Tuesdays.* Roseville, California: Prima Publishing, 2003.

Janis Mara. "Soapworks Cleans Up—In Healthy Way San Leandro Entrepreneur Sells Hypoallergenic Cleaning Products." Oakland Tribune. (August 10, 2003). HighBeam Research. 16 Dec. 2009 <http://www.highbeam.com>

Aquino, Corazon

"Corazon Aquino Speaks to Fulbrighters." <http://www.fulbrightalumni.org/olc/pub/ FBA/fulbright_prize/aquino_address.html>

Clyde Habermans. "Filipinos Pay Tribute to a Symbol of Opposition." *The New York Times,* 25 August 1983, A4.

Sandra Burton. "Corazon Aquino." *Time* (August 23–30, 1999). <http://www.time.com/ time/asia/asia/magazine/1999/990823/aquino1.html>

Ash, Mary Kay

Mary Kay Ash. *Miracles Happen: The Life and Timeless Principles of the Founder of Mary Kay Inc.* New York: Harper Collins, 1981.

William J. O'Neill. *Business Leaders and Success: 55 Top Business Leaders and How They Achieved Greatness.* New York: McGraw Hill, 2004.

Bader, Douglas

Paul Brickhill. *Reach for the Sky: The Story of Douglas Bader, Legless Ace of the Battle of Britain.* New York: Norton, 1954.

Bauby, Jean-Dominique

Jean-Dominique Bauby. *The Diving Bell and the Butterfly.* New York: Vintage, 1997.

Thomas Mallon. "In the Blink of an Eye." *The New York Times* (June 15, 1997) http:// www.nytimes.com/books/97/06/15/reviews/970615.mallon.html?_r=1

Beane, Billy

Michael Lewis. *Moneyball: The Art of Winning an Unfair Game.* New York: W. W. Norton and Company, 2004.

Creating Value through People: Discussions with Talent Leaders. Hoboken, NJ: Wiley, 2008.

Bennett, Tony

Tony Bennett. *The Good Life.* New York: Simon and Schuster, 1998.

John Lewis. "Tony Bennett." *AARP Magazine* (July–August 2003). http://www.aarp magazine.org/entertainment/Articles/a2003-06-18-bennett.html

Bleier, Robert "Rocky"

Rocky Bleier and Terry O'Neil. *Fighting Back*. New York: Stein and Day, 1975.

Gerry Faust, Roger Valdiserri, John Heisler, Bob Logan. *Gerry Faust's Tales from the Notre Dame Sideline*. Sports Publishing LLC, 2003.

Blige, Mary J.

Kevin Chappelle. "The New Mary J. Blige Tells How Drugs and Attitude Almost Ruined Her Sizzling Career." *Ebony* (January 1998): 60–64.

Keith Murphy. "Mary J. Blige." *The Vibe Q: Raw and Uncut*. New York: Kensington, 2007: 303–314.

Bloomberg, Michael

Maury Peiperl, Michael Bernard Arthur, N. Anand. *Career Creativity: Explorations in the Remaking of Work*. New York: Oxford University Press, 2002.

Roy C. Smith. *The Rise of Today's Rich and Super-Rich*. Washington, D.C.: Beard Books, 2002.

"Interview with Michael Bloomberg." *The Focus*. http://www.egonzehnder.com/global/focus/leadersdialogue/article/id/71500016

Bogle, John

Adam Smith, *Supermoney* (New York: John Wiley and Sons, 2006).

Norm Alster, "John Bogle Is at the Vanguard for Investors," *Investor's Business Daily* (June 10, 2009).

Boyle, Susan

Natalie Clark. " 'They called me Susie Simple,' but Singing Superstar Susan Boyle Is the One Laughing Now." *Daily Mail* (17 April 2009). <http://www.dailymail.co.uk/tvshowbiz/article-1171536/They-called-Susie-Simple-singing-superstar-Susan-Boyle-laughing-now.html>

Leigh Holmwood. "Susan Boyle: A Dream Come True." *The Guardian* (18 April 2009). http://www.guardian.co.uk/media/2009/apr/18/susan-boyle-britains-got-talent

Branson, Richard

Kateri Drexler. *Icons of Business: An Encyclopedia of Mavericks, Movers, and Shakers*. Santa Barbara: Greenwood, 2007.

Richard Branson. *Losing My Virginity*. New York: Virgin Books, 2007.

Brodsky, Joseph

Cissie Dore Hill, "Remembering Joseph Brodsky." *Hoover Digest* 4 (2000) http://www.hoover.org/publications/digest/3493691.html

Joseph Brodsky. "Nobel Lecture," 8 December 1987. http://nobelprize.org/nobel_prizes/literature/laureates/1987/brodsky-lecture-e.html

Burnett, Carol

Karin Adir. *Great Clowns of American Comedy*. McFarland, 2001.

"President Honors Recipients of the Presidential Medal of Freedom." White House <http://georgewbush-whitehouse.archives.gov/news/releases/2005/11/20051109-2.html>

Camus, Albert

Patrick McCarthy. *Camus, The Stranger: A Student Guide*. Cambridge: Cambridge University Press, 2004.

Herbert Lottmann. *Albert Camus: A Biography*. Berkeley: Gingko Press, 1997.

Carlson, Chester

David Owen. *Copies in Seconds: Chester Carlson and the Birth of the Xerox Machine.* New York: Simon and Schuster, 2004.

"Chester Carlson (Photocopier)." *Inventors and Inventions.* White Plains, NY: Marshall Cavendish Reference, 2008.

Carnegie, Dale

Dale Carnegie. *How to Win Friends and Influence People.* New York: Simon and Schuster, 1982.

Tom Sant. *The Giants of Sales: What Dale Carnegie, John Patterson, Elmer Wheeler, and Joe Girard Can Teach You About Real Sales Success.* New York: AMACOM, 2006.

Cheng, Nien

J. M. Coetzee. "A Prisoner of the Thought Police." *The New York Times* (May 31, 1987). <http://www.nytimes.com/books/98/12/06/specials/cheng-shanghai.html>

Norval Morris and David Rothman, eds. *The Oxford History of the Prison.* New York: Oxford University Press, 1995.

Nien Cheng. *Life and Death in Shanghai.* New York: Grove Press, 1987.

"Obituary: Nien Cheng." *Telegraph* (11 November 2009). <http://www.telegraph.co.uk/news/obituaries/politics-obituaries/6545847/Nien-Cheng.html>

Chihuly, Dale

Sheila Farr and Susan Kelleher. "Inside the Glass Empire." *Seattle Times,* August 8, 2006. <http://seattletimes.nwsource.com/html/chihulyinc/2003178395_chihuly06.html>

Gregory Burns. *Iconoclast: A Neuroscientist Reveals How to Think Differently.* Cambridge: Harvard Business Press, 2008.

Churchill, Winston

Martin Gilbert. *Churchill: The Wilderness Years.* New York: Houghton Mifflin, 1982.

Christopher Catherwood. *Winston Churchill: The Flawed Genius of World War II.* New York: Penguin, 2009.

Sebastian Haffner. *Churchill.* London: Haus Publishing, 2003.

Clark, James H.

Michael Lewis. *The New New Thing: A Silicon Valley Story.* New York: W.W. Norton and Co., 2000.

Goldberg, Michael. "Fire in the Valley." *Wired.* Jan. 1994. 14 Mar. 2003. <http://www.wired.com/wired/archive/2.01/sgi_pr.html>

Robinson, James. "Entrepreneur Clark Gives $150 Million for Bio-X." *Stanford Report Online.* 27 Oct. 1999. Stanford University. 13 Mar. 2003. <http://www.stanford.edu/dept/news/report/news/october27/bioxgift-1027.html>

Cleland, Max

Max Cleland and Ben Raines. *Heart of a Patriot.* New York: Simon and Schuster, 2009.

John D. Thomas. "Odyssey." *Emory Magazine* (Summer 1997). http://www.emory.edu/EMORY_MAGAZINE/summer97/max.html?

Coppola, Francis Ford

Peter Cowie. *Coppola.* Philadelphia: Da Capo, 1989.

Gene D. Phillips and Rodney Hill. *Francis Ford Coppola: Interviews.* Oxford, Mississippi: University Press of Mississippi, 2004.

Darwin, Charles
Frank Contosta. *Rebel Giants: The Revolutionary Lives of Abraham Lincoln and Charles Darwin*. Amherst, NY: Prometheus Books, 2008.
John Bowlby. *Charles Darwin: A New Life*. New York: W. W. Norton, 1992.

Deen, Paula
Paula Deen. *It Ain't All About the Cookin'*. New York: Simon and Schuster, 2007.
Julia Moskin. "From Phobia to Fame." *The New York Times* (February 28, 2007). http://www.nytimes.com/2007/02/28/dining/28deen.html

Disney, Walt
Neal Gabler. *Walt Disney: The Triumph of the American Imagination*. New York: Random House, 2007.
Kathy Merlock Jackson, ed. *Walt Disney: Conversations*, vol. 52. Oxford, Mississippi: University Press of Mississippi, 2006.

Dudley, Joe
Joe Dudley, Sr. *Walking by Faith, I Am! I Can! & I Will!* Richardson, Texas: Executive Press, 1998.
Sakina Spruell. "Joe Dudley, Sr., Dudley Products." CNNMoney.com (December 1, 2003).http://money.cnn.com/magazines/fsb/fsb_archive/2003/12/01/359890/index.htm

Einstein, Albert
Walter Isaacson. *Einstein: His Life and Universe*. New York: Simon and Schuster, 2007.

Ellison, Larry
Mike Wilson. *The Difference Between God and Larry Ellison*. New York: HarperCollins, 2002.
Matthew Symonds. *Software: An Intimate Portrait of Larry Ellison*. New York: Simon and Schuster, 2003.

Fertel, Ruth
Allen, Robin Lee. "Ruth Fertel: Tireless Entrepreneur." *Nation's Restaurant News* (September 21, 1992), 81.
McDowell, Bill, "Ruth's Chris Steak House." *Restaurants & Institutions* (August 1, 1994), 54.
Gregory K. Ericksen. *Women Entrepreneurs Only: 12 Women Entrepreneurs Tell the Stories of Their Success*. New York: John Wiley and Sons, 1999.

Fields, Debbi
Edward Horrell. *The Kindness Revolution: The Company-wide Culture Shift that Inspires Phenomenal Customer Service*. New York: AMACOM, 2006.
Kateri Drexler. *Icons of Business: An Encyclopedia of Mavericks, Movers, and Shakers*. Santa Barbara: Greenwood Press, 2006.
"Debbi Fields." The Online Encyclopedia. <http://encyclopedia.jrank.org/articles/pages/6203/Fields-Debbi.html>

Ford, Henry
Nathan Miller. *New World Coming: The 1920s and the Making of Modern America* (New York: Da Capo, 2003).

Frankl, Viktor
Viktor Frankl. *Man's Search for Meaning*. Boston: Beacon Press, 2000.
Anna Redsand. *Viktor Frankl: A Life Worth Living*. New York: Houghton Mifflin Harcourt, 2006.

Fuller, Buckminster

R. Buckminster Fuller. *Critical Path.* New York: St. Martin's Press, 1981.

Ronald Reagan. "Remarks at the Presentation Ceremony for the Presidential Medal of Freedom" (February 23, 1983). *American Presidency Project* http://www.presidency.ucsb .edu/ws/index.php?pid=40963&st=&st1=

Gabaldon, Guy

Allison Varzally. *Making a Non-White America: Californians Coloring Outside Ethnic Lines, 1925–1955.* Berkeley: University of California Press, 2008.

William Bennett and John Cribb. *The American Patriots' Almanac.* Nashville, TN: Thomas Nelson, 2008.

Gardner, Chris

Chris Gardner. *The Pursuit of Happyness.* New York: HarperCollins, 2006.

Scotty Ballard. "From the Streets to Corporate Suites: How Homeless Man Made Millions." *Jet* (July 31, 2006), 50–54.

Jia Lynn Wang. "'Happyness' for sale." *Fortune* (September 16, 2006). http://money.cnn.com/magazines/fortune/fortune_archive/2006/09/18/8386184/index .htm

Glennie, Evelyn

Harry Lang and Bonnie Meath-Lang. *Deaf Persons in the Arts and Sciences.* Santa Barbara: Greenwood, 1998.

Evelyn Glennie. *Good Vibrations.* London: Hutchinson, 1990.

Evelyn Glennie, "The Hearing Essay." http://www.evelyn.co.uk/Evelyn_old/live/hear ing_essay.htm

Goldberg, Whoopi

Laura B. Randolph. "The Whoopi Goldberg Nobody Knows." *Ebony* (Mar 1991): 110–115.

Amy Alexander. *Fifty Black Women Who Changed America.* Dafina Books, 2003.

Goldman, Jami

Jami Goldman and Andrea Cagan. *Up and Running.* New York: Simon and Schuster, 2001.

Audio interview with Bill Thompson. *Bill Thompson's Eye on Books.* <http://www.eyeon books.com/ibp.php?ISBN=0743424204>

Cecelia Goodnow. "World-class Runner's Career Began after She Lost Her Legs." *Seattle Post-Intelligencer* (January 10, 2002). http://www.seattlepi.com/lifestyle/53865_lost legs10.shtml

Grandin, Temple

Temple Grandin. *The Way I See It: A Personal Look at Autism and Asperger's.* Arlington, TC: Future Horizons, 2008.

Temple Grandin. "An Inside View of Autism," in Eric Schopler and Gary Mesibov, eds., *High Functioning Individuals with Autism,* 105–125. New York: Plenum Press, 1992.

Grant, Ulysses S.

Josiah Bunting and Arthur Schlesinger, Jr. *Ulysses S. Grant.* New York: Times Books, 2004.

Edward Longacre. *General Ulysses S. Grant: The Soldier and the Man.* New York: Da Capo Press, 2007.

Grove, Andrew

Andrew Grove. *Swimming Across: A Memoir*. New York: Warner Books, 2002.

Richard Tedlow. *Andy Grove: The Life and Times of an American Business Icon*. New York: Portfolio, 2001.

Gyatso, Tenzin

"Dalai Lama's Nobel Peace Prize Acceptance Speech." <https://ssl4.westserver.net/spiritual/peace/dalilama.htm>

Dalai Lama. *Freedom in Exile*. New York: HarperCollins 1991.

Olympics a Chance to Tell China of Rights." Reuters (March 27, 2008). http://www.reuters.com/article/latestCrisis/idUSSP154041

Hamilton, Bethany

Bethany Hamilton, Sheryl Berk, and Rick Bundschuh. *Soul Surfer: A True Story of Faith, Family, and Fighting to Get Back on the Board*. New York: Simon and Schuster, 2004.

"Latest News," Surf.Co.Nz, January 6, 2009 <http://www.surf.co.nz/news/local/news.asp?newsletterId=6915&archive=>

David Collins, "Bethany Hamilton Lost Her Arm to a Shark—Now She's Triumphed in Surf World Championships," *The Mirror*, January 12, 2009 <http://www.mirror.co.uk/sport/more-sport/2009/01/12/bethany-hamilton-lost-her-arm-to-a-shark-now-she's-triumphed-in-surf-world-championships-115875-21034238/>

Hawking, Stephen

Kristine Larson. *Stephen Hawking: A Biography*. Santa Monica: Greenwood, 2005.

John Boslough. *Stephen Hawking's Universe*. New York: Avon, 1985.

Hillenbrand, Laura

Laura Hillenbrand. "A Sudden Illness—How My Life Changed." *The New Yorker* (July 7, 2003) <http://tiny.cc/vEUJb>

Sally Jacobs. "Against All Odds." *The Boston Globe* (October 24, 2002), D1.

Jones, James Earl

Glenda Gill. *No Surrender! No Retreat! African American Pioneer Performers of Twentieth-Century American Theater*. New York: Palgrave-Macmillan, 2000.

"James Earl Jones." *Hollywood Hired Guns: Soldiers to Celebrities*. http://www.hiredguns.biz/profiles/jamesearljones.htm>

Kadeer, Rebiya

Rebiya Kadeer. *Dragon Fighter: One Woman's Epic Struggle for Peace with China*. Carlsbad, CA: Kales Press, 2009.

Paulette Chu Miniter. "Taking a Stand for China's Uighurs." *Far Eastern Economic Review* (July 8, 2009) http://www.feer.com/free-interviews/2009/july54/Taking-a-Stand-for-Chinas-Uighurs

Keller, Helen

Dorothy Herrmann. *Helen Keller: A Life*. Chicago: University of Chicago Press, 1999.

Helen Keller. *The Story of My Life*. New York: Grosset and Dunlap, 1902.

Kellogg, Will Keith

Laura Waxman. *W. K. Kellogg*. Minneapolis: Lerner Publications, 2007.

Doris Simonis, ed. *Inventors and Inventions*. Tarrytown, NY: Marshall Cavendish, 2007.

Robert Grimm. *Notable American Philanthropists*. Santa Barbara: Greenwood Publishing, 2002.

Kroc, Ray

Ray Kroc and Robert Anderson. *Grinding It Out: The Making of McDonald's*. New York: Macmillan, 1987.

Jacques Pepin. "Ray Kroc." *Time* (7 December 1998). <http://www.time.com/time/time100/builder/profile/kroc.html>

Kushner, Harold

Harold Kushner. *When Bad Things Happen to Good People*. New York: Random House, 1981.

Harold Kushner. *The Lord Is My Shepherd*. New York: Random House, 2003.

Lemieux, Mario

Filip Bondy. "Lemieux's Comfort Is Close-knit." *The New York Times*. January 16, 1993.

"Pittsburgh Honors Lemieux." *The New York Times*. November 20, 1997.

Bill Menezes. "Super Mario, Amazing Boy." *Boys' Life*. December 1993, 32–33.

Malcolm Kelly and Mark Askin. *The Complete Idiot's Guide to Hockey*. New York: Alpha Books, 2001.

Lincoln, Abraham

Richard Striner. *Father Abraham: Lincoln's Relentless Struggle to End Slavery*. New York: Oxford University Press, 2007.

Lombardi, Vince

David Maraniss. *When Pride Still Mattered: A Life of Vince Lombardi*. New York: Simon and Schuster, 2000.

Longaberger, Dave

Dave Longaberger and Robert Shook. *Longaberger: An American Success Story*. New York: HarperCollins, 2003.

Amanda Boyd. "Basket Case." *Cincinnati Magazine*, March 2001: 40–44.

Mai, Mukhtar

Mukhtar Mai. *In the Name of Honor: A Memoir*. New York: Atria Books, 2006.

Nicholas Kristof, Sheryl WuDunn. *Half the Sky: Turning Oppression into Opportunity for Women Worldwide*. New York: Random House, 2009.

Mandela, Nelson

Nelson Mandela. *Long Walk to Freedom*. Boston: Back Bay Books, 1995.

Tom Lodge. *Mandela: A Critical Life*. New York: Oxford, 2006.

Nelson Mandela. "Inaugural Speech." May 10, 1994. <http://www.africa.upenn.edu/Articles_Gen/Inaugural_Speech_17984.html>

Maradona, Diego

"Late Win Puts Argentina in World Cup Finals." CNN International (October 15, 2009). http://edition.cnn.com/2009/SPORT/football/10/14/football.samerica/index.html

Francesco Bonami, et. al. *The Human Game: Winners and Losers*. Ann Arbor: University of Michigan, 2007.

Marcus, Bernard

Jack Grimm, Clark Johnson, Rob Raines. *My One Big Break*. Sports Publishing LLC, 2004.

Bruce J. Avolio, Bernard M. Bass. *Developing Potential Across a Full Range of Leadership: Cases on Transactional and Transformational Leadership*. Lawrence Erlbaum Associates, 2002.

Maury Peiperl, Michael Bernard Arthur, N. Anand. *Career Creativity: Explorations in the Remaking of Work.* Oxford University Press, 2002.

McCain, John
"McCain: Change is Coming." Transcript of John McCain's acceptance speech at the 2008 Republican Convention. CNN.com (September 5, 2008) <http://www.cnn.com/2008/POLITICS/09/04/mccain.transcript/>
John McCain. *Faith of My Fathers.* New York: Random House, 1999.

Miller, Arthur
Arthur Miller. *The Man Who Had All the Luck.* New York: Penguin, 2004.
Martin Gottfried. *Arthur Miller: His Life and Work.* Philadelphia: Da Capo, 2004.
"Legacy of an 'American Titan.'" BBC (February 11, 2005) <http://news.bbc.co.uk/2/hi/entertainment/4258305.stm>.

Moses, Grandma
Jane Kallir and Roger Cardinal. *Grandma Moses in the 21st Century.* New Haven: Yale, 2001.
"Anna Mary Robertson 'Grandma' Moses." *Encyclopedia of American Folk Art.* New York: Routledge, 2004.

Murray, Liz
Thomas Hackett. "She's Giving It Her All." *New York Daily News* (January 21, 2001) http://www.nydailynews.com/archives/news/2001/01/21/2001-01-21_she_s_giving_it_her_all_over.html
Ron Sanders. "Homeless to Harvard Story Inspires Worcester Tech." WBZ TV (March 19, 2009) http://wbztv.com/local/worcester/homeless.to.harvard.2.963417.html

Obama, Barack
David Remnick. "The Joshua Generation." *The New Yorker* (November 17, 2008).
Michael Weiskopf. "Barack Obama: How He Learned to Win." *Time* (May 8, 2008).
Don Gonyea. "Obama's Loss May Have Aided White House Bid." National Public Radio, September 19, 2007.
Barack Obama. *The Audacity of Hope.* New York: Crown, 2006.
Barack Obama. *Dreams from My Father: A Story of Race and Inheritance.* New York: Random House, 2006.

O'Keeffe, Georgia
Roxana Robinson. *Georgia O'Keeffe: A Life.* Lebanon, NH: University Press of New England, 1989.
Lisa Mintz Messenger. *Georgia O'Keeffe.* London: Thames and Hudson, 2001.

Orman, Suze
Suze Orman. *Women and Money: Owning the Power to Control Your Destiny.* New York: Random House, 2007.
Lynn Andriani. "How a Waitress Turned Stockbroker Combined the Heart and the Wallet to Become America's Favorite Financial Guru." *Publisher's Weekly* (February 24, 2003). <http://www.publishersweekly.com/article/CA278785.html?display=archive>

Paine, Thomas
John Keane. *Tom Paine: A Political Life.* New York: Grove Press, 2003.

Pennebaker, James
Joann Ellison Rodgers. "Psychologists at Home." *Psychology Today* (September 1, 1993). <http://www.psychologytoday.com/articles/199309/psychologists-home-part-ii>

James Pennebaker. *Opening Up: The Healing Power of Expressing Emotions*. New York: Guilford Press, 1990.

Perot, Ross
Martin Fridson. *How to Be a Billionaire: Proven Strategies from the Titans of Wealth*. New York: John Wiley and Sons, 1999.
Peter Elkind. "Can Ross Perot Save America?" *Texas Monthly*. Vol. 16, No. 12 (December 1988), 99–102, 192–200.

Premji, Azim
Steve Hamm. "How This Tiger Got Its Roar." *Business Week*, October 19, 2006. <http://www.businessweek.com/globalbiz/content/oct2006/gb20061019_222233.htm?chan=top+news_top+news+index_global+business>
Vishwamitra Sharma. *Famous Indians of the 21ˢᵗ Century*. New Delhi: Pustak Mahal, 2007.

Rand, Ayn
Chris Sciabarra. *Ayn Rand: The Russian Radical*. University Park: Penn State Press, 1995.

Ray, Rachael
"Rachael Ray Revisits Her Past with TV Guide." *Everything Rachael Ray* (December 26, 2006) <http://rachaelrayblog.blogspot.com/2006/12/rachael-revisits-her-past-with-tv-guide.html>
Liza Hamm and Michelle Tauber. "All the Dish!" *People* (May 14, 2007). <http://www.people.com/people/archive/article/0,,20062211,00.html>
Jayne Keedle. *Rachael Ray*. Pleasantville, NY: Gareth Stevens, 2010.

Resnick, Judy
Gretchen Morgenson. "I Didn't Know I Was Oppressed." *Forbes* (March 15, 1993), 140–141.
Debora Vrana. "Ex-Drexel Duo Hits It Big: Neil Dabney and Judy Resnick's Brokerage Scores by Focusing on Troubled Firms' Equities." *Los Angeles Business Journal* (March 8. 1993).

Rodriguez, Juan "Chi Chi"
George Peper, Mary Tiegreen. *The Secret of Golf: A Century of Groundbreaking, Innovative, and Occasionally Outlandish Ways to Master the World's Most Vexing Game*. New York: Workman Publishing, 2005.

Roosevelt, Theodore
David McCulloch. *Mornings on Horseback*. New York: Simon and Schuster, 1982.
Desmond Morris. *Theodore Rex*. New York: Random House, 2001.

Rowling, J.K.
Sean Smith. *J. K. Rowling: A Biography*. London: Michael O'Mara, 2003.
"Harry Potter Author: I Considered Suicide." CNN.com (March 23, 2008) (http://edition.cnn.com/2008/SHOWBIZ/03/23/rowling.depressed/index.html)

Rudolph, Wilma
Tom Biracree. *Wilma Rudolph*. Holloway House Publishing, 1990.
David Maraniss. *Rome 1960: The Olympics that Changed the World*. Simon and Schuster, 2009.

Schultz, Charles M.
David Michaelis. *Schulz and Peanuts: A Biography*. New York: Harper, 2007.

Schwab, Charles R.
John Kador. *Charles Schwab: How One Company Beat Wall Street and Reinvented the Brokerage Industry*. New York: John Wiley and Sons, 2002.

Serlin, Marsha
Francine Knowles. "Top of the Heap in Scrap Metal." *Chicago Sun-Times* (5 May 1996).
Sharon Nelton. "A scrappy entrepreneur." *Nation's Business* (June 1997).
Jenna Goudreau. "Building a business on scrap." *Forbes* (May 1, 2009) http://www.forbes
   .com/2009/05/01/small-business-recycling-forbes-woman-entrepreneurs-careers.html"

Sinatra, Frank
Will Friedwald. *Sinatra! The Song Is You: A Singer's Art*. New York: Da Capo, 1997.

Smith, O. Bruton
"#317 O. Bruton Smith." *Forbes* (September 20, 2007) <http://www.forbes.com/
   lists/2007/54/richlist07_O-Bruton-Smith_HU32.html>
Peter Spiegel. "Life in the Fast Lane." *Forbes* (November 1, 1999) <http://www.forbes
   .com/forbes/1999/1101/6411266a.html>
Jeff Wolf. "Bruton Smith Makes Motorsports His Playground." *Las Vegas Review-Journal*
   (June 5, 2005) < http://www.reviewjournal.com/lvrj_home/2005/Jun-05-Sun-2005/
   sports/26631407.html>
John Davison. "Bruton Smith on Racing's Past, Present & Future." Fastmachines.com
   (May 6, 2005) < http://www.fastmachines.com/nascar/bruton-smith-on-racings-past
   -present-future/>

Stafford, Earl
"Earl Stafford." *Who's Who Among African Americans*. Farmington Hills, MI: Gale Group,
   2003.
Henry Penix. *Unwrap Your Gift*. Tulsa: PFC Press, 2005.
Michael Ruane. "Va. Man Spends $1 Million on Inaugural Package for Disadvantaged."
   Charlottesville Daily Progress (December 5, 2008). <http://www2.dailyprogress.com/
   cdp/news/national/article/va._man_spends_1_million_on_inaugural_package_for
   _disadvantaged/32403/>

Steinbeck, John
Catherine Reef. *John Steinbeck*. New York: Houghton Mifflin Harcourt, 2004.

Stockdale, James
James Stockdale. *Thoughts of a Philosophical Fighter Pilot*. Palo Alto: The Hoover Institu-
   tion, 1995.
James and Sibyl Stockdale. *In Love and War: The Story of a Family's Ordeal and Sacrifice
   During the Vietnam War* (2nd edition revised). Annapolis: Naval Institute Press, 1990.

Stovall, Jim
Amy Reid and Andrew Knox. "Jim Stovall: My Ultimate Gift." *CBN.com* (November
   16, 2007) <http://www.cbn.com/700club/features/amazing/Jim_Stovall111607.aspx>
Mike White. "Jim Stovall, Christian Businessman and Champion Weightlifter, Thrives
   Despite Being Blind." *Associated Content* (November 24, 2007). <http://www.associated
   content.com/article/453177/jim_stoval_christian_businessman_and.html?cat=9>
Jim Stovall. *You Don't Have to be Blind to See*. Nashville: Thomas Nelson, 1996.

Tada, Joni Eareckson

"Joni Eareckson Tada." *Life Stories: True Inspirational Stories of Faith and Life.* <http://joniearecksontadastory.com/jonis-story-page-1/>

Albert A. Herzog. *Disability Advocacy among Religious Organizations.* New York: Routledge, 2006.

Truman, Harry

David McCullough. *Truman.* New York: Simon and Schuster, 1992.

Tubman, Harriet

Kate Clifford Larson. *Bound for the Promised Land: Harriet Tubman, Portrait of an American Hero.* New York: Ballantine, 2004.

Sarah Bradford. *Harriet Tubman: The Moses of Her People.* New York: George Lockwood and Son, 1886.

Turner, Tina

"Tina Turner Tells How She Made It to the Top Alone," *Jet* (April 1, 1985), pp. 61–64.

Tina Turner and Kurt Loder. *I, Tina: My Life Story.* New York: HarperCollins 1987.

Andrew Perry. "Tina Turner: 20 Things You Never Knew," *Telegraph* (March 2, 2009).

Valladeres, Armando

Irving Louis Horowitz. *Cuban Communism.* New Brunswick, NJ: Transaction Publishers 1985.

Armando Valladares. *Against All Hope: a Memoir of Life in Castro's Gulag.* San Francisco: Encounter Books, 2001.

Warner, Kurt

Kurt Warner and Michael Silver. *All Things Possible: My Story of Faith, Football, and the Miracle Season.* New York: Harper-Collins, 2001.

Michael Silver. "The Greatest." *Sports Illustrated* (February 7, 2000). <http://sports illustrated.cnn.com/football/features/superbowl/archives/34/>

Weihenmeyer, Eric

Erik Weihenmayer. *Touch the Top of the World.* New York: Penguin, 2002.

"Statistics of 7summit Climber Weihenmayer." 7summits.com <http://7summits.com/info/stats2/index2.php?_=d&familyname=Weihenmayer>

Karl Taro Greenfeld. "Blind to Failure." *Time* (June 18, 2001) http://www.time.com/time/magazine/article/0,9171,1000120-1,00.html

Weinberg, Sidney

"Everybody's Broker: Sidney Weinberg." *Time* (December 8, 1958). <http://www.time.com/time/magazine/article/0,9171,864550-1,00.html>

"Sidney James Weinberg." *A Biographical Dictionary of American Business Leaders, vol. 4,* ed. John Ingham. Santa Barbara: Greenwood Publishing, 1983. pp. 1580–1584.

Williams, Michael Kenneth

Amos Barshad. "Michael Kenneth Williams' High-Wire Act." *New York* (November 29, 2009) <http://nymag.com/news/intelligencer/62355/>

Alex Altman. "Q&A: Actor Kenneth Michael Williams." *Time* (November 25, 2009) <http://www.time.com/time/arts/article/0,8599,1942833,00.html>

"Michael K. Williams: He's Only Playing Tough." *Fresh Air with Terry Gross* (January 22, 2008). http://www.npr.org/templates/story/story.php?storyId=18299087

Winfrey, Oprah

Janet Lowe. *Oprah Winfrey Speaks: Insights from the World's Most Influential Voice.* Hoboken, NJ: John Wiley and Sons, 2001.

Helen Garson. *Oprah Winfrey: a Biography.* Santa Barbara, CA: Greenwood Publishing Group, 2004.

INDEX

parental abandonment
    Gardner, Chris, 79–80
    Winfrey, Oprah, 201–2
parental disappointment
    Churchill, Winston, 47–48
    Darwin, Charles, 55–56
parents
    death of, 207
    influence of, 208
    childrens' illnesses, 7–8, 111–12
    See also death of parent
passion, importance of, 219–20
Pennebaker, James, 145–46
percussionists, 81–82
Perot, Ross, 147–48
persuasiveness, importance of, 223–24
philosophers
    Camus, Albert, 37–38
    Rand, Ayn, 151–52
philosophy, importance of, 206
phobias, 57–58
physical abuse
    Blige, Mary J., 23–24
    Gardner, Chris, 79–80
physical appearance, influence of, 211–12
physical disabilities
    Bader, Douglas, 13–14
    Bauby, Jean-Dominique, 15–16
    Cleland, Max, 51–52
    Glennie, Evelyn, 81–82
    Goldman, Jami, 85–86
    Hamilton, Bethany, 95–96
    Hawking, Stephen, 97–98
    Keller, Helen, 105–6
    Rudolph, Wilma, 163–64
    Stovall, Jim, 181–82
    Tada, Joni Eareckson, 183–84
    Weihenmayer, Erik, 195–96

political dissidents
    Cheng, Nien, 43–44
    Kadeer, Rebiya, 103–4
    Valladares, Armando, 191–92
political freedom, 204
    and artistic expression, 33–34, 37–38
political oppression
    Grove, Andrew, 91–92
    Gyatso, Tenzin, 93–94
    Rand, Ayn, 151–52
politicians, 218
    Aquino, Corazon, 9–10
    Bloomberg, Michael, 25–26
    Churchill, Winston, 47–48
    Cleland, Max, 51–52
    Grant, Ulysses S., 89–90
    Lincoln, Abraham, 115–16
    Mandela, Nelson, 123–24
    McCain, John, 129–30
    Obama, Barack, 137–38
    Perot, Ross, 147–48
    Roosevelt, Theodore, 159–60
    Truman, Harry, 185–86
poverty, impact of, 212–13
    See also childhood poverty; financial difficulties
pregnancy, teenage, 201–2
Premji, Azim, 149–50
prisoners, 213–14
    Branson, Richard, 31–32
    Gardner, Chris, 79–80
prisoners in concentration camps, 73–74
prisoners (political)
    Brodsky, Joseph, 33–34
    Cheng, Nien, 43–44
    Kadeer, Rebiya, 103–4

About the Authors

John F. Groom is the founder of Attitude Media, which publishes traditional books, ebooks, and Internet sites. Attitude Media also produces fine art and limited edition tee shirts. Groom started Attitude Media in 1996 when he began publishing the popular Internet site Positive Press, incorporating the Positive Quote of the Day email, which now has over 42,000 subscribers. Attitude Media's web sites and books have been featured in stories on CNN, Reuters, Playboy, the Boston Globe, USA TODAY, NPR, Fox News, and elsewhere. More information about these sites can be found at www.positivepress.com and www.attitudemedia.com.

Groom is also the author of the Living Sanely book series. The first book in this series was *Living Sanely in an Insane World: Philosophy for Real People*, followed by *Life Changing Advice from People You Should Know*. Groom has written for The Washington Post, Builder magazine, and a wide variety of other print and online publications.

David Noon is an associate professor of American history at the University of Alaska Southeast, where his main focus is cultural and social history. Dr. Noon received his PhD in American Studies from the University of Minnesota.